THE HARLOT AND THE STATESMAN

The Story of Elizabeth Armistead & Charles James Fox

I. M. Davis

THE
KENSAL
PRESS

British Library Cataloguing in Publication Data.

Davis, I.M.
   The harlot and the statesman: the story of Elizabeth Armitstead and Charles James Fox.
   1. Fox, Charles James — Relations with women   2. Fox, Elizabeth
   3. Statesmen — Great Britain — Biography   4. Statesmen's wives — Great Britain — Biography   5. Courtesans — Great Britain — Biography
   I. Title
   941.07'3   DA506.F7
ISBN 0-946041-45-8

Published by The Kensal Press.
Kensal House, Abbotsbrook, Bourne End, Buckinghamshire

Printed and bound in Great Britain by
Robert Hartnoll [1985] Ltd., Bodmin, Cornwall

Contents

List of Illustrations.

The Cyprian Corps

Mrs Armitstead, who was not married and whose name was not Armitstead, emerged from an obscurity so total that she might almost, like the goddess whose votary she was deemed, have risen fully nubile into existence. She was in her early twenties when a dissolute but discriminating nobleman encountered her in a brothel. Within three years she was the most celebrated courtesan in London.

In England the world of high harlotry, that in France a century later would be termed the demi-monde, reached its zenith in the late eighteenth century. The great courtesans were public figures. Not their liaisons merely, but their dress, the decoration of their coaches, even the flowers adorning the window-boxes of their elegant houses, were matters for chronicle. Occasionally the light-minded newspaper reader, skipping past such headings as 'Parliamentary Intelligence', 'Foreign Intelligence', and 'Shipping Intelligence', could even find the paragraphs recording such matters conveniently assembled under the heading 'Cytherean Intelligence'. For this age, that still took pleasure in draping its frivolities with the shreds of classical imagery, liked to deem these women the votaries of Aphrodite: they were Impures, but they were also Cythereans, Paphians, Cyprians. This last was the preferred designation, and collectively the leading harlots of the 1770s and 1780s were the Cyprian corps.

Their emergence reflected factors – demographic, economic and social – that had been developing throughout the century. Purchasable women were in abundant supply, and so was money. The national economy was already perhaps the strongest in the world. Production and prosperity increased year by year. British commerce encircled the globe, the fortunes of the West Indies and the East were coming to England for spending, and at home the return from land was rising with the spread of agricultural improvements. The concept still in some degree obtained that display was not merely a gratification but almost a duty of opulence; and how could pleasure and display be more agreeably combined than by flaunting an enviable mistress. The merchandise was forthcoming. Women could tap this widening river of wealth, otherwise than by inheritance, only through men. The range of employments open to them was narrow and poorly paid. Death from starvation was rare enough to attract shocked comment when it happened, but happen it still did; in 1763 a house-agent showing a prospective tenant over a supposedly empty house in Stonecutter Street found there three women dead from starvation and two more on the verge of death; another woman was found starved to death in the same district the following month; in 1774 a woman was found dead on a doorstep in Russell Street 'merely from want'. It was not coincidence that all these victims of utter penury were women.

For girls humbly born, neither marriage nor respectable employment, if obtainable, would ensure permanent subsistence. A husband might die or decamp, leaving the wife perhaps with children as well as herself to support. Domestic service, far the most extensive of female employments, offered its own gateway to prostitution, for the young and pretty especially; few servant-girls could withstand even if they wished to the lusts of the master, the son of the house, the male guest there or a superior manservant. Refusal could mean discharge. Compliance might also mean discharge – possibly pregnant – by the mistress of the house. For the servant-girl turned off without a character, for the deserted wife and for many another, prostitution was often not merely the easiest but the only means of self-support.

Temptation could be powerful where necessity failed. The penniless chaste plebeian could at best hope to earn herself, or to marry a man who would earn her, subsistence. Comfort, let alone luxury, was not for the poor. But the poor, especially in London, could observe their possible accessibility to the unchaste fair. The milliner's apprentice entering the satiny boudoir of Sophia Baddeley to deliver a hat into her diamond-flashing hands, the servant-girl watching from the street as Nancy Parsons was armed into the theatre by a Duke who was also Prime Minister, could reflect that these women had been born to circumstances scarcely superior to their own. The highest rewards of whoredom exceeded any earnings possible in respectable employments open to women save at the topmost levels of the theatre and the opera, and those summits could be occupied by fewer than half a dozen at a time. Even at the two patent theatres an actress playing second leads was fortunate to earn £14 a week; but in 1782 it was reckoned that the eight leading courtesans of the day, foremost of a throng in which a dozen more were living at a rate only slightly less flamboyant, were spending on their ordinary expenses an average of £3,000 a year each. This was at a time when a skilled workman might earn perhaps a pound a week, a labourer two-thirds as much, and a minor government clerk £50 a year.

Lazy or ambitious or driven by need, the daughters of the poor flooded in to the one trade that required neither skill nor investment and that to the fortunate few could bring immense returns. They swarmed the streets. They filled brothels, from the opulent establishments in King's Place and Marlborough Street that catered for the nobility and gentry down to the hovels where a few poor drabs congregated for company and to pool the drawing-power of such attractions as they had. While young and fresh, and if possessed of a lodging to which clients could be taken, they might be among those whose price, according to the *Covent Garden Magazine,* 'for a flying leap is half a crown and for a night's lodging five shillings; likewise a bottle of wine is expected.' Many would join before long the host of streetwalkers 'who will satisfy your wishes for three pence and a dram and give more than you desire' on the journey whose likely end was the pauper's grave, beside perhaps a chaste sister whose progress thither had been as rapid and uncheered by the fun and the wine. Those who were healthy, prudent and lucky might prosper, amassing from savings capital enough to start a business (sometimes brothel-keeping, the trade best known to ex-whores and most accessible to poor and independent women with entrepreneurial talent), or to serve as dowry in marriage to a man looking, as men of all classes did, for a bride with more to offer than herself. Very occasionally one of these girls, lucky enough to captivate a man sufficiently rich and amorous to take her into comfortable keeping, would start the climb that led to the heights of opulent celebrity.

For the plebeian, however, the way to the top was beset with competition from those better equipped to charm and to hold the men of birth, wealth and taste whose patronage alone could establish the harlot at the head of her profession. Its ranks were not recruited from the humble only. From every class the tributaries poured in to swell the flood of purchasable women.

Marriage, as Jane Austen observed, must be for well-educated young women of small fortune their pleasantest preservative from want. That preservative was now however in shorter supply than the numbers of marriageable males might suggest; throughout the century the upper-class marriage rate appears to have been low. Sexual morality was lax. The widespread piety of the previous century had faded into indifference. Wesleyanism affected few outside the lower classes, and its geographical spread was patchy. Many men would agree with Bunyan's Mr Badman: 'Who would keep a cow of their own that can have a quart of milk for a penny.' As a respectable outlet for male sexuality marriage was seldom essential save to men who needed legitimate heirs to titles, property or both, and they, with much to offer in marriage, normally expected to gain in return. Gain was expected too by lesser men who saw in marriage a means of advantage, in a wife well-dowered according to their own status in life, or well-connected. 'No-one here [England] thinks of marrying without money', wrote the Irish Betsy Sheridan; housekeepers and bedmates could be secured without sacrificing what might be the future asset of matrimonial availability. Love-matches indeed there were, but the brides were not necessarily virgins. Though the late eighteenth century witnessed a number of true Cinderella stories, Cinderella was often already the mistress of the Prince, nor was he always her first lover.

As men grew warier of marriage without a bonus, the number of women equipped with graces to allure the eligible increased. A use often made of new-found prosperity by people of the middle class – farmers, small merchants, master tradesmen – was to buy their daughters such education as might, they imagined, lead to advantageous marriages. All over the country there were springing up 'boarding schools . . . which, for ten, twelve or even fourteen guineas a year, will undertake to instruct *young ladies* in every accomplishment . . . Replete with affectation and ignorance, or in the school phrase FINISHED, Miss is brought home . . . and having no company or conversation but what arises from the parents' connection, she soon thinks every Macaroni a gentleman and elopes with the first pretty white-legged fellow she meets.'* The accomplishments taught by these boarding schools, however inadequate to secure the hoped-for hypergamous marriage,

---

*The *Gazetteer and Daily Advertiser,* 24 August, 1774. The wearing of white stockings by a man was an outward sign of being, or claiming to be, a gentleman.

might at least prove assets in the career likely to follow such elopements – which itself might, rarely, end in such a marriage as had been the object of the education.'

Nor were these 'finished' Misses the only merchandise available to gentlemen seeking mistresses graced with the manners and accomplishments of women of their own class. Virgins of that class too could sometimes be bought. Well-bred but dowerless girls, though unlikely to starve if orphaned, might find no respectable subsistence but as a poor relation or a companion to some autocratic dowager, fates to which comfortable keeping by an agreeable lover might well appear – particularly to those with no close family to be distressed by the lapse – vastly preferable. Such girls, especially if they were fortunate enough to get a chance of displaying their still unpossessed charms on fashionable promenades such as Ranelagh and Vauxhall, might well secure as their first clients the men of wealth and position whom any *Impure* must capture if she sought to rank as courtesan rather than whore, and so enter their profession at the top. So too might leading actresses and opera-dancers seeking the greater rewards of the Cyprian, and bringing to this second career the cachet that, for men desirous of flaunting covetable mistresses, enhanced their personal charms.

Even women so well armed for the fray, however, had to compete with those of higher rank and greater prestige yet. The distinction of the courtesan lay not merely in her price but in her marketability among men desirable in terms of person as well as rank and wealth. In captivating such lovers, however, the Cyprians faced competition unknown to the hetairas of ancient Greece, the geishas of Japan, and all others who plied their trade in societies which kept respectable women secluded and ignorant. The young noblemen of their day moved among, and would frequently hope for access to the beds of, socially liberated, educated and accomplished women of their own rank. Upper-class society was more permissive than in any subsequent generation until the mid twentieth century. The double moral standard was not invariable, and where it did obtain the gap between the standards set for men and for women was far less than it would be a century later. The sexually liberated married woman was indeed so conspicuous a figure that a term was coined for her: demi-rep. 'This order, which seems daily increasing upon us', observed the *Town and Country Magazine* when defining the word in 1781, 'was first instituted by some ladies eminent for their public spirit, with a view to raising their half of the species to a level with the other in the unbounded licence of their enjoyments . . . It is absolutely necessary that every lady of this order should be married.' The slackness of English usage soon destroyed the precision of the term, which within a few years was being used interchangeably with 'courtesan'. The phenomenon however continued, while some ladies of the order themselves became interchangeable with courtesans.

For not all husbands were complaisant, and those initially so could change their minds. The demi-rep sometimes found herself a divorcee. Co-respondents, if themselves unmarried, and particularly if they had been the lady's only lover, usually did the honourable thing: there were indeed so many divorces and remarriages at this period that Horace Walpole once observed: 'ere long a quarter of our peeresses will have been the wives of half our peers'. The co-respondent might however himself be married, or fail in his duty, in which case it was not unknown for the lady to take full advantage of her de-married state and even to become a professional. These noble divorcees would no doubt have repudiated any such designation as Cyprian, but some of them, like Lady Grosvenor, certainly forfeited amateur status; they took money from their lovers.

Thus for the man who added to rank and wealth youth and personal attractions, London was virtually a seraglio enjoyed in common with those who could match his endowments. The finished Misses turned professional, the dowerless gentlewomen ready to enter unsanctified keeping, the peeresses willing to cuckold their husbands, the ex-peeresses whose husbands had objected to their horns, were most of them available on his courtship. Yet still, against all competition, the occasional low-born harlot – aided often by the intelligence for which her time offered women few outlets and no comparable rewards, powered perhaps by a determination unmatched among those who had never known real poverty – fought her way to the summit from which she could choose among such men. Among all the courtesans of the day none was to command a more resplendent clientele, as none was to have a more remarkable destiny, than the nobody who chose to be known as Mrs Armitstead.

CHAPTER ONE

That Celebrated Thais

Elizabeth Bridget Cane had been born on 11th July, 1750, the date established by an entry in the journal she kept in later life, her name by the record of a land purchase. Her parentage and place of birth are alike beyond trace. According to the *Public Advertiser,* which on 29th June 1781 recorded the alleged birth dates and birth places of six then famous courtesans, she was born at Greenwich, but no surviving Greenwich church register for the relevant period contains the name. This does not disprove the attribution, for not all registers survive, but the statement of the *Public Advertiser* cannot in itself be relied on, particularly as it errs on her year of birth.

If her origins are lost to record, the loss would probably accord with her wishes. She appears to have blotted out of her own memory all recollection of her childhood and youth, for in her later journals, and in such letters from her as survive, not one of many references to the past recalls her early days. None indeed relates to any period before her mid-thirties – when what to her was her real life began – save for occasional allusions to the commencement of some still subsisting friendship. Her friendships were lasting, for she was an affectionate creature, and it is the more remarkable therefore that no attachment from her childhood survived into adult life. The earliest link she would mention was with 'one who befriended her when she was a helpless girl of eighteen', a reference suggesting that at that age some loss or rupture may have sundered her for ever from family and childhood connections.

This blank – which, unlike many courtesans, she never sought to fill with romantic stories – left an empty sheet for the creation of journalistic fantasies about her origins. These varied, the only common factor being the ascription to her of humble birth. By one account she was the offspring of a market porter and a herb-vendor, by another the child of a shoemaker turned Methodist lay preacher, while Samuel Rogers understood her (at a time before they were personally acquainted) to have been at one period waiting-woman to the actress Mrs Abington. Insofar as the soil may be deduced from the fruit, the adult Elizabeth – tall, beautiful and robust, and apparently literate from childhood – was an improbable product for the uneducated, undernourished, ill-housed labouring classes. Her origins may well have been in the respectable class of the skilled artisans.

Equally unknown with her own origin is that of the name by which she chose to be known. She did not acquire it by marriage, for in 1784 she would still be legally 'Elizabeth Bridget Cane, spinster'. Nor indeed did the title 'Mrs' at this period necessarily denote either the married state or a pretence of it. Until the early part of the century this had been the standard style for untitled women, married or single; 'Miss', when first employed as a mode of address, had been used exclusively to or of young unmarried gentle-women, and it was only in the middle years of the century that this style first began to be used for unmarried women of all ages and of all but the servant classes. A woman of Elizabeth's age and likely social class may never have called herself or been called 'Miss'. As for the name 'Armitstead', she may have taken it simply because she liked it (the *Town and Country Magazine* once observed that some of the lesser Impures varied their names as often as they did their lodgings), though names taken from fancy are seldom those that lend themselves to mis-spellings as 'Armitstead' did; pronounced 'Armistead' or 'Armstead', it was so frequently spelled thus that use of the correct spelling would become virtually a token of personal acquaintanceship with the lady.

What is perhaps most likely is that, like many another girl, Elizabeth made her first entry into her profession by way of keeping, and that Mr Armitstead was a keeper whose name, as was common at the time, she took, to retain thereafter. 'Keeping' was a frequent custom of the day, and insofar as it was practised by young men unable or unwilling to marry, and of decent girls, tended to evoke the approval of all but the strictest moralists, as healthier than resorting to whores. Nor was it for dowerless women significantly riskier than marriage without a settlement. Some keeping arrangements ended in marriage, and in the majority that did not the woman, if she was constant to her keeper and he was both decent and solvent, could expect that on leaving her he would make adequate provision for her and for any children she might have borne him. If he failed, as many did, her position was little worse than that of an abandoned wife; the women who on the ending of monogamous connections had no recourse but to prostitution had by no means all been unmarried within them.

However she came by the name of Armitstead, Elizabeth was using it in 1771 if – as from the rarity of the name seems probable – she was the Mrs Armitstead referred to in Sir Joshua Reynolds's appointments book for that year. In these diaries Reynolds entered his sitters' appointments on the left-hand pages, jotting down on the otherwise unused right-hand pages odd notes - of social engagements, of pictures to go to the framers – on matters of which he wanted reminders. On the right-hand page for the week starting 8th June, 1771, appears the entry 'Mrs Armitstead, at Mrs Mitchell's, Upper John Street, Soho Square.' The purpose of the notation does not appear; conceivably Reynolds had seen a potential model in the tall and beautiful girl. But whatever her success, if any, as artist's model, Elizabeth was to become in the next year or so a professional whore. From a spell of association with one of London's selecter brothels she would emerge to take her place among the supreme practitioners of the trade she mastered there.

Which whorehouse reaped the profit of her charms is unknown. According to the *Town and Country Magazine* of several years later, it was Mrs Goadby's celebrated establishment in Marlborough Street, but that source – as will be seen – cannot be relied on in any account of occurrences, other than public events, preceding by more than a few months the date of writing. Certainly the brothel in question was, if not Mrs Goadby's, one that like hers catered for the nobility and gentry.

'Mrs Goadby, that celebrated Lady Abbess' wrote the *Covent Garden Magazine* in 1773, using a euphemism so general that it had virtually ceased to be such, 'having fitted up an elegent Nunnery in Marlborough Street, is now laying in a choice stock of Virgins for the ensuing season . . . She has disposed of her Nunnery in such an uncommon taste, and prepared such extraordinary accommodation for gentlemen of all ages, sizes, tastes and caprices, as, it is judged, will far surpass every seminary of the kind yet known in Europe.' Had any of the girls on offer been genuinely virgin, Mrs Goadby would (according to the same source) have secured fifty guineas, then the median annual stipend of a curate, from the first man to enjoy her; and even after this deflowering the girl's price would, if she proved good at her work, drop only gradually to the five guineas commonly charged in such estalishments as this. The girl herself would probably see little of this money. Notoriously the Abbesses kept control of their 'nuns' by retaining possession of the clothes they wore in public and by running up against them alleged bills for board and lodging. Of Charlotte Hayes, Mrs Goadby's chief rival, it was said that, whenever she suspected a nun was on the point of leaving, 'she made out such enormous demands as compelled the poor girl either to stay or to retire into a prison.' A few years later the newspapers reported that another, unidentified, madam, quarrelling with one of her inmates, had turned the girl literally naked into the street.

Yet, if the brothel had for the inmates features of a debtors' prison, the superior ones combined with these some of the advantages both of a good hotel and of the seminaries to which they were often jocosely likened. The furnishings were handsome and the beds – necessarily – comfortable. There was no need to trouble oneself with household management, and there was always company available for hours of leisure. Life in a brothel could indeed be so pleasant that some self-supporting courtesans, and women maintained by regular protectors, chose to live in one rather than have the bother as well as the independence of managing their own establishments.

The company could be excellent, and for gauche or ill-educated girls improving in the social if not the moral sense. Of the exquisite Harriet Powell, at one time an inhabitant of Charlotte Hayes's 'nunnery', it was said that she allowed no ribaldry into the conversation and that her society was so delightful that men paid for the sole privilege of talking or playing cards with her. (This girl, the daughter of an apothecary, passed into the keeping of, and eventually married, the Earl of Seaforth.) Nor was the improvement of the graceless in manners and accomplishments necessarily left to association with the better graced. The superior Abbesses knew that their more lucrative clients preferred harlots capable at choice of assuming the manners and deploying the skills of their patrons' social equals, and saw to it that suitable girls were adequately groomed. The ability to make music in particular was – in the times when all music must be made in the listener's presence – an accomplishment most gentlemen approved in their doxies, and one possessed by many of the superior courtesans; Dr Johnson's friend Bet Flint was aping her professional as much as her class superiors when she bought a harpsichord she could not play, and put herself in fine attitudes, and drummed. Fine attitudes and drumming were not good enough for the clients of such Abbesses as Mrs Goadby and Mrs Hayes, and it may well have been in a brothel that Elizabeth Armitstead first learned, not only to assume the manners of her clients' sisters, but to play a musical instrument and to use to the best advantage her pretty singing voice.

The resemblance to a seminary was enhanced by the occurrence of outings for the inmates, and if the purpose – the attraction of new custom – was not educational, the venue on at least one occasion was. In July, 1773, according to the *Covent Garden Magazine,* some of the Abbesses took down coach-loads of their girls to the Encaenia festivities at Oxford. There 'M-tch-ll's family amused themselves one afternoon upon the Isis with some *bons vivants,* and made the banks echo with the chorus of ''Lord have mercy, my bubbies'' and ''Lord have mercy, my bum''.' More frequent were excursions to the London centres of public entertainment, and increasingly, as their advantages became realised, to subscription balls and masquerades.

The intensifying appetite for pleasure, and the increase of wealth to spend on it, had in Hanoverian England little satisfaction in the court life which in contemporary Continental states afforded the principal arena for enjoyment and display, and such gratifications as the Opera, the theatre and private parties could offer had long been found inadequate. Throughout the century the number, range and attractions of public entertainments had been expanding. In summer the pleasure gardens, particularly Ranelagh and Vauxhall with their elegant promenades, concerts and dances, did much to satisfy the demand, but their entrance charges were too low for those who desired a measure of exclusivity, and their winter appeal was limited. By mid-century the purveyors of public enjoyment had begun to cater for a more expensive taste, for subscription balls and, even more, masquerades, those much enjoyed and much criticised functions that added to the pleasures of dancing and eating, of dressing up and seeing others dressed up, the delights of incognito encounters permitting flirtation, or more, with strangers. The former singer Mrs Cornelys was the first fully to exploit this demand. 'At first', wrote Horace Walpole of the subscription balls she organised at Carlisle House,'they scandalised, but soon drew in both righteous and ungodly. She went on building, and made her house a fairy palace, for balls, concerts and masquerades.' Soon her success inspired rivalry, and in 1771 the Pantheon ('imagine Balbec in all its glory', exclaimed Walpole) was built in Oxford Road.

The prospects Carlisle House offered of attracting new custom had quickly been recognised by the more prosperous Abbesses. They were well able to afford several times over the guinea or even (for the more opulent functions) two guineas subscription for each person, and soon the nuns of King's Place and Marlborough Street were brushing their domino skirts against those of peeresses as impeccably virtuous as the Duchess of Hamilton or the Countess of Hertford. The Pantheon organisers, determined to prevent any such invasions of their palace, announced on its opening that no women of doubtful character would be admitted, an injudicious attempt in that the exclusion sought was not of the 'nuns' only but of the independent Cyprians. They and their protectors could be expected to resent it, and did. The beautiful Sophia Baddeley arrived at the Pantheon's door attended by her current lover and a troop of his friends wearing – conventionally – swords and indicating that they were – unconventionally – prepared to use them if the lady were denied admission. Mrs Baddeley entered and in her wake there duly followed Mrs Goadby, Mrs Hayes and Mrs Mitchell, each with her bevy of nymphs alert for purchasers.

All in all, if the brothels run by women such as Goadby and Hayes constituted for the inmates prison that might be left for good only under the protection of a man the Abbess preferred not to offend, they afforded unique opportunities for learning how to attract such a man, for meeting him, and for leaving the brothel for a life more opulent than that experienced before entering it. These opportunities Elizabeth had and took. Her deliverer, the second Viscount Bolingbroke, was no Prince Charming, but it was he who launched her into what became an independent and triumphant career.

A brothel was a likely place to meet Lord Bolingbroke. Gross in all his appetites (he ate like a boa constrictor, said the Earl of Egremont, and drank to excess), he was notorious above all for sexual voracity. He had been, declared the *Town and Country Magazine,* 'early initiated into all the mysteries of Venus under those celebrated practitioners, a G-dby, a F-rguson, a P-ham and a H-yes . . . We might introduce the whole alphabet of initials in giving a list of his Dulcineas; the reader cannot suggest a Cleopatra to whom he was not an Anthony.' His temper was no more appealing than his conduct. 'Bad health and pain', wrote Egremont, 'had soured a naturally cynical temper and converted him into a sort of devil upon earth.'* His friends' nickname for him was Bully, and his wife, Lady Di Spencer, had found it all too apt; so determined had she become to end their marriage that she got pregnant by another man and told Bolingbroke, to coerce him into divorcing her, which he duly did. (On marrying the co-respondent, Topham Beauclerk, she found him nearly as unpleasant a husband as Bully.) Yet this greedy and ill-tempered creature had a host of friends that included some of the most talented and popular men of the day; his friendship with Lady Di's brother, Lord Robert Spencer, survived the divorce; and even Egremont admitted that 'a man who could make himself agreeable to persons of such opposite minds, characters and habits as Charles Fox and George the Third must have had something in him beyond the ordinary specimens of the animal.'

At the time he first encountered Elizabeth, Lord Bolingbroke was attached to a lady later identified by the *Town and Country Magazine* (June, 1776) as 'Miss R-d', one of those middle-class girls whose ambitions led her to despise men of her own class. 'She had an utter aversion to tradesmen and mechanics, and thought it less dishonourable to be the mistress of a nobleman that the wife of a plebeian . . . Lord B- first discovered this *penchant* of Miss R-d in favour of nobility, and availed himself of this predilection . . . but variety, dear variety, at length prevailed, and his lordship being struck with the charms of the enchanting Mrs A-st-d, he relinquished Miss R-d for this lady.'

Elizabeth was not, then, the finished article she had become by the time those words were written, but Bolingbroke had the perception to recognise in her a potential that he desired – for the time being – to monopolise. He set her up in lodgings, displayed her about the town, and introduced her to his friends; and also to his two young sons, one just in, the other approaching, his teens. He further, it would appear, suggested to her that she might venture her luck upon the stage, and introduced her to the managers of the Covent Garden theatre.

The London patent theatres served a small audience with a constant appetite for novelty, if not in type of play – the sentimental comedy and the heroic tragedy had reigned almost unchallenged for half a century – at least in plays and in performers. For the winter season of 1774 the Covent Garden management had unfortunately no new plays, and was

*British Museum Additional Manuscripts 51725, from which all quotations from Egremont are taken. These reminiscences were written at the request of Lord Holland in 1832; see page 200.

trying to attract custom by the display of new performers. A pretty novice, sponsored by Lord Bolingbroke, was worth trying out. Cast as the heroine, Indiana, in Steele's *The Conscious Lovers* and theoretically incognita (she was billed as 'A Young Lady (who has never appeared on any stage)', this qualification being deemed an attraction), she made her first appearance before an audience, visibly quaking with stage-fright, on October 7th, 1774.

The Conscious Lovers, still popular after half a century, had been one of the first of the sentimental comedies that so long and so monotonously portrayed to fashionable audiences conduct singularly unlike their own.

'Thalia, once so ill-behaved and rude,

Reform'd, is now become an arrant prude;'

Richard Fitzpatrick would justly write in his prologue to Sheridan's 'The Critic':

'Retailing nightly, to the yawning pit,

The purest morals, undefiled by wit.'

Such necessarily were the morals of Indiana, a heroine of the then approved comedy type, misunderstood, ill-used, chaste, and accidentally mislaid in childhood by a parent since come to wealth who discovers his long-lost child in the nick of time and in the fifth act. As the plot requires that at the outset of the play she is being financially supported, in perfect chastity, by the equally virtuous hero, and as Indiana's purity is apparently matched only by her simplemindedness, her first speech – to a confidance less pure in mind – is: 'Will you persuade me there can be an ill design in supporting me in the condition of a woman of quality? attended, dress'd and lodg'd like one, in my appearance abroad and my furniture at home? every way in the most sumptuous manner, and he that does it has an artifice, a design in it?' For a young woman in Elizabeth's circumstances, and conscious that these were known to a good many of the audience, it must have been a nerve-racking commencement.

She got past it safely if with little diminution of nervousness, to judge by the *Westminster Magazine's* review of the Covent Garden novices: 'A young lady was next brought forward in the character of Indiana. Her figure and apparent sensibility appeared to *promise* much, but she has as yet *performed* but little; so greatly did her fears subdue her powers of utterance and expression. She is said to have made her way to the stage under the patronage of a noble Lord. Though her person is rather lusty, her figure is by no means inelegant. In stature she is about Mrs Bulkley's height, with a side-face and plaintive voice very much resembling the late Mrs Cibber's'. This last at least was praise, for Susannah Cibber had been noted both for her beauty and for her success in pathetic parts.

Elizabeth played Indiana twice more that month. In November she appeared as Perdita in 'The Winter's Tale', her performance being now billed as 'by the Lady who plays Indiana' and 'with the Sheep-shearing song' (this presumably being included to make use of her singing voice), and in January she made one more appearance. No re-engagement followed, however, in the next season, by which time Elizabeth had presumably realised that for her advancement was likelier in a profession to which even successful actresses had recourse, as more profitable than their own. If on the stage she portrayed indifferently the chaste and modest heroines preferred by the time, it was otherwise with her performance on the promenades of Ranelagh or in the ballroom of the Pantheon as a fashionable courtesan. This she was now perfecting, as month by month she advanced in mastery of the arts of display and enticement. Within a year the signs of elegance discerned by the *Westminster Magazine* had flowered into elegance itself, the lustiness of person had softened into voluptuous allure, and 'the enchanting Mrs A-st-d', swept forward by the whim of fashion, had become the most courted harlot in London.

At the upper levels of harlotry, as always where conspicuous expenditure is at work, the influence of fashion did much to regulate demand. 'I have known several gentlemen', wrote a correspondent of the *Covent Garden Magazine,* 'turn off a first mistress merely because she was not sufficiently well known, for the sake of a celebrated woman of the town, a dancer or an actress.' Conversely, mere réclame could so elevate a woman as to convince fashionables and would-be fashionables that she must be the most desirable in the country, or at least that if they did not profess that opinion they would be contemptibly out of mode. Such celebrity was now Elizabeth's.

She was not a great beauty, but it was her fortune that her looks entirely conformed with the requirements of current taste. This, while approving girlish freshness, saw nothing to please in girlish slenderness. Fashion in dress favoured maturity of figure: height to carry off spreading hoops and high-piled hair, a bosom to justify deep decolletage under the seductive veiling of a kerchief the snatching away of which was the amorous male's first move towards conquest, a bearing of stately ease despite the weight of hoops, the grip of tight-lacing and the burden of the lofty coiffure. (Small slight girls were in this generation singularly unlucky; swamped by such modes when young, they aged as fashions grew younger, to confront as stout matrons the nymphet styles of the Directory.) Fashion demanded and fashion displayed the fine woman, and Mrs Armitstead, younger in face than her years but tall, deep-bosomed and superb in bearing, was now reckoned one of the finest women in England.

It was her good fortune too that several of the young men who were Bolingbroke's friends and had now become hers were fashion-setters for the would-be modish. Most of them were members of the Whig club, Brooks's, and Elizabeth's first encounter with them – which occurred before Bolingbroke set her up in lodgings – had been of a rather disconcerting nature. A visiting Frenchman* being entertained at the club one night, some members took him to a bawdy-house, and on arrival discovered 'that Bully as they called him was in bed with a Lady and they kicked the door open and she was the Lady.' This episode however represented one aspect only of the young bloods of Brooks's, who included some of the most urbane and cultivated young men of the time. Lord Robert Spencer, younger brother of the Duke of Marlborough, James Hare, 'the Hare with many friends' and Richard Fitzpatrick were notable in a group reckoned by the Duchess of Devonshire to be 'the set of men in England most deserving to be known . . . they united good sense, wit, wonderful quickness and a *ton* of *persiflage* that, tho' it made them to be fear'd by some, when they chose it render'd their society wonderfully pleasant.' The appearance of such men as these in Elizabeth's train was evidence that here was a woman to be desired by any man capable of discernment. 'There is a fashion in intrigue', declared the *Town and Country Magazine*. 'As a man of taste, to establish his reputation, must have a mistress as well as a man-cook, the degree of his gusto is determined by the happiness of his choice. Who then so proper to establish a man's virtu in his amours as Mrs A-st-d, who can claim the conquest of two ducal coronets, a

---

*Egremont says it was Lafayette, but his memory must have misled him, as Lafayette did not visit England until 1777. The Duc de Lauzun, who was in England in 1773 and was of a nature to appreciate the entertainment offered, may have been the visitor in question.

marquis, four earls and a viscount.'

The identity of these conquered peers, other than Viscount Bolingbroke and possibly the Duke of Dorset, is beyond conjecture. Not all among them and their less noble rivals would have attained the lady's bed. Some no doubt seriously aimed at it and were bidding for the position of her accepted keeper; a Cyprian's first celebrity placed her well for forcing up the bidding for a temporary monopoly of her embraces. Others perhaps, unable to compete for the distinction of supporting her entire living expenses, offered for briefer pleasures, or if young, handsome and hard-up sought to buy, with their own charm, charms on offer at a price beyond their purse. Some, probably, were not in the market at all, having joined the lady's train of suitors only to show themselves no less capable than the Brooks's Club trend-setters of admiring what was admirable. Whatever the personal causes of these attachments, their multiple effect was beneficial in the extreme to Elizabeth's pocket and her career. The more numerous and richer the bidders at the auction, the higher the price of the ware, while the period during which tenders were under consideration brought incidental benefits in such hopeful offerings as diamond rings, rouleaux of guineas or gloves which, drawn on, revealed banknotes tucked inside.

In such references as she made to this period of her life in her much later journals (in which they are few and always related to the start of some still subsisting friendship), Elizabeth always described herself in the same, remarkably euphemistic, words: 'I was then a foolish giddy girl.' Giddy, in the sense of pleasure-loving, she may have been, but foolish she certainly was not. Her acumen was manifest in the choice of her next protector, patently made with prudential considerations in mind. He was General Richard Smith, and he was a Nabob.

Smith, allegedly the son of a cheesemonger, was one of the many poor boys who had gone to Bengal in the service of the East India Company to make a fortune, and one of the conspicuous few who had made it, survived and returned home to spend it – and in so doing add to the dislike and suspicion the Nabobs inspired. English society, exceptionally open by the standards of the rest of Europe, had a long tradition of commercial wealth marrying or buying its way into the ranks of the gentry and aristocracy, but the Nabobs were a different matter. Their dissociation from known social groups, the suddenness and immensity of their fortunes, the rumours of questionable methods of acquisition and the inflation (inter alia in the price of Parliamentary seats) caused by their use of money to storm the strongholds of the establishment had no precedent and aroused widespread resentment. This was illustrated by Samuel Foote's play, *The Nabob*, first produced in 1772. The Nabob of the title is half a figure of fun, half an outright villain – an improbable cross between M. Jourdain and Sir Giles Overreach – who, in the intervals of learning from waiters how to comport himself in gentlemen's clubs, purchases boroughs, tricks a simple country squire into debt, and demands the heroine's hand as the price of not ruining her father. Foote called his Nabob Sir Matthew Mite, and either the name with its suggestion of cheesemites or some correspondence between the conduct of the fictional and the real man led, despite Foote's disclaimers, to the wide-spread identification of Sir Matthew Mite and General Smith. It was as Sir Matthew Mite that the General figured, with 'that celebrated Thais Mrs A-st-d, who for some time had been the reigning toast in that line in the *haut ton*', in the *Tête à Tête* in the *Town and Country Magazine* for July, 1776.

The Tête à Têtes had begun in 1769 with an account of the affair (actually a then secret marriage) between the Duke of Gloucester and Lady Waldegrave. They were now the most popular feature of the magazine, the circulation of which they were said to have raised to the improbable – considering the size of the literate population – number of 14,000. Each Tête à Tête recounted an intrigue in which one party at any rate, usually the man, was a public figure, prefacing the story with a brief biography of each partner. This was normally roughly correct where the person concerned belonged to a prominent family, but where this was not the case, gaps in knowledge tended to be filled by invention. Elizabeth's past being all gap (the writer having apparently been unaware even that she had appeared on the stage), she was supplied with a market porter for father and a herb-vendor for mother, and for first seducer a friseur who had beguiled her by undertaking to dress her hair in the extravagant and costly mode of the day; after whose abandonment of her and a brief liaison with 'a Levite', she suddenly and inexplicably became the rage. It had probably been only on her first becoming fashionable that the journalist noticed her existence. He may however have been near the mark in opining that her being the fashion was the source of her attraction for General Smith, who shared with the fictional Sir Matthew Mite a craving to establish himself in modish society.

The *Tête à Tête* does not describe the bargain Elizabeth was believed to have driven with General Smith, beyond remarking that 'he makes her a very handsome allowance'. This is unlikely to have been all. During her career she apparently acquired two settlements,* and while there is no clue to the grantor of the first, General Smith is the most likely candidate. The securing of a settlement from a keeper or would-be keeper was the objective of any prudent harlot, and while many men adjudged the making of settlements unwise, as conveying a security permissive of infidelity, women able to force up the bidding for their exclusive favours frequently insisted on this price.

It was while Smith was her keeper, and doubtless at his expense, that Elizabeth became a householder. In the Westminster Rate Book of 1776 she appears as the occupier of a house in Bond Street with the then very substantial rental value of £40. The move to occupancy of one's own house (which must of course be in the supremely fashionable quarter bounded by the Oxford Road to the north, Bond Street to the east, St James's Park to the south and to the west the still extending development towards Mayfair) represented the final step to Cyprian independence. Some even among the successful courtesans never took it, preferring to live literally as kept women – their dwellings, carriages and servants provided and their household bills paid by their keepers – rather than assume with the dignity the anxieties of managing their own households. The running of such an establishment as befitted a leading Impure was no trivial job even for a woman bred to it. For plebeians who had grown up with no knowledge (save for any acquired as a servant) of the organisation of a large household, who had never observed a mother or an aunt at the task, and who started with no nucleus of trained servants from the parental or other family home, the prospect could be formidable. Even in a London house, with no outdoor servants but stablemen, 'there was much to be done, especially by women who – as Elizabeth did – liked to entertain. There were the domestic staff to organise (Sophia Baddeley had three men and five women servants); there were kitchen supplies and menus to plan; while the wine-cellar must – unless a protector assumed this duty himself – be carefully stocked as to both quantity and quality with the clarets, the

---

*'Her two annuities, from – and –,' *Morning Post*, 2 July, 1784. Their amounts are nowhere indicated. *The Town and Country Magazine* mentions courtesans as securing settlements of £400 and of £600 a year, and the former amount is also mentioned in 'The Memoirs of Mrs Sophia Baddeley'.

ports and the brandies her guests would approve. Another responsibility sometimes taken over, even for the independent, by the current keeper, was the stable. More than one Tête à Tête mentions the gentleman's provision for the lady of an 'equipage' (which for the self-respecting Cyprian preferably should be two equipages, a closed carriage for comfort and an open one for self-display in the Park), a convenience for the lady balanced by the probability that termination of the affair would mean withdrawal of the equipage.

Acceptance of the exertions involved in managing her own house and stable gave the Cyprian an independence enjoyed by few other women of her time. It also entailed risk, for the bills came in and the servants – and the lady – must be fed whether a lavish keeper was to hand or not: it was between keepers that even the topmost Cyprians occasionally had to descend to one-night stands.* Yet to the more energetic and independently minded among these women the risk was worth taking for the freedom it conveyed; to break with a lover if you wished without having to move house, to bed with a friend from affection, to live for a time without men if funds permitted, to run two or three lovers simultaneously, or to convey a temporary grant of exclusive favours which they were as free as the men to terminate unilaterally.

Smith had secured such a grant from Elizabeth, but he was not to enjoy it long. Its termination was the incidental consequence of his activities in another sphere. The acquisition of high-priced mistresses was only one among the desires of nabobs; much commoner was the hankering for seats in Parliament, those enviable possessions of the nobility, which opened prospects both of further social advancement and of access to the levers of power. Their invasion of the Commons had begun decades earlier, and was said to have raised the price of a seat from £1,400 – 1,500 in the reign of George I to £4,000. By now the administration had taken alarm, and scrutiny of the proceedings at elections was closer; only a few years earlier another nabob, Francis Sykes, having secured election for Shaftesbury by means of bribery, had been unseated on an appeal by the defeated candidate. If Smith gave

---

*Reports of the charges a leading Cyprian might levy for one night range from £50 to £500. According to the *Covent Garden Magazine,* Polly Kennedy, a notable courtesan of the 1760s, once successfully charged £2,000 for a single visit, but this story perhaps was not meant to be credited.

thought to Sykes's disappointment when he set about purchasing his own election for Hindon, he doubtless foresaw at worst no more serious a consequence. He had underestimated the increasing resentment evoked by open manipulation. In June, 1776, he and his fellow-candidate, found guilty of corrupt practices, were fined 1500 marks (£1,000) each and condemned to six months' imprisonment.

It was at this juncture in Smith's affairs that the *Town and Country Magazine* recorded his connection with 'Mrs A-st-d', reporting that despite his incarceration 'Sir Matthew' continued his allowance to the lady. 'But if some can be believed, she avails herself of his situation to increase the splendour of her conquests; that at least may be judged from the number of her attendants and admirers at Vauxhall and other public places.'

Of those admirers who convoyed Mrs Armitstead as she sailed the promenade at Vauxhall, who squired her to theatres and masquerades and looked in at Bond Street to pass an hour in her drawing-room – or perhaps several hours in her bedroom – some had already found more to attract them than beauty and allure. If Elizabeth lacked wit, she was an intelligent and sympathetic listener; if uninformed, she was appealingly eager to learn; and she was blessed in exceptional degree with the always attractive gift of vitality. And the more perceptive among her admirers may already have begun to sense in a woman outwardly made for passion an inward genius for friendship.

Elizabeth liked her fellow-beings. She took pleasure in their society, she liked promoting and witnessing their happiness. 'How delightful it is to see people about one happy', she would one day write, 'and how easy it is to make most of them be so.' Such a disposition could easily have helped to precipitate her unsanctified loss of virginity, but could hardly have contributed towards advancement in the career that ensued, and the probability is that, suppressing her natural inclinations in connections she saw as primarily commercial, she expressed them the more freely in other relationships. It is indicative of the bias of her nature that her friendship with Bolingbroke's sons was to endure more decades than her liaison with their father had years. From Bond Street she maintained affectionate ties with people who had nothing to do with her gilded public life; with Mr and Mrs Marston, one of whom had been kind to a friendless girl of eighteen, with a respectable middle-class matron called Mrs Payne, who to the young Elizabeth appeared an old woman but who still had forty years to live and who would be still Elizabeth's friend at the end of them. Now ties of friendship were forming with some of the young bloods who had helped to raise her to the heights of fashion. It was probably at about this time that the foundations of her long association with Richard Fitzpatrick were laid.

The eighteenth century had its own concept of the complete man. To dance, to drink, to whore, to gamble, even to ride and to shoot as well, were parts only of the full life. The man of true fashion should be equally capable with these of informedly discussing the achievements of the admired Old Masters, of turning a neat verse in more languages than his own, and of debating, preferably from his seat in one or the other House of Parliament, the political issues of the day. In virtually all required endowments, save those that pertained to outward appearance, the archetype and cynosure of the day was Charles James Fox, and in the solar system of which Fox was the sun no planet outshone Fitzpatrick; whose friendship with Elizabeth was by early 1777 sufficiently well rooted to survive by correspondence when in March of that year he was ordered to America with his regiment.

A younger son of the first Earl of Upper Ossory, an accomplished writer of light verse, a competent professional soldier and an MP, Fitzpatrick came near to incarnating the approved type of his day. 'His person tall, manly and extremely distinguished', wrote Nathaniel Wraxall, 'set off by his manners which, though lofty and assuming, were nevertheless elegant and prepossessing, these endowments added grace to the attractions of his conversation. No man's society was more eagerly courted among the highest orders by persons of both sexes.' Nor courted in vain as far as beautiful women were concerned. Fitzpatrick was a womaniser, and his friendship with the lovely and purchaseable Mrs Armitstead was probably an *amitié amoureuse*. But she was a woman who when not exclusively committed to a protector might open her arms to a friend at less than market rate, he a man who would prove capable of maintaining a lifelong affectionate tie with a former mistress;* for both of them friendship could encompass a bout of love-making and outlive changes of bed-mate on both sides.

Elizabeth indeed had acquired before Fitzpatrick left England a new

*Notably with Lady Caroline Price who, according to her cousin Lord Egremont, had been his mistress in youth.

protector, and one whose patronage afforded the prestige that Smith had sought rather than bestowed. The distinction of the courtesan from the prostitute lies not only in her price but in her ability to sell at that price favours other women would happily grant free. Elizabeth's next capture proved her right to the title; there was hardly a woman in London not otherwise enamoured or resolutely chaste, but would have jumped when the Duke of Dorset dropped the handkerchief. He was the man who had everything: youth, beauty, health, a dukedom, wealth by any standards but those of nabobs and other English dukes, and, to cap it all, an imcomparable attraction for women. 'I have always looked upon him as the most dangerous of men' wrote the young Duchess of Devonshire, herself a noted charmer, 'for with that beauty of his he is so unaffected, and has a simplicity and persuasion in his manner that make one account very easily for the number of women he has had in love with him.' Horace Walpole was intrigued by the potency of his charm into trying to analyse it. 'He was unusually handsome, well made, and had an air of sentimental melancholy which more than atoned with women for his want of sense. His silence had the air of amorous absence, and he looked so ready to sigh that it served him instead of sighing: it seeming charity to afford him that pity which he was formed to repay so delightfully.'

Before departing on the Grand Tour (at the rather late age of twenty-five) Dorset had wreaked havoc enough to establish his reputation as King of Hearts. His departure proclaimed it. He took with him Nancy Parsons, the then reigning Cyprian, and he left weeping behind the beautiful Lady Betty Hamilton, who had dreamed of becoming his Duchess. Nancy Parsons had for some years before that time been the mistress of the Prime Minister, the Duke of Grafton, seeming to exercise over him a sway so absolute that it was seriously supposed that Grafton's divorce of his Duchess (for adultery with Fitzpatrick's brother Lord Ossory) would be followed by his marriage to Nancy; when it was not, and she went abroad with Dorset, even the worldly Walpole believed that she had chosen to be the younger Duke's mistress rather than the older one's Duchess. As for Lady Betty, on whom her mother was pressing the suit of the Earl of Derby, she consented, in tears, to the match. They were not the last tears she was to shed for Dorset.

Dorset and Nancy had continued together throughout their three years' tour of the more elegant cities of Europe, but their return to London was followed by a rupture. Nancy in due course captivated, and married, the young Viscount Maynard, and Dorset, filling in the time with desultory liaisons, looked about him for a worthy replacement. Survey of the Cyprian field identified the current occupant of Nancy's former throne. For Dorset, only the best, and the best now was clearly the finest woman in London, Mrs Armitstead. A proposition from such a quarter could not but be acceptable, and Dorset was granted temporary licence to the enjoyment of the house in Clarges Street – no less fashionable, no less expensive than that in Bond Street – to which Elizabeth had lately moved, and temporary exclusive rights to the favours of its mistress.

For the professional courtesan, a new liaison could entail more than a change of bedmate. The incoming lover might move, though at the same social level, in a different social group, to which the Cyprian must now accustom herself; so now, Dorset being insofar as he interested himself in politics at all, a supporter of Administration, Elizabeth must see less of the young Opposition Whigs she had hitherto found congenial. He might have tastes or interests new to her which it now became her business to study – a necessity not always disadvantageous to an ill-educated, intelligent woman, who might benefit from her lovers' contributions to her education as well as to her living expenses. In one respect her association with Dorset did open to Elizabeth access to knowledge in which no woman aspiring to accomplishment should be totally deficient: of the visual arts. Of these she was ignorant, inevitably at a time when the lack of public galleries confined classical painting and sculpture to the private collections to which even so celebrated a courtesan as Mrs Armitstead had normally no access. But Dorset, a bachelor who wanted no female relative to act as housekeeper or hostess for him, was free to take his mistress down to Knole, where his forbears had gathered what they found beautiful and where he in his turn had disposed the English nobleman's traditional Grand Tour assemblage of art to extend the ancestral collection.

He was not the first Sackville to take to Knole living as well as pictured beauty. Like his taste for art (and for his second interest, cricket, a plebeian game his father had been the first nobleman to play regularly), Dorset's taste for women had ancestral precedent. The Sackvilles indeed had a talent for amours with beautiful women destined to be famous for later associations with other men. The fourth Earl of Dorset had been the lover of 'that celebrated and beautiful courtesan' Venetia Stanley, who afterward married Sir Kenelm Digby; his grandson the sixth Earl had preceded Charles II with Nell Gwyn. Had Elizabeth been a fanciful woman she might, considering such histories, have imagined in them auguries for her own future: a royal lover? a happy marriage? In fact she was a practical creature, and any speculations she now indulged about her future were probably focused on her next source of supply. The connection with Dorset was not going to be long-lived.

Entered into, as it seems to have been on both sides, from considerations chiefly of prestige, it could indeed have proven a lasting relationship only if some ground for sympathy if not affection had been discovered. This however was lacking. Elizabeth, already accustomed to the society of intelligent and conversable men, may have found that Dorset's air of sentimental melancholy did not long atone for his want of sense. Such a defect could no doubt have been overlooked, in a more than creditable keeper capable of maintaining her in the state to which she preferred to be accustomed, had the Duke been inclined to constancy; but he was not. Dorset had now been, and been observed by the world to be, the temporary monopolist of two reigning Cyprians, and his thoughts were turning to that other seraglio in which a man of his rank and qualities might – indeed for the sake of his reputation occasionally should – find a mistress: the world of married noblewomen.

It seemed sensible for Elizabeth to re-advertise her charms, and how better than by a fresh appearance on the stage. This was, as the *Morning Herald* observed a few years later, 'a situation that adds fascination to beauty, and affords such opportunities of *sporting* the *graces* as seldom fail to captivate even *Rival Lotharios.*' George Colman, in 1774 head of the management under which she had appeared at Covent Garden, was now running the Theatre Royal in the Haymarket and was willing to present her again. There was no reason to suppose that her acting abilities had increased in the interim, but her fame certainly had, and – though once again anonymously billed, this time as 'A Gentlewoman' – she could be relied on for some drawing-power. When on 5th May 1777, she appeared in Colman's own comedy 'The English Merchant' (a rendering of Voltaire's 'L'Ecossaise'), as the heroine Amelia, another chaste, misfortunate, long-lost daughter, it was noted that, though the pit was poorly attended, a considerable part of the 'coach-gentry' was present. The *Morning Chronicle's* review made it plain that the reason for their presence was understood; more than half of it was devoted to her. 'The young Lady who played the character of Amelia is Mrs Armitstead, who a season ago performed *Indiana*, in the Conscious Lovers, at Covent Garden Theatre. She last night, at first coming on, appeared to be much embarrassed and frightened; the candour and applause of the audience, however, greatly dissipated her fears; and it is but truth to say, that she spoke the pathetic speeches with remarkable sensibility, and demeaned herself throughout the play, with that striking air of diffidence and modesty, which particularly marks the character she represented.'

Even so kind a reception failed to encourage Elizabeth into pursuing further a career for which she was plainly ill-suited. She appeared in one more production the following month, Colman's farce *'The Deuce is in Him'*, and thereafter entered a theatre only as a member of the audience.

In June, the month of Elizabeth's last stage appearances, Dorset was engaged with the Earl of Derby in arranging a cricket match at Derby's Surrey property, The Oaks. The event was made, as were most functions organised by the wealthy and pleasure-loving Derby, the occasion of lavish entertainment, in the course of which Lady Derby proposed, arranged and took part in the first recorded ladies' cricket match. So enthusiastic an endorsement of his favourite sport could not but evoke Dorset's approval. In August, Dorset and the Derbys' were fellow-guests at a house-party at Castle Howard. In the autumn, rumour began to hint that Lady Derby still preferred Dorset to the man she had married.

It is not known when the liaison between Dorset and Elizabeth came to an end. If the *Town and Country Magazine* – always a doubtful authority on events more than a few months old – can be believed, the break was for her followed by a period of financial stress. This allegedly was so great that she was compelled sometimes to hire herself out to the King's Place brothels obliged to consort with 'Captain Toper' (Captain Roper, notorious for his bibulousness and his destructiveness when drunk), himself so hard up that he could raise only such sums 'that would scarce be a breakfast to our heroine'; and had to stoop even to 'a Jew from Throgmorton Street' for support of the order necessary to sustain the expenses of the house in Clarges Street.

If there was any substance behind these stories, its implication is that the severance from Dorset occurred in the autumn, when Parliament was in recess and the friends on whom Elizabeth would normally rely for support between keepers were at Newmarket or enjoying country-house shooting-parties. By February of 1778, when the fashionable world was again assembled in London, she was once more playing off against each other candidates for the pleasures associated with maintaining her. By this time too it was beginning to appear, to those personally acquainted with Lord Derby, that the emergent Derby-Dorset triangle might develop into a quadrilateral. On February 23rd, in a letter to Fitzpatrick in America (with which he enclosed one from Elizabeth), Charles Fox wrote: 'I . . . dine at nine o'clock at Derby's who is become a great vagabond and is desperately in love with Mrs Armitstead.'

This promising seed of scandal did not immediately burgeon. For several months Elizabeth spread her favours, with Lord George Cavendish most prominent among the contributors to her support. Rumours that the Derbys' marriage was under strain spread more widely, but the Earl and Countess still appeared together in public from time to time. Then, with summer, came a threat of invasion, consequent on France's declaration of war in support of the American insurgents, that sent the more active of the younger noblemen into camp with the militia. On 27th June, in a letter to George Selwyn, James Hare described Lord Derby's provisions for his comfort on service: 'Derby is gone into camp near Winchester, and has built a kitchen, and a stable for twelve horses, while Lady Derby is living away at Brighthelmston. He does not, however, think his establishment complete without a declared mistress, and he is therefore to take Mrs Armstead from Lord George, that he may have the privilege of supporting her expenses entirely to himself.'

When with autumn the risk of invasion receded and the camps broke up, Lord and Lady Derby returned to the Grosvenor Square mansion Adam had designed for him, but their living together now was merely a matter of sleeping under the same roof, and it was said that as soon as Derby left the house Dorset entered it. In November the Earl at last secured evidence of his wife's infidelity and confronted her with it, and she left his house for good. The amorous exchange was complete, and all the Sneerwells and Backbites whom Sheridan had typified in his masterpiece of the previous year could delight in recounting how Lord Derby and the Duke of Dorset 'played their ladies into each other's hands.'

So newsworthy an imbroglio could not be ignored by the *Town and Country Magazine,* which in March 1779 duly presented a *Tête à Tête* between 'Lord Champêtre' (Derby had celebrated his engagement to Lady Betty Hamilton with a fête champêtre of inordinate and unforgotten splendour) and 'the celebrated demi-rep Mrs A-ms-d'. The swap at the core of the story had of course to be preceded by the usual brief biographies, and from Elizabeth's it is plain that the magazine's disregard of sources extended to its own back numbers. This time, she was represented as the child of a shoemaker turned Methodist lay preacher, whose enthusiastic pursuit of his new calling led to neglect both of his trade and of his daughter who, thus left 'deserted and distressed', fell into the hands of Mrs Goadby. 'She was at this time not above nineteen', she had actually been about twenty-four when she first came to the notice of the fashionable world, 'tall and genteel, with a beautiful face and most captivating eyes'. Mrs Goadby, continued the *Tête à Tête,* procured her to Lord L-n, to whom succeeded 'the young Duke of A-r' (by whom evidently the fourth Duke of Ancaster, who had inherited the title only the previous year, was intended). Him however she allegedly betrayed with 'a lieutenant of a marching regiment', who got her with child, on discovering which the Duke cast her off; her delivery was rapidly followed by her lover's being ordered to America; and 'the Noble Cricketer' – Dorset – entered her life.

The extent to which journalists employed pure fiction, in producing the histories of those courtesans they celebrated, could hardly be better revealed. Of the contemporaneously recorded facts of Elizabeth's career not one appeared, while the 'biography' of 1779 places her alleged attachment to the marching-lieutenant and pregnancy at the very period when, according to the contemporary account of 1776, she was conspicuous at places of public resort with a train of noble suitors. The child she was said to have borne remains subsequently unaccounted for even in this story; it is in fact probable that Elizabeth Armitstead, like most of the successful Cyprians, was barren.

On current affairs the *Town and Country Magazine* tended to be less unreliable, and there is no reason to question its authority for the fact that Elizabeth's connection with Derby entailed, besides the usual adaptation to new interests, the necessity of acquiring a new physical skill. Derby's passion was for horses. His addiction to racing would, the following year, attach his name to the most famous of flat-races, but his hippophilia was not confined to the race-course. His carriage-horses and hacks were the best money could buy, so must his mistress's be, and what he provided she must of course use. In short, Elizabeth now had to learn to ride. Though she retained the Clarges Street lease, Derby took for her a house in Hampstead (perhaps so that she might surmount in the solitudes of Hampstead Heath the inelegances of commencing equestrianism), and: 'they may frequently be seen riding ensemble in Hyde Park on a fine day, or on the road to Hampstead. They seem perfectly well pleased with each other', concluded the *Tête à Tête,* 'and his lordship has had so complete a surfeit of matrimony, that this probably may be a lasting alliance.'

That was a reasonable supposition. Derby, to whom his wife had supplied an heir before her passion for Dorset was renewed, had no desire to re-marry, and the separation was not followed by the widely expected divorce. On the contrary, the Earl, learning that Dorset had sworn to marry the Countess as soon as she was free, resolved that she never should be. This uncharacteristic vindictiveness ensured the ruin of what hope of happiness remained to her. Dorset inevitably was unfaithful, transferring his devotion within two years to the dancer Giovanna Bacelli, and the unhappy Countess, who had no taste for the promiscuous amours enjoyed by so many well-born adulteresses, drifted forlornly about Europe or her brother's estates until her death in 1797. By then Derby had long, for his own sake, regretted his failure to divorce her while he could, but for the present he had no desire to take another wife, being perfectly satisfied with his delightful Armitstead.

The connection must have seemed one the lady would wish to maintain. Elizabeth was now in her late twenties, an age at which the taking of thought for the morrow would suggest the advisability of a permanent liaison, and a more suitable partner than Derby could scarcely be imagined. He was of her own generation (in fact, two years the younger), good-natured, generous and immensely wealthy. He was moreover a fundamentally monogamous man who, disappointed in a marriage that on his side had been for love, could still be recognised by a discerning woman as in quest of an enduring and exclusive attachment.

Good sense would have directed Elizabeth to establish herself as the partner in such a union; but, calculating as she could be in her professional relationships, she was not always ruled by sense. A later episode in her career suggests that the prospect of permanency in a sexual relationship may itself have been alarming to a woman distrustful of the constancy of any masculine ardour – and besides, she seems not to have cared greatly for riding. Whatever the reason, at some time not long after the *Town and Country Magazine* had prophesied a lasting alliance, she parted from Derby and resumed the embraces of Lord George Cavendish.

Here there would be no question of a permanent attachment. Lord George had to marry. His sister-in-law, the lovely Duchess of Devonshire, had borne no child in six years of marriage, and it was the general opinion that, in George Selwyn's words, 'the Cavendish family must be continued from his loins'. Already he had been spoken of as a possible husband for Lady Betty Compton, the heiress of the day, but currently it was towards Elizabeth Armitstead that his loins inclined him.

Lord George was reckoned a typical member of a family noted for its taciturnity, its probity, and its phlegm. He was also rich, having besides his patrimony as a Duke of Devonshire's younger son a share in the wealth of his maternal grandfather the late Earl of Burlington, whose title would many years later be revived for this grandson. He could be relied on to treat even so expensive a mistress as Mrs Armitstead with the generosity she deemed fitting, and it was indeed he who, according to 'The Jockey Club', provided her with her second settlement. It may also have been a point in Lord George's favour with her that he was a supporter of Opposition. Though the lethargy then common in the family meant that few were active in politics (Lord George's uncle Lord John Cavendish being currently an exception), the Cavendishes regarded as proper a silent but vote-wielding concern, entailing membership of the Commons for younger sons. Lord George sat for Derby. In recent years, and partly through the instrumentality of Duchess Georgiana, they had lent their support particularly to the Foxite group, several members of which were already Elizabeth's friends. Her ties with them, slackened in Dorset's time, had been resumed when it ended, and strengthened during her liaison with Derby who, shortly before his separation from his wife, had reinforced with political association his long-standing friendship with Fox and Fitzpatrick.* Now that Elizabeth was Lord George's again, he was content for her to apply his wealth, as Georgiana did the Duke's, to entertaining these friends, and those who one day dined amid the splendours of Devonshire House might sup the next at Elizabeth's house in Clarges Street.

These old friends might now be accompanied by younger if not always newer ones. The men whom Elizabeth had met first in Bolingbroke's day as the flower of youthful fashion were now in or approaching their thirties, and a younger generation was joining them at Brooks's or behind the standard of Charles Fox on the benches of the Commons. John Townshend was one, adjudged by Wraxall 'one of the most gallant, accomplished, highly informed individuals of his day', and by Duchess Georgiana to have 'great parts'. Another who had great parts in Elizabeth's view was George St John, Bully's elder son – 'a pretty-looking man with a beautiful face', wrote his cousin Lady Spencer, 'but not tall and inclined to be fat' – of whom, with the partiality perhaps of old affection, she expected great things. Less partial judges might have preferred the prospects of his distant cousin, St Andrew St John, younger brother of Lord St John of Bletso, also now taking his place in the Commons and also to be met with where Foxites were gathered together to expound political issues into the ears of beauty.

For the themes that engrossed Parliament were carried outside. They were debated in Devonshire House, in Cumberland House, in Melbourne House, and in Elizabeth's drawing-room, and it was probably now that she began to take an interest not only in politicians but in politics. The political atmosphere had never been more exhilarating. Factional fighting and manoeuvre, for long the stuff of politics, were now overshadowed by issues of principle weightier than at any time since the Revolution of 1688. The domestic conflicts arising from the American Revolutionary War, the demand for electoral reform, the suspicion of royal encroachment on the independence of Parliament, all activated the Opposition, and especially its younger members, with an energy that could not be confined to Parliament.

---

*In indirect consequence of Burgoyne's surrender at Saratoga. Burgoyne, returning to England on parole, associated himself with the Opposition's attacks on Ministers' conduct of the war, and Derby, who was Burgoyne's nephew by marriage and much attached to him, crossed the floor of the Lords to support him.

Wherever they were, discussion would arise, and women were welcome to join in. The notion that in talking to a woman 'from politics, it was an easy step to silence' was undreamed of by these amorous young aristocrats who, delighting in the society and the conversation of women, saw no reason why what interested them should not interest a Duchess or a Cyprian. Elizabeth's first guide into politics may have been Fitzpatrick (now returned from America and even less sympathetic to Administration's policies than when he left); many years afterward, and when a greater politician swayed her life, she maintained an immense respect for Fitzpatrick's judgment. By the end of 1780 she was so closely associated with the Foxite Whigs as to be reckoned politically one of them. The association was not without its risks for one who must tread carefully if she desired not to incur the scurrility of the Press.

The newspapers of the day were both careless and venal. Paragraphs offered by any correspondent, known or unknown to the editor, would if newsworthy enough be inserted unchecked (any that provoked contradiction being followed next day by the contradiction) unless their trend was contrary to editorial policy; and that this was for sale was something of which sophisticated Londoners had little doubt. The sub-villain of Colman's 'The English Merchant', in which Elizabeth had appeared in 1777, is a journalist who introduces himself to a wealthy man with the offer: 'If I can be of any use to you – if you have any friends to be praised, or any enemy to be abused; any author to cry up, or Minister to run down; my pen and talents are entirely at your service.'

Currently the readiest purchaser and most generous paymaster of such talents appears to have been an Administration in more than common need of a good press and with less than common prospect of unsolicited commendation. The principal targets of Press obloquy were thus those who vexed Administration, and above all Fox, whose incomparable and too often unanswerable oratory rendered him uniquely capable of orally hitting Ministers where it hurt. His supporters collectively shared in the abuse. They were, from their adoption of the colours of the American Revolution, 'the buff and blue junto'; they were 'The *Patriots*', the italics denoting a facetious intent, unnecessarily, for at this period the term 'Patriot' almost automatically carried the pejorative significance of, in Dr Johnson's words, 'a factious disturber of the government'.

The largesse of Administration was however unlikely to be conveyed to the editors of unread newspapers. The public must be pleased; and about 1779 some of the less reputable editors – having perhaps reflected on the continuing success of the *Town and Country Magazine* – decided that the affairs of courtesans were selling material. From the occasional listing of notable Impures as among those present at masquerades, or the recording of some particularly newsworthy liaison, the coverage grew until by 1780 readers could follow the activities of some conspicuous Cyprians as closely as those of the foremost politicians or the leaders of the *ton*. This practice indeed afforded an early example of the creation of 'media personalities', and for this reason it is difficult to judge whether the early 1780s in fact represented a vintage period for harlots, or whether the newspapers simply made it appear so.

Two of the women thus celebrated would probably have been notable at any period. One was Mrs Mary Robinson, that Perdita whose beauty and whose conquest of the young Prince of Wales would inevitably have attracted attention. The other was Grace Dalrymple Eliot, the only Cyprian of the time who could compete with Elizabeth Armitstead for the length of her reign and the splendour of her clientele. Grace was one of the well-bred whores who had entered the profession at the top. The daughter of a Scottish lawyer and a distant relative of the Earl of Stair, but dowerless, she had been married at seventeen to John Eliot, a fashionable physician eighteen years her senior. Prosperous and devoted, Mr Eliot was nevertheless too old, too short, too busy and too solemn to be a fit match for a tall, beautiful and pleasure-loving teenager. There was however no shortage of fashionable beaux ready to make good any lack in Mr Eliot, and in 1774, in the third year of her marriage, Grace was detected in an amour with Lord Valentia. Eliot proceeded to a divorce – securing it, to Grace's irritation, only a few weeks before he received the knighthood that would have made her Lady Eliot – but the already married Valentia could not make an honest woman of her. In the traditional sense of the term, no man could have done it. Grace would gladly have remarried could she thereby have gained a title, but she was a natural demi-rep. High-spirited, amorous, and independent, she enjoyed promiscuity, she revelled in luxury, and she found it an excellent arrangement for the former to pay for the later. 'Miss Dalrymple', as she preferred to be called in default of 'Lady Eliot', had the advantage of bilinguality, having been educated in a convent in

Flanders, and was one of the few courtesans of the time to pursue her calling with equal success in London and in Paris. (Another was Rosalie Duthé, who had first come to England as one of Lord Egremont's souvenirs of the Grand Tour.) In France the Duc de Chartres was Grace's most frequent partner, and in England the Earl of Cholmondeley. Harlotry was her game, and she played it as long as the other players would let her; in 1800, at the age of forty-six, she had a brief liaison with one of Bonaparte's brothers, and when on her return to England her friends asked why, said: 'c'était par curiosité, et pour avoir quelque chose à conter en arrivant ici.'

If 'Miss Dalrymple' liked talking about her amours, so did the Press. She and Perdita were however only two of the many to figure in the columns of the *Public Advertiser,* the *Morning Post,* and above all the *Morning Herald,* which recorded their lovers (under coy disguises meant for penetration), their bons mots if any, the colour of their carriages and the whereabouts of their absences from London. With a pretence of intimacy not inappropriate to such subjects, the newspaper correspondents referred to the ladies by their Christian names or by sobriquets, Grace's being 'Dally the Tall'. Perdita's, deriving from the stage part in which the Prince had first seen her and by the name of which he had courted her, was deemed peculiarly apposite for its meaning, which stimulated references to her as 'the Perdita'.

Some Impures seem to have courted both the Press and the more pleasing of the appellations it could bestow. Mrs Irvince, when she had a swan painted on the panels of her carriage, may well have hoped to secure, as she did, the alluring designation of 'The White Swan'. Avian nicknames – the White Crow, the Greenfinch, the Water-Wagtail – were indeed common; the most frequent in appearance being 'the Bird of Paradise'. This denoted another well-born demi-rep, Gertrude Mahon, niece of the Earl of Cavan and half-sister of the Earl of Kerry, who had made a foolish marriage in her teens and drifted into prostitution after separating from her husband; the well-born Cyprians were usually married before starting their careers, the plebeian ones tended to marry, if at all, on ending them. The Bird of Paradise, so nicknamed from her passion for bright colours, was a particularly popular theme with the 'Cytherean Intelligencers', who heavy-handedly pursued the metaphor with such items as: 'the little *Bird of Paradise* is said by some to have been moulting, by others to be laid up with the pip', or: 'the Hen of Paradise, though no larger than a canary, can swallow gold and silver with the facility of an ostrich'. Though paragraphs of this kind may not have pleased Mrs Mahon, the frequency of references to her at this time suggests that she encouraged Press attention, while Perdita was subsequently accused (and, the improbable frequency of panegyric upon her suggests, with justice) of arranging for the insertion of laudatory paragraphs about herself.

One great courtesan disdained such advertisement. Elizabeth Armitstead seems, throughout her career, to have held herself aloof from the Press. She acquired no sobriquet, nor was she ever called by her Christian name, which indeed, from the total absence of newspaper or magazine use of it, she seems to have kept wholly private: it, unlike her surname, was her own. The period when the newspapers first began to follow the doings of Cyprians was one in which she had no need to trawl for lovers by advertising herself, and she had outgrown any youthful pleasure in attending balls and masquerades for their own sake. During the first eighteen months or so of 'Cytherean Intelligence' she was scarcely mentioned, the principal reference to her being one to suggest that she was now extremely selective in the entertainments she patronised.

This occurred in June, 1779, when Lord Cholmondeley organised at the Pantheon an unusually expensive fête – the subscription fee was three guineas – designed to be as magnificent as it was costly. Press coverage was extensive, retailing in detail the scope and splendour of the enjoyments offered. They began with a sumptuous supper, accompanied by catches and glees by the Opera House band, at which the patrons were regaled with a variety of hot and cold meats, a profusion of fruit and a choice of seven wines, while there was 'to every plate a most elegant nosegay of the rarest flowers and at the back of each chair was a wreath of flowers'. Supper concluded, the party adjourned to a tea room below, decorated to represent a thick wood and equipped with a Magician, a Hermit playing water glasses, and a company of opera-dancers disguised as a 'Sicilian band'; and on return to the supper room a performance of 'the Four Seasons' was given by another group of opera-dancers before the patrons themselves began to dance. In fact the whole thing was, according to Horace Walpole, a dreadful flop. 'The subterranean apartment . . . was laid with mould, planted with trees and crammed with nosegays, but the fresh earth and the dead leaves and the effluxia of breaths made such a stench and moisture that they were suffocated; and when they remounted the legs and wings of chickens and remnants of ham poisoned them.' Even Walpole however did not question one point generally agreed concerning this feast; the company had been distinguished in the extreme. 'No person of distinction absent that was in town', wrote the *Morning Post,* 'the company truly brilliant and select'. The *Morning Chronicle,* in evidence of that selectivity, further informed its readers that 'Mrs A-d was the only *avowed Impure* who found admittance, and she conducted herself with a very becoming modesty and address in a situation that must have been rather embarrassing.'

Modesty and address were necessary, in a courtesan known to be attached to members of the buff and blue junto and believed to be attached to their opinions, if the gibes heaped on them were to be avoided. For a professional beauty however, even one who disliked Press notice, there could be more important objectives. At some time in 1780 Elizabeth learned, probably through her buff and blue friends, that the liaison between the Prince and Mrs Robinson might be approaching a rupture. This knowledge could not but suggest an opportunity irresistible to ambition. Now awful beauty did on all its arms and, late in 1780, the celebrated 'Mrs Armstead' sallied forth to the capture of the Heir Apparent.

CHAPTER TWO

The High Priestess of Patriotism

Though in August, 1780, he had attained his eighteenth birthday, and so by royal custom come of age, the Prince of Wales had as yet neither an income nor an establishment of his own. He had however been provided with his own household – chosen by his father – and, after a childhood and adolescence compulsorily spent in almost total seclusion, been allowed to some extent the disposal of his own time. Even before then, and certainly before the light ladies of London had reason to suspect how he differed from his painfully continent father, he had fallen in love with the beautiful actress Mary Robinson, whom he first saw playing the part of Perdita, and – after a salvo of love-letters signed Florizel – conquered the willing prize.

The rapturous affair that followed was one only of the tokens of his emancipation. In the tradition of Hanoverian heirs apparent, he cultivated the society and drank in the teachings of Opposition members -- above all of Charles James Fox –, while also establishing close relations with his uncles, the Dukes of Cumberland and of Gloucester. These were the princes whose marriages to commoners had enraged George III into requiring the introduction and passage of the Royal Marriage Act, and their Duchesses were not received at court. The hospitality of Cumberland (far livelier than that of Gloucester, whose household had the stuffiness of court protocol without the benefit of court advancement) was particularly welcome, for Cumberland was going through an opposition phase, and at Cumberland House the Prince could enjoy the double pleasures of meeting his politically reprehensible friends under the roof of his morally reprehensible uncle.

Cumberland, however pleased to irritate his brother, had no desire to see that irritation exacerbated to rage by the Prince's involvement in a really serious scandal. As the day approached when the Prince must be granted his own income, the Duke grew uneasy about his nephew's continuing attachment to the married Mrs Robinson. Cumberland had his share of Hanoverian stupidity, but he could learn from experience. Some ten years previously, before his marriage, he had in consequence of his liaison with Lady Grosvenor found himself the defendant in a suit for criminal conversation – during which the court and so the public were regaled with his notably puerile love-letters – brought by the hitherto supposedly complaisant Lord Grosvenor. With the £10,000 damages awarded Grosvenor, Cumberland had purchased two lessons: a husband's continuing complaisance could never be relied on; and a royal lover should be cautious about expressing himself in writing. He dropped a warning in his nephew's ear.

A year earlier, in the first fever of his passion for the bewitching Perdita, the Prince would have scorned such cautions. Now he was more receptive. He was beginning to realise that constancy to one woman, however beautiful, was a waste of the opportunities open to a young, handsome Prince. The world was full of lovely women. He saw them everywhere, at balls, at hunting-matches, at the Opera. One in particular – tall, elegant, voluptuously mature – seemed to catch his gaze wherever he went in public. Who could she be? 'Florizel made enquiry about her, and was informed by a trusty page that she was among the number of come-at-ables. Egad, rejoined Florizel, she is a fine woman, I should like to have a Tête à Tête with her. The page took the hint, waited upon Mrs A-mst-d, and an appointment was made for next evening at a certain inn in the neighbourhood of Bushy Park. Unluckily Florizel was obliged to attend his father that evening to the play, and the appointment was put off till next day, when the parties met and an enclaircissement ensued that can easily be conjectured.'*

If the Memoirs of Mrs Robinson, written many years after these events, may be relied upon, the abandoned mistress herself witnessed one of the approaches to Bushy. The Prince had the previous day brutally terminated their affair by sending her a letter saying merely that they must meet no more. Perdita, the first though not the last woman to experience the suddenness and heartlessness with which he could break off an attachment, understandably could not credit this dismissal,

---

*Town and Country Magazine, March, 1781. The story of Cumberland's warning comes from the same source, but has some support in Horace Walpole's statement ('Last Journals') that: 'The Duchess of Cumberland and the Luttrells (the Duchess's family) openly countenanced the amour of the Prince of Wales and Mrs Armstead.

and set out for Windsor in an attempt to see and plead with him. After, she recounts, a frightening drive over Hounslow Heath, in which a footpad tried to intercept her, she reached a small inn called the Magpie, where 'a circumstance soon after arose that did not tend to quiet my emotion. This was the appearance of Mr H. Meynell and Mrs *******. My foreboding soul instantly beheld a rival, and with jealous eagerness interpreted the hitherto inexplicable conduct of the prince, from his frequently having expressed a wish to know that lady.'

This was in August, said Perdita, erring at least as to date, for all other indications are that the affair between the Prince and Elizabeth Armitstead began in late December or early January. The Prince seems to have been in the first flush of enthusiasm over her when, according to the Duchess of Devonshire, he buttonholed Fox at the New Year reception to enthuse about her. From the same source we learn that in her eagerness to capture the new love Elizabeth had neglected the preliminary of being off with the old. 'About this time a ridiculous event happened with Ld George Cavendish and the Prince of Wales. Ld George was returning one night to Mrs Armistead's, rather drunk. In going into her room he perceiv'd some unaccustomed light in another, and much against her entreatys went in. The room seem'd empty, but willing to examine everywhere he soon found there was a man conceal'd behind the door. He stretched out his arm with the candle in his hand close to the person's face, and to his great surprise found it was the P. of Wales. As he was drunk he might very easily have not been quite so respectable as he ought, but it had luckily another effect – he burst out a laughing, made his R.H a low bow and retir'd.'

Perdita, still unwilling to resign herself to the loss of her royal lover, was making every effort to allure him back. While those close to the Prince and to Elizabeth knew of the change of mistress, the outside world could see only that a combat had apparently begun for the Prince's person between two of the most notable Cyprians of the day. The newspapers, enchanted, brought from the scenes of battle constant bulletins in which Elizabeth normally got the rough side of their pens. This might seem inevitable, and indeed deserved; a mature harlot employing her arts to seduce a very young man from his first love can hardly expect a sympathetic Press. The singular feature was however that the duel was represented as politically orientated. 'There has been a *severe contest*', wrote the *Public Advertiser* on 16 January, 'whether a very

Great Person shall have the honour of participating in the embraces of the *patriotic* Mrs A-d or the *courtly* Mrs R-n.' The attacks on Elizabeth portrayed her as the instrument of a political faction, the most remarkable line being that taken by the *Morning Herald,* which persisted in declaring that the liaison between the Prince and 'Mrs A-d' was pure fabrication. 'There cannot be stronger proofs of the miserable shifts to which opposition are driven than the reports they so industriously circulate of a connection between that *High Priestess* of Patriotism, Mrs A-d, and a certain heir apparent,' declared that newspaper on 24 January; and a few days later, in reporting a masquerade at which the Prince had been conspicuously engrossed in the lady, the *Morning Herald* announced that the seeming Prince had been a friend of hers dressed to resemble him.

The Prince enjoyed the masquerade so much that at his request another was held the following week at which, throughout, he kept a masked lady at his side; a man dressed as a butcher approaching him and offering to buy his heifer at his own price, the Prince declared she was above all price. On another newspaper's identifying the masked treasure as Mrs 'Armstead', the *Morning Herald* nearly burst a blood vessel. 'These words were so very forcible that it plainly proved Mrs A-d was not the lady he attended thither. Had she been anything in that *stile,* the *unremitting attention* he paid to his *fair companion,* from whom not anything could draw him, would indeed have been surprising. It is a most shameful affair that such *cattle* as the A-d (to answer perhaps some vile purpose) should dare, without *the least foundation of truth,* to join their names with the highest and most *innocent* characters in the kingdom, and to whom *they are not even known.'* Unfortunately for the *Morning Herald,* even a subsidised newspaper must, to continue worth its subsidy, retain some credibility, and by now it was, at least to London readers, quite plain that the Prince and Mrs Armitstead at any rate knew each other.

A popular venue for observing the direction of the princely interest was the Opera House. This, the last purchaseable bastion of selected public entertainment, had fallen the previous autumn, when Mrs Robinson and Mrs Mahon contrived to secure boxes. They were quickly followed by Elizabeth, and by several other high-ranking Cyprians. By the start of 1781 the Cyprian corps was sufficiently well represented in the Opera-House for the Prince to pursue his new interest there, and 'much speculation' recorded the Duchess of Devonshire 'was occasioned by the bent of his R.H.'s lorgnette.'

This was particularly noticeable at a performance of *Mitradate* on 17th February, after which even the *Morning Herald* had to recognise that its preferred Paphian was not holding her own. 'Mrs R-n sat in a box over against the P-'s; Emily' probably Emily Roberts 'took her station nearly opposite, from which side Mrs A-d also directed her artillery. His Highness in surveying them round met in an upward glance the eyes of Mrs R-. They scarce exchanged a look, when his attention was riveted by Mrs A-d, who, during the momentary victory over her competitor, drew a glove from a beautiful hand and seemed to hold it as a gauntlet to her R-l admirer.' By the end of March, the *Morning Herald* had had to admit that the victory was more than momentary, and was blandly declaring that: 'Notwithstanding all the interested assertions to the contrary, Mrs Armst-d is indisputably the *reigning sultana* of a certain royal paramour.'

Inevitably the reigning sultana was a prime object of interest to all who, by way of the Press or otherwise, followed the progress of the Cyprians. If she drove in Kensington Gardens it was recorded, together with the fact that she condescended to 'press the verdant carpet', with her feet, presumably, 'for about ten minutes': her attendance at a masquerade, 'in a cloak of sky-blue silk, not deigning to unmask all evening', was noted even though the Prince was not present. When her carriage broke down the fact was committed to print, as was the identity of her companion, the dashing Colonel Banastre Tarleton, 'whose gallantry inspired her with such spirits that she soon forgot the danger she had been in; Elizabeth was shamelessly a physical coward, 'and laughed at the incident that had at first greatly alarmed her.' In May she sat for her portrait, and Lord Pembroke wrote to tell Sir William Hamilton how 'Sir Joshua Reynolds is now painting Armstead sacrificing to the God of the Garden, round whose middle he had made a garland of flowers very perturberant, mais elle ne s'en doute point, which is very extraordinary considering that, besides a closely followed up suite of acquaintance with the rural God, she has been on the stage, where a little reading knowledge is generally picked up by its votaries.'

Lord Pembroke evidently over-estimated the extent to which Elizabeth had ever been a votary of Thalia. It was not a common error. To her acquaintance, and to the newspaper-reading public, she was once again the supreme votary of the Cyprian goddess: 'The Arm-d, who now unquestionably holds the *cestus*.' Only Perdita still sought to vie with her, if no longer for the Prince (who had there been succeeded – as some believed, he had been preceded – by Lord Malden) at least in conspicuous expenditure. If one week 'Mrs Armstead' appeared in a phaeton drawn by four cream-coloured ponies, the next Mrs Robinson sported a team of matched chestnuts; but which of the rival beauties first set the fashion for brimstone-yellow carriages, nobody could determine.

The *Morning Herald* had been right at least in observing that 'Mrs Armstead' was the reigning sultana of a harem rather than a sole consort. The Prince, having discovered the Cyprian pastures, was rampaging through them with an enthusiasm that, together with inordinate drinking, brought on, wrote the Duchess of Devonshire, a violent fever 'which soon however spent itself in a hideous humour in his face. Undeterred, he resumed his enjoyments as soon as he was sufficiently recovered' and, astonishingly, it began to appear that Mrs Armitstead was encouraging his polygynous propensities by introducing to him those who might seem her rivals. The *Town and Country Magazine* thought it had the explanation of this conduct. 'Mrs Arm-d, finding that her charms were rather too antiquated and that Florizel languished after youth and variety, was resolved, at least, to a due regard to the main chance; and as she was acquainted with some who might attract the attentions of the hero . . . administered to his appetites.'

In fact – though it would be long before even the Prince's friends realised this – Elizabeth's seniority must from the start have been an element in her charm for a man whose lusts were most strongly excited by women older than himself. Her real reason for encouraging the Prince's interest in other courtesans was one which, if scarcely more creditable to her, reflected a shrewder awareness of the main chance than the *Town and Country Magazine* realised. She now wanted the affair ended, but not by her. Her problem – as the betrayed Lord George noted with amusement – was that the Prince did not pay.

Mrs Robinson could have told her that, but Mrs Robinson had a natural turn for extravagance and a disregard for the morrow that were not shared by her successful rival. Mrs Robinson moreover had, during her liaison with the Prince, looked forward to the day when Parliament would grant him a lavish income from which he would pay all her debts and redeem the bond for £20,000, payable when he came of age, that he had given her at the height of his passion. The bond was legally worthless, but its existence was an embarrassment to the Prince, as was (Cumberland's forebodings having been partly justified) that of some indiscreet letters he had written to her. The retrieval of these documents having become necessary, and the Prince preferring not to meet his discarded mistress, Fox was asked to help negotiate a settlement; as eloquent in private as in Parliament, he negotiated Perdita into parting with the letters and the bond for an annuity of £500, and took advantage of the necessary meetings to negotiate himself into her bed.

Mrs Armitstead could not expect a repetition of the folly that had given an unremunerated mistress material for blackmail, and her prestigious and politically useful liaison was becoming inconvenient. Bills for capital items such as the cream-coloured ponies and the brimstone-yellow carriage doubtless went to, to be left unpaid by, the Prince; but Elizabeth had to pay for the stabling of the ponies and the oats they ate, and the food and the ale and the wages of the coachman who drove them, and of all the servants in the house in Clarges Street, not to mention the delicacies and the wine consumed at the *petits soupers* there. These seem to have been more popular than ever, with the Prince's young military friends such as Colonel Tarleton and Colonel St Leger mingling with 'buff and blue junto' whose interests may have been among the considerations that deterred her from breaking off the affair herself.

The Prince's failure to pay for his pleasures soon became public knowledge, understandably affording much amusement to the *Morning Herald*. Mrs A-d's financial position in its columns varied according to the views of the correspondent who had most recently submitted a paragraph, so that at one time she was ruining herself for the buff and blue junto and at another living in Poppaean luxury on their subventions. Thus in February: 'the luxuries of the time are so great, says a correspondent, that a certain female, not many miles from Clarges-Street (thanks to the Leverets, the Lord Georges and the Lord Johns),* absolutely paid the bright star Vestris, ten guineas, to teach her

*The Leveret is Hare, though it is doubtful if he was ever Elizabeth's lover; for one thing he was, unlike her identified lovers except the cuckolded Derby, married. The identity of Lord John is uncertain; Townshend's father was not at this date a marquess. Lord John Cavendish may be intended. He was not a patron of the Cyprians, but he almost certainly knew Elizabeth, and a man's being seen to visit her regularly would cause him to be reckoned by some her lover.

to make her entrée in her box at the opera.' Later however, when the lady had set off on a Continental tour, 'the principal cause of her going abroad was that ill-founded patriotism, which led her to sacrifice so much of her time to the heroic members of opposition, without the receipt of a single guinea.' Though it is improbable that Elizabeth paid Vestris to teach her to to enter her opera-box (she may, like the Duchess of Devonshire and Lady Melbourne, have taken dancing lessons from him), the first paragraph was nearer the mark as regards her financial position. For all the Prince's inability to support her, she was contriving to keep out of debt. Though her royal lover, however numerous his secondary connections, expected to keep a lien on his charming Armitstead, he did not insist on a monopoly; when not required to pleasure him she was free to sell her favours elsewhere. Lord George, forgiving or fond enough to return, took advantage of this to enjoy with her a last spell of freedom before submitting to matrimony, and she appears at this time also to have entered into a brief rapprochement with Lord Derby. (The Earl had already begun the long attachment to the actress Elizabeth Farren which would, on his wife's death, culminate in a singularly happy marriage; the association however was, the lady always declared, a chaste one, and if so Derby may have found it necessary to satisfy his sexual needs elsewhere.) Nevertheless, it may have been the impossibility of terminating, by means short of herself provoking a rupture, the eagerly sought and now inconvenient connection with the Prince that moved Elizabeth to decide on a tour abroad. Before departing, in July, she had the satisfaction of knowing that a potential replacement had arrived in London; Grace Dalrymple Eliot, having quarrelled with the Duc de Chartres and heard that a royal prize was available in England, was back at home.

Elizabeth's success in maintaining her income that summer is attested by the fact that during it she extended her commitments by leasing a second residence. It was a little house in Surrey, near Chertsey, standing on and taking its name from the modest eminence called St Anne's Hill. Lord Robert Spencer may first have introduced her to it, for the property of which it formed part belonged to the estates of the Dukes of Marlborough, and the house had been occupied until her recent death by his aunt by marriage, Lady Trevor. It may have been Lord Robert too who, finding that Elizabeth had set her heart on the house, helped her with an introduction to the agent for the estate, whom she rapidly charmed into granting her a lease. The enjoyment of St Anne's Hill was however for the future. In July the property's new mistress left for Paris.

Paris, already the capital of fashion and of pleasure (and, thanks to the strength of the pound sterling, offering these delights at less cost than London imposed), was almost inevitably the first objective of English men and women travelling abroad. The appeal of a shopping spree alone was often enough to tempt the elegant and would-be elegant into visiting a city so geared to the tourist trade that the well-breeched visitor need not even speak the language. Foreigners arriving at the better inns found courier-interpreters competing for their patronage, while, for those who preferred not to remain indefinitely dependent on go-betweens, language-teachers were ready with their services. At this period of her life Elizabeth may have been ignorant of French, still the second language of the aristocrats with whom she habitually consorted; if so, however, it was probably now that she began to acquire the knowledge that in after years enabled her both to speak and to read the language.

The attractions of Parisian merchandise and Parisian prices were not, many visitors thought, matched by those of Paris itself, the dirtiness of which in particular was apt to strike visiting foreigners. Horace Walpole called it 'the ugliest, beastliest town in the universe', a condemnation later unconsciously concurred in by Francis Burdett, who saw there: 'such a mixture of pomp and beggary, a filth and magnificence as may truly be said to beggar all description. Suffice to say, it is the most ill-conditioned, ill-built, dirty, stinking Town that can possibly be imagined.' Whether Elizabeth's now refined senses were likewise offended, or whether she was disappointed in such hopes as she may have entertained of securing there the kind of support to which she was accustomed, her stay was not prolonged. On 26th September the readers of the *Morning Herald* – which kept track of her even when she was out of the country – were informed that: 'The Armsted has made an excursion to Spa, some say with the sole view of recruiting her health, which was much impaired by her *patriotic* exertions during the last Sessions of Parliament; some on the other hand think she is making the *trip pecuniary,* as the Spa is well known to contain, at this time, not only the *warmest affections* but the *longest purses.*'

Spa was indeed a resort for the wealthy. Its architectural, scenic and social attractions rendered it a favourite gathering-place for the well-born and well-off who sought to combine the pursuit of health and of pleasure with the enjoyment of international society. Whatever her purpose in going there, Elizabeth spent two months at Spa before leaving (in consequence, said the *Morning Herald* of 'an unexpected fracas between her and her quondam noble enamorato of D-y') for Geneva. She did not leave alone. 'The Lords *Cholmondeley* and *Coleraine*, though not immediately in her suite, saw her no small part of the way, and mean to winter in the same city as their *fascinating countrywoman*.'

In the competition here implied, Cholmondely had the advantage over his rakehell Irish rival. If this large, bouncy, athletic young man had little in his handsome head beyond pleasure and fashion, such political opinions as had found lodgment there were satisfactory buff-and-blue. A liaison with him at the present juncture had also the charm of appropriateness, for he had long if intermittently been the lover of Grace Dalrymple Eliot, now taking Elizabeth's place with the Prince. Their situation abroad also gave him an advantage, for a passion for travel – the Grand Tour had merely whetted an appetite frequently gratified by whisking about Europe at a speed that astonished his great-uncle Horace Walpole – had endowed him with experience helpful to a lady making her first extended Continental tour.

Cholmondeley prevailed, and it was doubtless he who persuaded Elizabeth out of her first intention to winter in Geneva (an odd choice indeed, for Geneva offered little in the way of public entertainment), and to venture the crossing of the Alps. Considerable encouragement must have been needed to induce so timorous a creature to embark in December on a journey then difficult and even dangerous at any season, but Cholmondeley was successful, and before 1781 was out the two had crossed into Italy. There, he kept her on the move ('he pursues her through every town in Italy like the stricken deer with an arrow in her side', declared the *Morning Herald* picturesquely, too delighted with its own simile to consider why a lady of the Armstead's profession should flee the approaches of a handsome young Earl), and if Elizabeth was denied the chance of acquainting herself thoroughly with any place visited, at least she seems to have covered a great deal of ground.

In February the two turned north again, and early in March reached Paris, picked up mail from England and learned exciting news. Lord

North had fallen, Lord Rockingham had been asked to form an administration, and the buff-and-blues were coming into office. Cholmondeley, wishing to be on the spot when appointments were in the making, set off immediately for London, expecting Elizabeth to follow at a more comfortable place, but soon. His expectations were disappointed; she lingered in Paris, her stay being perhaps not unconnected with the arrival there of Lord Coleraine the day after Cholmondeley's departure. She did not return to England until 10th May, and then, by one account, only because the Prince had written to summon her back to London.

She returned to find her old friends rejoicing in their accession to office under Lord Rockingham's leadership, and her first task the delightful one of congratulating them on their success. On 11th May Fox, now Secretary of State, wrote to Fitzpatrick, now in Dublin as secretary to the Chief Secretary for Ireland: 'Mrs. Armitstead arrived yesterday from Paris and seems to be quite well, tho', he ungallantly continued with some ironic cupid looking over his shoulder, 'she certainly looks (one can not conceal it) a little old. She desires me to give her love to you.' If Elizabeth, now nearly thirty-two, was beginning to look her age, it did not lessen her charm for the Prince; her nine months' absence had not obliterated her from his memory, and soon he was eager to resume the pleasures she had withdrawn. Elizabeth had reservations. Possibly she now realised that the Prince's attachment to the buff-and-blues, and in particular to Fox, was too strong to be affected by any woman's grant or withholding of her favours; certainly she was no longer prepared to make these available to him gratis. Payment for services rendered was now, as far as the heir apparent was concerned, her motto, and such were her tact and her sexual accomplishments that – to the great indignation of the *Morning Herald* – she got it. 'The *Armstead*, with very subordinate personal attractions, has contrived to out-jockey the whole *stud* of first-rate *impures*, by the superiority of her understanding, – for she has not only outstripped them in the *race amorous* for a certain *Royal sweepstakes*, but has contrived to *touch the plate*, which none of the others could do.' By August the Prince was, Lady Sarah Napier observed, visiting her every morning.

Her achievement was the more impressive in that she was neither selling nor receiving an exclusive service. The Prince continued to disport himself with other Cyprians (including, though with diminishing interest, Grace Eliot, who in May had borne a child she declared was his), while Elizabeth maintained her association with Cholmondeley. He had been appointed ambassador to Prussia, and the newspapers made merry with the picture of an embassy led by this rattle and accompanied by 'the Armstead'. 'the *athletic Lord* and his *fair* amanuensis are likely to be very acceptable at Berlin; it being apparent what a *congeniality* this exhibits with the manners of Frederick.' A not dissimilar thought had struck Horace Walpole, who opined that his great-nephew's propensities would have rendered more appropriate an accredition to Catherine the Great. Cholmondeley however was not destined to go to Berlin. Early in July the strains on Administration that followed Rockingham's death and Shelburne's succession to him led to Fox's resignation and that of his friends, and soon afterward Cholmondeley too gave up his appointment.

The inconstancies of politics seemed matched by the inconstancy of the amorous. The comparative decorum of transient but temporarily exclusive pairings appeared a thing of the past, that summer of 1782, as the Prince, his lovers and his friends entangled themselves in a network of multiple liaisons. The Grand Chain of the Cytherean dance seemed broken up into an orgy of promiscuous hands-across: the Prince and the Armstead, the Prince and Dally; Dally and Cholmondeley, Cholmondeley and the Armstead; Fox – now dubbed by the Press the Ex-Secretary – and Perdita, Perdita and Banastre Tarleton. Amidst this confusion of couplings there unsurprisingly occurred, some time in August or September, the Ex-Secretary and the Armstead.

The season was over now and the *ton* dispersing, to country seats, to watering-places or inland spas, or – in the case of many of the gentleman – to Newmarket and then to shooting-parties. The wealthier Cyprians also left town, to pursue such of their prey as could be found at the more exclusive resorts. Elizabeth was not among those recorded as having taken lodgings at Ramsgate or at Brighthelmstone, and it is probably that that autumn she went to Chertsey, to enjoy there for the first time the rural pleasures of her second home at St Anne's Hill. In December, however, with the resumption of Parliament, the *ton* returned to town, and so did 'the Armstead'.

The amorous wind had shifted yet again. The Prince at last was temporarily sated with the pleasures offered by the professionals. Like Dorset before him, he turned his desires towards peeresses; the Duchess of Devonshire and her no less alluring sister Lady Duncannon proved disappointingly virtuous, but Lady Melbourne appeared more compliant. Grace Dalrymple Eliot and Lord Cholmondeley resumed their long if intermittent connection. Perdita was yielding ever more totally to her ultimately ruinous passion for Tarleton. And the Armstead? 'The A-d had always policy enough to have *many* strings to her bow,' the *Morning Herald* had written only four months previously, and that policy, it seemed, she still practised. Early in January she was announced to be passing her mornings 'in a *platonic* kind of passion with the tranquil Mr D-e' (possibly Peter Delmé, a friend of the Prince's), and later that month she was observed at a masquerade, in one of the boxes, 'giving audience to her various inamoratos'. A couple of weeks later, the *Morning Herald* got hold of and published a list of subscribers to the Opera, from which it could be seen that, while Mrs Robinson and Colonel Tarleton had a box to themselves, Mrs Armitstead had in hers no less than four fellow-subscribers: Lord Foley, Mr Wyndham, Mr Monson, and Mr Fox. The attention this might have evoked was lessened by the rapidly ensuing discovery that Mrs Robinson's box had, at the lady's expense, been lined with pale pink satin and fitted up with looking-glasses, suggesting 'a kind of Paphian sanctuary'. (Perdita, always easily drawn, hurriedly arranged the insertion of a paragraph declaring that such arrangements were high fashion in Paris, and that the object of the looking-glasses was to extend the occupants' view of the stage.) Elizabeth got off with a few gibes at having her box 'pretty well manned'. What none of these sedulous Cyprian-watchers had yet realised was that her bed, now, was not. There was only one man in it: Fox.

Their first association had perhaps been casual, almost incidental. Elizabeth had long been on friendly terms with Charles Fox, she was probably fond of him, she knew him to be loved and looked-up to by men who were her own loved and respected friends, and she seems always to have been ready, her commercial relationships permitting, to admit friends to her bed on uncommercial terms. The dangers to a harlot of affairs of passion were well known – and Elizabeth could never have maintained her position so long and so successfully had she not eschewed them – but friendship must have seemed safe. How natural therefore than when Charles sought a share in her embraces she should grant it to him, and how delightful was the companionship she enjoyed in consequence. Notoriously bankrupt as he was, he could not support her as she liked to be supported (though she had doubtless had a share of the £3,000 he had won at Newmarket in November), but when the connection began she had had two other paying lovers, and if they had now gone elsewhere, they could, like their predecessors, be replaced. The entertainment of Mr D-e and the interviews at the masquerade perhaps represented a desultory vetting of candidates. If none was selected, more would doubtless present themselves. She knew, or thought she knew, the power of her enchantment. What she had still to learn was that she had now under-estimated it.

The connection between the Armstead and the Ex-Secretary seemed no less natural to the outside world. 'Mrs Armstead' was notoriously the especial Impure of the buff-and-blues, sometimes written of almost as her collective lover, and what was more predictable than that sooner or later their leader would share in her widely distributed favours. The only oddity in the affair was that so hard-headed a woman should be awarding so large a portion of these to an inamorato so impecunious. The Press sought for an explanation, and found one. 'The terms of the pacification are said to have been these, that Mr F- shall have free egress and regress into the privy chamber of the fair one, without fee or reward, on condition that when he assumes the reins of power he shall appoint her *purveyor* of *chickens* to the P- of W- at Carlisle House.' Elizabeth, in short, was supposed to be speculating on Fox's return to office.

Quite possibly she herself rationalised the attachment in this way. She was a practical woman, she dreaded debt, and her present lack of any remunerative lover must have given her some qualms, but as the factions in Parliament shifted and re-grouped, and Fox and North put out tentative feelers towards each other, the prospects of Charles's resuming office appeared increasingly bright. Meanwhile, with the constant society of the most enchanting companion of his day, she had the excitement of feeling herself at the hub of affairs. At Clarges Street Charles's friends gathered to discuss the next moves in Parliament or in negotiations with Lord North, and thither when the Commons had been sitting he came late at night or in the small hours of the morning to tell her what had happened and what had been said and, if he had spoken himself, how he thought he had done. 'He always knew when he spoke well himself', she told his niece long afterward, 'and when he had come from the H. of Coms. at five or six o'clock in the morning used to say, so so, or very well indeed, as he knew how it delighted me to hear these words.'

Their hopes were fulfilled. At the end of February Shelburne resigned, Fox and North reached agreement and, after a month during which the King struggled to evade the necessity of appointing the only administration that could command a majority in the Commons, the coalition took office with the Duke of Portland as Prime Minister and Fox as Secretary of State. It was most unpopular in the country, Fox being widely assailed for his cynicism in allying himself with the man whom for years he had been attacking, and Elizabeth came in for her share of the mud slung. She would probably have been spattered in any case; it was generally supposed that any harlot whose lover was a Minister would exploit the position by selling offices in his grant. 'The *Armstead* is in tip-top spirits on the late barefaced *Coalition*. She now says, in the frank Exultation of her heart, "Choose what office you will in the Land." '; and again: 'The Man of the People [Fox] and the Woman of the People, Mrs A-, yet continue in union blind and mercenary; yet cordially hoping to feed and fatten on *the people between them*.' It was soon alleged that Fox had settled on her the fantastic income of £1,000 a quarter, a settlement that would have entailed a capital outlay of £80,000.

In reality, any expectations she might have entertained of his being better able to support her when in office were soon disappointed. Fox was rigorously opposed to making any profit from office, while as Secretary of State responsible for foreign affairs he felt himself obliged to entertain foreign ambassadors to an extent his salary was insufficient to cover, so that office was actually running him farther into debt. His duties did not however sever him from Elizabeth. Though his social as well as his official activities necessarily divided them, as much as possible of the time he had to himself was spent with her. Whatever concerned him, he wanted her to know; when he was troubled, he wanted her to comfort him; when he was happy he wanted her to share his joy.

He permeated her life. When, on Parliament's rising, she went down to St Anne's Hill, he accompanied her there. He himself had taken, and used for official entertaining, a house at Wimbledon, near enough to Chertsey for him to ride there and back within the day. He brought his nephew Lord Holland, a plain, slightly lame, intelligent and entirely charming nine-year-old, to visit her. He talked with pleasure of St Anne's Hill and its suitability as their country home. His entire assumption was, as at last she realised, that they were going to spend the rest of their lives together.

At this point, it seems, some time in the late summer or early autumn of 1783, Elizabeth took stock, and took fright. She was in debt. She had no wealthy supporter, and the close season, when potential keepers were out of London, was starting; and perhaps too she now recoiled from setting out on the old hunt. She had let herself slip into attachment to a man, and all her knowledge of the world told her that one day he would want the association ended. Elizabeth's experience was that sexual ardours in the male were transient, and while she did not necessarily doubt the sincerity of oaths of eternal devotion, she knew too that no man can give a bond for his future affections. Her long avoidance of affairs of the heart may have been dictated by fear of hurt no less than of financial ruin, and both fears may have dictated the step she now took. Whatever her reasons – and she was perhaps too worried for reasoning – she decided that she and Charles must part.

She did not tell him so face to face. Possily she could not bring herself to do so; possibly she tried and failed; possibly she feared that his incomparable persuasiveness would undermine any arguments from her. In October he left her, following his usual autumn routine, for the Newmarket races and then a round of shooting-parties, and when he had done so she wrote to tell him that the affair must end and that (perhaps because she saw no other means of ensuring its termination) she meant to leave the country and settle abroad.

The response was distraught. 'It is impossible to conceive how miserable your letter has made me. No my dearest Liz you must not go indeed you must not, the very thought of being without you so sinks my spirits that I am sure the reality would be more than I can bear. To talk of favours received from me is ridiculous, are not our interests one? do I live but in you? no my dearest Angel you must not abandon me you must not – As to the difficulties you speak of they are to be sure very vexatious but not in my opinion at all insurmountable. Sell your House and furniture in town; and I by no means despair of being able to bring you enough from this place together with what I know I can borrow in town and with *some* help from the Prince which I think we may certainly have to pay all your debts; but pray my dearest Life take no rash resolution. I would be with you immediately if I did not know that my not attending the Prince to Ld. Townshend's and Mr Coke's would be taken ill by both him and them. I will certainly be with you the 2nd or at farthest the third of Nov'r till when pray my dearest friend decide nothing. Pray write to me directly and give me some comfort. You shall not go without me wherever you go. I have examined myself and know that I can better abandon friends country everything than live without Liz. I could change my name and live with you in the remotest part of Europe in poverty and obscurity. I could bear that very well, but to be parted I can not bear, but I will compose myself. Pray wait till you see me. All my money here is so engaged that I can not send you any at present, but in a day or two I hope to be able to send you a little for immediate use. Adieu, my happiness depends upon you entirely, surely you will not deliberately make me miserable – adieu. P.S. Pray do not think any of the expressions in this letter the expressions of passion or romantic exaggeration. I have examined myself more than once upon this subject and know that I can not live without you.'

Nor could she, after that, bring herself to make him try. She gave up the struggle and accepted that, whatever the outcome for herself, her fate was to devote herself, for as long as he wanted her, to the well-being and the happiness of Charles Fox.

CHAPTER THREE

Fox

Charles James Fox was the talking-point and wonder of his time. Like some mythic hero destined for glory, he had in his very infancy been the theme of tongues; indeed, it might be said, pre-natally, for he was born of the most talked-of marriage of its day. In May, 1744, polite society had been astounded to learn that Henry Fox, a thirty-nine-year old M.P. of recently respectable but undistinguished ancestry, had secretly married Lady Caroline Lennox, the beautiful twenty-one-year-old daughter of the Duke of Richmond. The Richmonds were appalled, the Treasury bench was shocked, the gossips were delighted, and the offending pair were and continued supremely happy.

The sense of social inferiority hammered into him by the critics of his marriage may nevertheless have helped impel Henry Fox towards the course that was to steep him in infamy. Ancestry to match his wife's he could not gain, wealth he might. Reckoned at the time of his marraige among the foremost of younger statesmen and the only real rival to the elder Pitt, he soon began to direct himself, with a thoroughness unmatched even in an age when gain was a recognised object of office, to self-enrichment. In 1757, having already served as Secretary for War, he secured the less dignified but more lucrative office of Paymaster to the Forces. It was then accepted that funds voted for Government purposes might, between vote and often long-delayed appropriation, be invested by and for the benefit of the Minister. Pitt when Paymaster had refused to avail himself of this custom; Fox now exploited it to a degree that shocked even contemporaries. Worse followed. When the accession of George III was followed by the ending of the Seven Years War on conspicuously disadvantageous terms, Fox was reckoned the only Minister cynical enough to undertake and able enough to carry through the negotiations necessary to buy Parliamentary endorsement of the peace treaty. He took on the job, stipulating for a peerage and retention of the Pay Office, abandoned his colleagues, carried the operation through and emerged Lord Holland and the target of public opprobrium for the rest of his life and beyond. Charles grew up in the knowledge that to the outside world his father was 'the public defaulter of unaccounted millions'.

He grew up also in a happy home. Domestically Henry Fox was a loving and beloved husband and a father devoted to all his three sons, but not equally; Charles – the third and second surviving son, born in January 1749 – he adored. Lively, sweet-tempered and precocious, Charles was hardly more than a toddler when his father began to make of him not a pet merely but a companion, and it was to Charles in particular that Henry Fox applied the theories on upbringing that so startled contemporaries. A decade before Rousseau published 'Emile', a century and a half before the founding of Summerhill, Charles received what would now be called a permissive education. 'Let nothing be done to break his spirit', said his father, and soon amazed acquaintances were exchanging stories of the indulgences deemed necessary to preserving Charles's spirit unbroken. He had been let wash his hands in a bowl of cream; the demolition by explosion of a wall having been performed in his absence albeit he had been promised he should witness it, Fox had the wall rebuilt and blown up again for Charles's sake: he had smashed a watch to pieces while his father looked on saying: 'Well, if you must, I suppose you must.' Some of these stories may have been invented or distorted, but it was no invention that Charles was allowed the direction of his own education.

So allowed, he proved the progressive educationist's dream, a child who, not compelled to learn, sought learning and absorbed it with facility and delight. Taught at home by his mother until he caught her out in a mistake in Roman history and, at the age of seven, insisted on going to school, he was given the choice between Eton and a small fashionable private school. First he opted for the latter, but in due course decided on a transfer to Eton, There, enthusiastic both in work and play, he rapidly drew to him the first nucleus (at its heart Fitzpatrick, then and ever after his fidus Achates) of the admiring, adoring, ever enlarging group of friends that was to surround him all his life. His love both of friends and of learning was so strong that when in 1763 his father withdrew the fourteen-year-old for a pleasure tour abroad, he insisted after a few months on returning to Eton. The following year he continued, again at his own wish, to Oxford, where without neglecting pleasure he studied so devotedly that his tutor wrote telling him: 'Application like yours requires some intermission; and you are the only person, with whom I have ever had connexion, to whom I could say this.' In after years Charles used to carry this letter with him for production to and confutation of any person who charged him with irredeemable idleness, needing the testimonial not because he was ever idle when industry was justly called for, but because he was to prove that rare and almost incomprehensible being, a man capable both of intensive work when it was called for and of total indolence when it was not.

His University career endured only two years. In 1766 Lord Holland summoned him away for the Continental tour deemed essential for the polishing of any aspirant to success in high London society. The next two years were spent abroad, wintering with his parents in Italy or the south of France, touring Italy in summer with friends of his own age, lapped everywhere in luxury, received by the most exclusive society wherever he went, gambling, whoring, improving his already notable command of French and mastering the Italian language and, with delight, its literature. By 1769 the process of education was deemed complete. Charles returned home (as an M.P., his father having bought seats for his elder boys and arranged their return at the general election of 1768 albeit Charles was both abroad and under age), and London society and the House of Commons were enabled to view the product of Lord Holland's theories on the education of a promising child.

If the process had shocked, the product moved wonder. Charles was the multiple superlative of his generation. He was the most dazzling of orators, the most dandiacal of dandies (one role he early abandoned), the most reckless of gamesters, the most enchanting of companions, and his vitality seemed inexhaustible. Simultaneously and at full stretch, as if living three men's lives at once, he was the rake, the socialite and the Parliamentarian, and not his elders only but his coevals were left gasping behind as Charles hurtled exuberantly from sphere to sphere. 'After a night of the greatest intemperance', wrote Egremont long after, 'which lasted till quite late in the morning and after which everybody else was sick and stupid, he would go down the house [sic] and make a long and most brilliant and energetic speech upon a subject the details of which he perhaps knew little about except what he could pick up just before or during the debate.' Horace Walpole, who speedily saw in him 'the meteor of our days', in 1773 was drawn despite a previous abjuring of Parliament to hear the meteor speak. 'The object answered; Fox's abilities are amazing at so early a period, especially under the circumstances of a dissolute life. He was just arrived from Newmarket, had sat up drinking all night, and had not been in bed. How such talents make one laugh at Tully's rules for an orator, and his indefatigable application. His laboured orations are puerile beside this boy's manly reason.'

To suggest that Charles's greatest energies were directed into his Parliamentary activities would be misleading – his greatest energies were directed into whatever he was doing at the time – but it was early plain that his seat in the Commons was the launching-pad of a career. Initially indeed careerism seemed his objective. Established in the Commons by a father to whom public office existed for private advantage, he immediately adhered to Administration, and soon was to be heard defending such measures as the exclusion of Wilkes from Parliament. The value of a brilliant orator apparently possessed of his father's time-serving qualities was soon evident to Lord North, and in 1770 Charles was appointed a Junior Lord of the Admiralty. His services proved all that had been expected, but Administration had hardly enjoyed them for two years when the introduction of the Royal Marriages Act proved that Charles could follow his father in directions less pleasing to the Treasury bench.

The elder Fox, hero of a marriage that the Marriage Act of 1753 would have precluded, had abandoned his normal careerism to oppose that measure with all his power, and now the son resigned office to oppose a Bill militating yet more strongly against the freedom of individuals, however few, to follow the matrimonial dictates of their hearts. They were however mistaken who supposed that filial duty alone directed this course. Charles's opposition to anything that hindered the freedom of young people to marry as they chose was personal and profoundly felt. In 1781, when Lord Holland had been seven years dead, he attempted the repeal of the 1753 Marriage Act, assailing with a fervour that impressed even opponents the impediments raised by family pride and wealth to the union of persons of dissimilar rank and condition, extolling the social benefit and personal happiness – 'the most able and tranquil felicity' – secured by marriages of choice and firmly declaring that 'passion, not reason, is best capable of promoting our felicity in wedlock.' However dubious his thesis, his sincerity was total. Charles believed ardently in the wisdom of the heart.

Between his first crusade for freedom in marrying and his second, Charles had held office again. He was appointed to the Treasury Board in 1773, his intransigence of the previous year having been forgiven as a piece of youthful impulsiveness – which would not of course be repeated. It was. As if overweeningly confident in his value to Administration, their fear of the nuisance he could prove in opposition, or both, he became an ever more difficult team member, alternating between disregard of collective policy and pursuit of it to an excessive degree. At last, in February 1774, Lord North discarded him with the brief missive: 'His Majesty has thought proper to order a new Commission of the Treasury to be made out, in which I do not see your name'

Charles's recent erraticism in office may have reflected personal distress. The happy family in which he had grown up was nearing its dissolution. In July, 1774, Lord Holland died, to be survived a few weeks only by his wife. By the end of the year his heir Stephen, the second Lord Holland, had followed his parents to the family vault, leaving (by his wife Mary, Richard Fitzpatrick's sister) a daughter and a one-year-old son, the child 'like a second Messiah', said Charles, 'who came to foretell the ruin and dispersal of the Jews', whose birth had come between Charles and the prospect – on which his creditors had reckoned – of the still immense Holland fortune, but who was to become one of the great delights of his uncle's life.

Charles's current gambling debts were paid from the estate of his father, who had while living already paid out a small fortune on the first enormous batch. 'Lord Holland is dying, is paying Charles Fox's debts, or most of them, for they amount to ONE HUNDRED AND THIRTY THOUSAND POUNDS', Walpole had written in 1773; and already there were more. Even a society used to wild gambling was staggered by the magnitude of such losses, and the unconcern with which the loser regarded them. Modern commentators, aware that gambling can be an addiction, have classified Fox as a compulsive gambler. This diagnosis ignores both his ability to stop gambling totally when he chose and the nature of his gambling. He played as if his object were not to win money but to lose it. A skilful card-player, he neglected whist and picquet for games of pure chance; reckoned one of the best handicappers of horses in the country, he chose to run his own racing stable and bet on his own horses, which usually lost. ('My horses can run very fast', he once said, 'but they do not like to tire themselves.') Charles's gambling – like his conduct in office, from which he never made a penny beyond his salary – may in fact have expressed his real and unadmitted feelings concerning his father's much stigmatised wealth.

However his gaming might tell against him with the public at large, neither this nor any other conduct of his could diminish his friends' devotion. Few men have been so beloved. 'A man made to be loved,' Burke said of him once, and Gibbon, 'Do what he will, I can't help loving the dog.' Only one man to whom Charles was personally known ever wholly withstood the bewitchment of his personality, but this – unfortunately, it was to prove, for Charles – was the King, who both disapproved his political conduct and viewed his happy licentiousness with all the resentment of a repressed and joyless nature for a joyous and uninhibited one. For most people it seems to have been this spontaneity that – allied as it was with sweetness of disposition and brilliance of mind – was at the heart of Charles's charm. Greville related how, when Charles had been many years dead, that old sophisticate Talleyrand 'delights to dwell on the simplicity, gaiety, childishness and profoundness of Fox', and indeed he retained all his life the naturalness of a nice child, so openly pleased with and interested in other people that few could fail in response. (In his fortunately rare dislikes he showed the same naturalness, simply turning his back on anyone he did not want to talk to.) It is indicative of the affection he evoked that in a highly formal age he was generally referred to by his Christian name; even Walpole, to whom it came naturally to speak of a child of ten as 'Miss Hotham', would in his letters refer to Mr Secretary of State Fox as 'Charles'.

His charm owed nothing to his looks. A representative member of a short, stout, swarthy family, he was five foot seven and a half inches tall (as later measured by the painter Opie), pear-shaped, and so hirsute that a Thames waterman, observing the youthful Charles naked on the river bank after a swim, had called a mate to 'look at Nebuchadnezzar come up from grass'. Yet intelligence and vitality redeemed all. 'It was impossible', wrote the Pittite Wraxall, 'to contemplate the lineaments of his countenance without instantly perceiving the marks of genius . . . His figure, broad, heavy and inclined to corpulency, appeared destitute of elegance and grace, except the portion conferred on it by the emanations of intellect, which at times diffused over his whole person, when he was speaking, the most impassioned animation. In his dress, which had constituted an object of his attention earlier in life, he had then become negligent to a degree not altogether excusable in a man whose very errors and defects produced admirers and imitators . . . in 1781 he constantly, at least usually, wore in that assembly [the Commons] a blue frockcoat and a buff waistcoat neither of which appeared in general new and sometimes appeared to be threadbare.'

The significance of these garments lay not in their wear but in their colours, those of the American Revolutionaries. It was in his response to the rebellion of the American Colonies that Fox's public and private natures had seemed at last to coalesce. North's dismissal of 1774 had meant that the outbreak of war found Fox free of all ties with Administration, and so free to consider, criticise and attack. That he should have opposed the conduct of American affairs by an Administration with which he was anyway at odds was perhaps inevitable, but soon his defence of the insurgents was a matter less of contrariety than of conviction. Now, as if his natural propensity to like and think well of everyone he met was extending itself outward to unmet millions, he began gradually to manifest the opinions that eventually would transform him into the supreme exponent, in his day and country, of every man's right to life, liberty and the pursuit of happiness.

Like feelings perhaps moved him four years later, when in 1779 the pressure for Parliamentary reform manifested itself in the reform associations, to indentify himself with their demands; and to express his sincerity, at the general election of 1780, by abandoning his pocket borough to stand for the open constituency of Westminster. It was now that he declared himself, in the sobriquet that was to be turned against him and his mistresses, the Man of the People. Returned for Westminster, he continued to assail both Administration's policies towards America and their conduct of those policies with a force and shrewdness that gathered behind him the supporters who were to become the Foxites, and rendered him one of the chief Parliamentary spearheads of Opposition.

Outside Parliament, his way of life continued unchanged, in all but dandyism, from that he had pursued for more than a decade. He, who had so extolled the joys of marriage, had never been moved to sample them (old Lord Holland, asked about a rumour that Charles was to be married, had said; 'I wish it were true, for then he would go to bed one night at least'), nor was there any decline in the energy he poured into his bachelor pleasures. Still at thirty-two he lived as if he had three lives at his disposal: 'still the hero in Parliament, at the gaming-table, at Newmarket. Last week he passed four-and-twenty hours without interruption at all three', wrote Walpole in 1781, 'or on the road from one to the other; and ill the whole time, for he has a bad constitution, and treats it as if he had been dipped in the immortal river.' Walpole erred in supposing Charles to have had a bad constitution; had he not been exceptionally robust he could not long have survived such courses. But they were beginning to tell on him, and Wraxall noted that now his autumn round of shooting-parties served to restore health 'lost in St James's Street and in the House of Commons'. It is likely that by now he had already sown, long delayed though they would be in germination, the seeds of the disease that was to kill him.

This was the period of his life at which his magnetism first attracted to his side the young Prince of Wales, and by so doing petrified into hatred the unchanged disapproval of the King. 'The anguish to a mind [the King's] that had from the Prince's childhood anticipated jealousy rendered the already conceived antipathy to Fox a rankling ulcer,' wrote Walpole. The King's dismay at North's fall in 1782 was thus reinforced by the knowledge that the Administration replacing him could scarcely fail to include Fox. No Prime Minister capable of engaging adequate support in the Commons could ignore Fox's achievement or the strength of the Foxites, and when Lord Rockingham took office in March of that year Charles was duly appointed one Secretary of State.

Less unwelcome to the King, despite his sincerely sustained opposition to North's American policies, was the other Secretary of State, the Earl of Shelburne. To Fox however no harness-mate could have been more repugnant. Shelburne was one of the few human beings he positively disliked. Though filial piety may have been a factor here – Shelburne and the first Lord Holland had been gravely at odds – the real distaste stemmed from Shelburne's seeming incarnation of the quality most odious to the open-hearted Charles: duplicity. The Earl in fact was no less honourable than any other politician of the day, but he was cursed with a personality irredeemably suggestive of insincerity. 'His falsehood was so constant and notorious that it seemed rather his profession than his instrument,' wrote Walpole. 'His plausibility was less an artifice than a habit; and his smiles were so excited that, like the rattle of the snake, they warned before he had time to bite.' The same recorder makes plain that it was not Fox alone who believed his colleague was intriguing against him. 'The material features [of the Administration] were the masterly abilities of Charles Fox and the intrigues of Lord Shelburne. The former displayed such facility in comprehending and transacting all business as charmed all who approached him . . . While Fox thus unfolded his character so advantageously, Shelburne was busied in devoting himself to the King and in traversing Lord Rockingham and Fox at every point.' The suspicions of Shelburne's detractors seemed confirmed when, scarcely three months after forming his Administration, Rockingham died; it was Shelburne the King invited to take his place.

Fox was already at odds with Shelburne over the question whether the independence of the United States should (as he considered it must) be recognised before negotiations for a treaty began. With his opponent now his master he must lose his point and, rather than be associated in what he saw as a foredoomed attempt to secure some concession from the victors, he resigned, dismaying many of his supporters and enabling his critics to declare that he had acted solely from dislike of Shelburne. He had waited eight years for office, had held it little more than four months, had proved himself superbly competent in it, and now was idle once more. Idleness, however, allowed more time for pleasure. It was not long before the Press learned with glee that the Ex-Secretary had commenced a liaison with the Perdita.

The talked-of Charles Fox had naturally been talked of with women since first he returned from the Grand Tour. Even then he was sexually well experienced. Among the many stories about Lord Holland's upbringing of his favourite son there was one relating how he had selected a first mistress for the adolescent Charles, who, enjoying the pleasure more than the partner, had speedily replaced her. Certainly he had written to Fitzpatrick from Italy: 'I have had one pox and one clap this summer. I believe I am the most unlucky rascal in the universe.' Returning to London to become the darling of drawing-rooms no less than gaming-rooms, he had ascribed to him a plurality of intrigues with society women; 'but', observed the *Town and Country Magazine* in a *Tête à Tête* ascribing the dancer Heinel to 'the Young Cub' as mistress, 'most of these reports breathe the voice of scandal rather than truth'. One, circulating soon afterwards, certainly did so; that he was the lover of his beautiful young aunt Lady Sarah Bunbury, who as Lady Sarah Lennox had once moved the youthful George III to contemplate marrying a subject.

He attracted women, certainly, not by allure of the Dorset variety (all else apart, he lacked the looks), but as he did men, by his vitality and by the warmth of his interest in the person he was talking to. He pleased, and for the pleasure he gave was pursued. Plain as he was, the mistress most frequently assigned him by gossip was the young peeress reckoned the most charming woman of her day, the enchanting Georgiana, Duchess of Devonshire. That gossip almost certainly was ill-founded, despite their mutual and obvious attachment. Georgiana had not yet achieved that essential qualification for licence in the well-bred would-be adulteress, the provision of a legitimate heir to her husband, and it is doubtful whether if she had Charles would have sought or she opened her arms; there seems to have been between them a measure of temperamental affinity which rendered their affection liker that of brother and sister than of would-be lovers. The one woman of rank Charles did pursue with adulterous if vain intent was the beautiful Mrs Crewe, and even for her his passion was scarcely overwhelming if we may judge by the self-consciously elegant declaration thereof to Fitzpatrick: 'Je suis amoureuse de Mme Crewe . . . Je n'aime plus cependant l'annee passee en heros de roman, j'aime en homme du monde, j'ai de la passion sans en etre la dupe'. But Mrs Crewe was obdurately virtuous, and there is no evidence that Charles ever otherwise pursued, let alone prevailed upon, a woman of birth. His sexual appetites were slaked with obscure women, two of whom had borne him children, and he was known to have a regrettable taste for cheap street-walkers.

Even at the height of his extravagance he had never mounted any of the great courtesans as his mistress; it was as if his need to waste money precluded the acquisition in return even of so transient an asset as the enjoyment of an expensive whore. But Perdita's favours to him were not bought. His liaison with her seems to have originated in the discovery, during his dealings with her over the Prince's bond, that this publicly deserted woman was ready to yield herself free to a kind and attractive man who wanted her. That she had nothing from him was notorious. The Press rejoiced in the spectable of this extravagant *Cyprian* bestowing her embraces gratis on the ruined Ex-Secretary, and his aunt Lady Sarah Napier* declared: 'I long to tell him he does it to show he is superior to Alcibiades, for *his* courtezan foresook him when he was unfortunate, and Mrs Robinson takes *him* up.

Perdita offered more than the assuagement of desire. Intelligent as well as beautiful, she was as conversable and as ready to learn politics from Charles's lips as the ladies of the aristocratic drawing-rooms he frequented, and as her lover he began to enjoy the association of mental with physical intercourse. When therefore the lady's fancy turned away from him (Colonel T-n has delightful hopes of carrying Fort *Perdita*', wrote the *Morning Herald* on 26th September, 1782, when probably that fort had already fallen) it was more than a yielding body that Charles wanted to replace. His first amorous approaches to Elizabeth Armitstead may simply have reflected the thought that if one expensive Cyprian had granted him her favours free, so might another.

He had known Elizabeth for years, probably ever since Bolingbroke had first displayed her about town, certainly since the days when she and Fitzpatrick had been close; he had forwarded her letters enclosed with his own to Fitzpatrick in America. All her known lovers except Smith and Dorset had been his friends, and more than one had made him confidant of the ardours she inspired. He knew her as a woman not only lovely (albeit now looking 'a little old') but intelligent, sympathetic and responsive in conversation, conveniently a Whig, and kind. Perhaps she would be kind to him. She was.

By the beginning of 1783, the year in which Fox's public and private lives were both to reach their turning-points, the Ex-Secretary and the Armstead were approaching an exclusive attachment. The settlement of his amorous life may still as yet have been a minor concern to Fox. Far from having abandoned with office his interest in office, he was actively scheming to resume it, not from want of power or profit but because only from office could he get things done. The American war now ended, his thoughts were reaching ahead to his next objectives, the regulation of the East India Company, and Parliamentary reform. This approach to politics solely in terms of ends promoted a dangerous

---

*Lady Sarah Bunbury, some years after her elopement from Sir Charles Bunbury with Lord William Gordon, married Colonel George Napier.

unconcern with the significance of means, in handling which he could show, as he was soon to prove, a serious lack of judgment. He was thirty-four years old, and seemingly robust, he might have thirty years or more of political life ahead of him, but he could not wait. He wanted office now, in an Administration excluding Shelburne, but as this could be reached only through control of the Commons it was attainable only by joining his group's voting strength with that of a leader powerful enough to command, with him, an assured majority; and the only leader of a group sufficiently numerous was the man Fox had for years mocked, reviled, condemned as both misguided and incapable, Lord North.

Fox saw in this past no reason why they should not in the present unite. To him, political combat was wholly separate from personal animosity (a detachment not shared by William Adam, who in 1779 had in consequence of a speech of Fox's forced on the surprised orator his only duel – in which he, unlike Adam, refused to fire). With North personally Fox had formerly got on well. North had a like capacity for separating personal and political attitudes, and he too desired to return to office. Early in 1783 he put out, through intermediaries, cautious feelers towards Fox. They were not rebuffed. On 17 February signs of a juncture were discernible when the two, each arguing from different grounds, combined to oppose the terms of the treaty with the United States and to defeat Administration. By the end of the month Shelburne had resigned.

For six weeks manoeuvring went on towards the formation of a new Ministry, as Fox and North dickered on programme, on appointments, and on choice of head of Administration. Fox never wished to be himself Prime Minister; his chosen role in Government was the effective one, negotiater with foreign Governments and putter-through of reforms. The management of business, the making of minor appointments, the deployment of patronage were odious to him, all the more perhaps because it was in these his father had excelled and grown infamous in excelling. This distaste may also have nurtured his choice – reckoned highly amusing in the self-professed Man of the People – of candidate for the job. Fox's preferred Prime Minister was always a nobleman as conspicuous for the wealth that placed him above corruption as for the probity that disdained it. Currently, it was the Duke of Portland.

The London drawing-rooms were naturally abuzz with rumours and counter-rumours over the manoeuvring of the politicians. In March Lady Hertford gave a ball to which she invited the leaders both of the fallen Administration and of Opposition. Charles Fox was the man of the hour and, said the Duke of Devonshire, twenty ladies kept themselves disengaged in the hope of having him for a partner. But Charles was not present. There was metal more attractive in Clarges Street, and when early in April he and North at last came to an accommodation, it was to Clarges Street he hurried with the news.

On 8th April the coalition took office, with Portland at the head, Fox and North as Secretaries of State, Lord John Cavendish as Chancellor of the Exchequer, Burke as Paymaster to the Forces, Sheridan as a Secretary to the Treasury, and Fitzpatrick as Secretary for War. The King, said John Townshend, when Fox kissed hands 'turned back his eyes and ears like the horse at Astley's when the tailor he had determined to throw was getting on him'. But Fox believed he could not be thrown. Ahead of his time in this as in much else, he thought it now established beyond dispute that control of the Commons spelt an authority to govern that bound even the monarch.

The King was not alone in his distaste for the coalition. Its emergence unloosed a flood of Press obloquy on all concerned, but primarily on Fox. His conjuncture with the man he had so long, so publicly and so variously condemned, of whom (as he was now constantly reminded) he had once said that should he ever make terms with him 'he would rest satisfied to be called *the most infamous of mankind*', was inevitably presented as, and by most people not personally aquainted with Fox believed to be, the outcome of cynical ambition. Even among his own friends and supporters several, like Thomas Coke, questioned his wisdom while understanding his motives. Fox himself, abandoning the gaming-tables and buckling down to work, regretted the contumely but accepted it as inevitable. He was accustomed to the opprobrium of the Press. He had been its target for his opposition to the American war, and time had proved him right. Why therefore should he have regard to what the Press said now. 'I know I am right,' he wrote to Elizabeth a few months later, 'and must bear the consequences, tho' I dislike unpopularity as much as any man. Indeed my dearest Liz it is no hypocrisy in me to say that the consciousness of having always acted upon principle in public matters and my determination always to do so is the great comfort of my life . . . I have the weakness of disliking abuse, but that weakness shall never prevent me from doing what I think right.'

At work again, plunged in negotiations over the treaties with the United States, France and Spain, he showed all the industry and ability he had revealed the previous year. 'He is now as indefatigable as he was idle', wrote Walpole, and Wraxall: 'Fox, during that brilliant but transitory portion of his life, fulfilled with universal approbation . . . all the essential no less than ostensible functions of Secretary of State . . . [Foreign ambassadors] who were never weary of his conversation, respected his talents while they admired the immense variety of his information on all diplomatic points.' Yet with all the pressures of office, Parliament, official entertainment and public social life, he could make time for the private life in which increasingly he experienced his fullest joy.

In Elizabeth he was finding all he needed in a woman; the sexual ease of the street-walkers with accomplishments unknown to them, the friendship, intelligence and political awareness of Duchess Georgiana together with a stability she would never attain. Elizabeth moreover was caring for him in the literal as well as the figurative sense. There were scores both of women and of men, who loved him and delighted in his society, but she was perhaps the first person since his childhood to concern herself over such matters as whether he was eating properly, and getting enough sleep, and had all his buttons sewn on. That care perhaps it was that enabled him, with an intuition that for himself justified his exaltation of passion over reason, to divine in this *poule de luxe* the one woman who could both evoke and assuage his inward need for loving domesticity. Here at last was the companion with whom he could endure anything, without whom he could enjoy nothing.

His certainty of his total need for her, expressed in the distraught letter with which from Newmarket he responded to her effort to break with him, overcame, if not her fears, at least her determination to act on them. It is likely that he received from her some promise never to leave him against his wishes, either in answer to that letter or when in October he returned from East Anglia to spend at St Anne's what he called, in a letter to Lord Northington, 'the few moments of idleness one has just before the opening of the most terrific session of Parliament that ever was held.' It was in the happy knowledge that Elizabeth was his that he went up to the opening of Parliament.

The principal business of this session, the first great achievement of the coalition, was designed to be the passage of the East India Bill. The cause taken up might well have been – and it might have been well if it had been – the reform of Parliament so ardently advocated by Fox in 1780, but the better regulation of the East India Company was dear to the heart of his political mentor Burke, and precedence was therefore given to this measure. A principal provision of the Bill was for the placing of the government of Indian affairs under the control of a board of seven Commissioners, to be appointed by Parliament; that was, by the coalition; that was, in the eyes of an already dubious public, by Fox. He had already enabled his enemies to portray him as a ruthless cynic scrambling to office over his own violated declarations; he now added material for the painting of a ruined gambler recouping his losses by arrogating to himself patronage richer than any wielded by the Crown.

For to the whole country the coalition was Fox's Administration. Portland was Prime Minister, but Portland was Fox's nominee. North, a former Prime Minister and commander of the larger Commons following, was now seen as Fox's henchman; soon he would be caricatured as a bewildered elephant being ridden down Leadenhall Street (seat of the East India Company's headquarters) by 'Carlo Khan'. Indeed, in the eyes of his followers, of Parliament, and of the public at large, Fox was the driving force of Government. At thirty-four and after fourteen years in Parliament, he stood at the summit of power. 'Here is a man who has divided the kingdom with Caesar', declared Dr Johnson, 'so that it was in doubt whether the nation should be ruled by the sceptre of George the Third, or by the tongue of Fox.' Only two people knew that the wielder of this power would have abandoned 'friends, country, everything' rather than part with Elizabeth Armitstead.

The new session opened on November 11th, and a fortnight later Fox moved the Second Reading of the East India Bill. His speech on the motion was deemed one of the finest ever heard even from him, being adjudged by one reporter: 'One of the completest performances ever heard in Parliament, both for accuracy, in the part of it dependent on arithmetical statement, as well as for the finest energy of thought and expression.' But the finest energy of thought and expression could not reconcile the Bill's opponents. Fox himself was well aware of its unpopularity, and his own. To Elizabeth who had remained at St

Anne's Hill when he returned to London, he wrote: 'They are endeavouring to make a great cry against us, and will, I am afraid, make us very unpopular in the City . . . Whether I succeed or not, I shall always be glad I attempted, because I know I have done no more than I am bound to do, in risking my power and that of my friends when the happiness of so many millions is at stake.' It was in connection with the East India Bill that, to the rhetorical question, 'What is the end of all government?' he answered: 'Certainly the happiness of the governed.'

His cohorts, with North's, could carry the Bill through the Commons; the test would come in the House of Lords. The King knew it, and saw his chance to unseat his hated riders. He let it be known that those who supported the bill in the Lords would no longer be regarded as his friends. Such still was his command of patronage that of those who believed in the Bill only the disinterested or the altruistic could ignore the implied threat. They were not enough. On 17th December Administration was defeated in the Lords, and the same day, writing hastily to tell Elizabeth the news, Charles remarked: 'We are not yet out, but I suppose we shall be to-morrow.' They were; and on 19th December the twenty-four-year-old William Pitt became Prime Minister.

Profoundly cast down despite his certainty that no government was possible without control of the Commons, Charles was in desperate need of Elizabeth. She had decided against accompanying him to London on the ground that she feared to go there (her fear being possibly of arrest for debt), and though she had proposed joining him after Christmas she then changed her mind and apparently went to pass the dark days of the solstice at some unidentified resort. The disappointment was more than he could bear. 'I can not have a moment's happiness or rest until I see you again', he wrote to her. 'I had so set my mind upon seeing you now that I can not wean myself from it, and I know I shall be so nervous and out of spirits if you are not here till the 12th that I shall disgrace myself and be thought to be oppressed by the accidents of fortune, which God knows is not the case. On the contrary I think things look well, and if they did not I think I should have courage enough to dispise them; but I can not bear the disappointment of your not coming. Pray come even if you should think it wise to go away again, and come immediately. You may be here by the 7th or 8th. Indeed I do not doubt your affection for me, but if you love me you must come.' She could not resist him; she went.

During the first months of 1784, while Fox and North inflicted defeat after defeat on Pitt in the Commons, Elizabeth remained in London to comfort and cheer her Ex-Secretary. He evidently took the opportunity of her presence there to commission her portrait by Reynolds, whose sitter's book for the year records appointments with her on the 24th, 26th and 30 January and the 2nd and 5th of February. (The resulting portrayal was probably the profile head and shoulders which, though its later history is unknown, survives in an engraving made by S. W. Reynolds in 1825 and titled 'Mrs Fox'.) Charles had need now of his love's sustaining presence, for all the while the tide was running against the coalition leaders; in division after division, the majority against Pitt decreased.

Charles believed himself ambitious, or had done so once. 'I am certainly ambitious by nature,' he had written to Fitzpatrick a few years earlier, 'but I really have or think I have totally subdued that passion.' Even then, probably, he had no idea what that passion could mean, least of all in a man who, like Pitt, had no thought, no interest, no life almost but in his career. Horace Walpole, as delighted by comparisons as Plutarch and with better contemporary material to suggest them, contrasted the two great statesmen of his old age with a vividness to achieve which he disregarded his own earlier tributes to Fox's industry in office. 'The one [Fox] trusted to his natural abilities, and, whenever he wanted, never found them fail. Pitt, on the contrary, attended to nothing but the means of gratifying his abilities. His application was not a moment relaxed . . . No juvenile avocations diverted from his studies, nor left reproaches from the grave on his character. Fox seemed to leave pleasure with regret, and to bestow only spare moments on the government of a nation; Pitt to make industry and virtue the ladders of his ambition. Fox's greatness was innate; and if he had ambition, it was the only passion which he took no pains to gratify.'

Pitt's industry, his resolution, and his careful assessment of his prospects were paying off. When on 18th February Fox moved to postpone the discussion of supplies, the majority against Administration fell to twelve; by 8th March it was down to one. On 24th March Parliament was dissolved, and Fox faced with the prospect of defending his record on the hustings.

Now the electorate had the opportunity of expressing its opinion of the coalition, and now at last Fox realised that the distaste for his actions proclaimed by the Press had not been confined to the Press. In open seats throughout the country supporters of the coalition, 160 in all, lost their seats, and within a couple of weeks Fox himself was struggling to retain his. What he was fighting, however, was not merely the odium of the coalition – indeed, so powerful were his personality and his oratory that this he could have overcome, and Walpole said that if he had been able to fight every seat in the country personally he would have won them all – but the implacable determination of the King and the obedient willingness of the King's servant Pitt to humiliate him by unseating him.

In an election to continue for forty days unless terminated earlier by mutual agreement, there were three candidates for the two Westminster seats; Fox, Admiral Hood – a popular hero who was certain to be returned whatever happened – and Sir Cecil Wray, an undistinguished adherent of the court party. The object of the King was that Wray should be elected with Hood, and to promote it he used every means at his disposition. 'The court exerts itself against him [Fox] in the most violent manner', wrote Walpole, 'by mandates, arts, etc. – nay, sent at once a body of two hundred and eighty of the Guards to give their votes as householders.' So flagrant indeed were the King's tactics as to promote a counter-swing of sympathy for Fox, even the normally subservient Press opining that the King had gone too far. But sympathy would not bring in votes.

To Elizabeth, who had returned to St Anne's Hill soon after the election began, Charles sent a daily bulletin on the state of the poll. On 3rd April:

'The Poll now is

Hood 2185
Wray 1973
Fox 1923

I hope to get up my ground to-morrow, & by Tuesday night should be able to form a judgment. Plenty of bad news from all quarters, but I think (and you won't suspect me of boasting to you) that misfortunes when they come thick have the effect rather of raising my spirits than sinking them. There are few against which I can not bear up and much the greatest of those few it is in your power to prevent ever happening.'

On 7th April:

'Worse & Worse

Hood 4458

Wray 4117

Fox 3827

but I am afraid I must not give up tho' there is little chance indeed.'

On 8th April:

'Hood 4797

Wray 4420

Fox 4126

I must not give up tho' I wish it. I have serious thoughts, if I am beat, of not coming in to Parliament at all, but of all this I will talk with you more as soon as this Business will let me go to you.'

On 9th April, Good Friday:

'The Poll to-day was for one hour only and we had six majority [i.e. of votes cast that day]

Hood 4877

Wray 4489

Fox 4201

'If Sir Cecil does not beat me to-morrow which I think he will not do, I must go on tho' much against my inclination . . . I hope you have had some cross buns to-day. Oh how I do long to see my Liz.'

Now however the balance was beginning to swing against Wray, for now it was that the practice of Charles and his friends of treating women as intelligent beings reaped its reward. Now Westminster beheld the incursion of women into democratic politics, as the Duchess of Devonshire, with her sister and her friends, moved in to canvass for Fox and to win the seat for him and for herself the title of 'Fox's Duchess'. No doubt it was her beauty and her charm that prevailed – together with the flattery of being talked to by a duchess, and carried to the poll in her coach – rather than her reasoning,* but they were great and those of Lady Duncannon scarcely less so, and Administration, looking hastily round for counter-attractions, was forced to realise that the loveliest women of London society were Foxites.

Charles did not tell Elizabeth (who, once wholly committed, could

---

*She did not, as so often alleged, sell kisses for votes. After the election, she wrote to her mother Lady Spencer: 'My Sr and Ly [illegible] were both kiss'd, so it's very hard I who was not sh'd have the reputation of it.'

be jealous) the cause of the upswing in his votes, but he continued to notify her of the rising poll. By 27 April he was in second place.

'Hood 6468

Fox 5827

Wray 5806

I gained 21 to-day and am now as you see 21 ahead . . . I really believe we are quite sure here, but there may be a scrutiny which will be troublesome beyond measure. Adieu my dearest Liz, it is a great part indeed of my pleasure in my triumph to think my Liz will be pleased with it.'

By the start of May he was in hopes of an early finish to the poll, but longing for a visit from Elizabeth ('I have been quite spoiled with seeing you so much this year and begin to [grow] quite uneasy when I am three days without you') and vexed at being absent in the spring, not only from her but from St Anne's. 'Have you any leaves out? or any signs of spring? are you learning Italian or anything else? I hope not reading Herodotus.' The election dragged on its full forty days, for Wray would not concede (and when Parliament resumed Pitt was indeed petty enough to demand a scrutiny) but on 17th May Hood and Fox were declared elected. Fox's victory was celebrated by a triumphal procession, joined by the Prince in Fox's colours of buff and blue, by a breakfast given by the Prince at Carlton House the next day and by a dinner the same evening given by Mrs Crewe. The hero of these triumphs was eager only that they should be over. As soon as he could he left for St Anne's Hill, to renew the enjoyment of the union in which he – the most loved and by many the most esteemed man of his time, the superior in rank, immeasurably the superior in talents – never saw himself as anything but a gainer.

CHAPTER FOUR

The Lady of the Hill

The house that stood on the south-eastern slopes of St Anne's Hill, and took its name therefrom, was a modest dwelling, undistinguished in appearance and with rooms adjudged by some dark and poky. Its charm lay in its situation and environs. Of the ninety-odd acres attaching to the property some two-thirds, of pasture and arable on the lower slopes of the hill, were sub-let to a local farmer, but there remained about the house a demesne of garden and woodland that, crowning and circling the summit, afforded both an immediate pleasure-ground and an outlook over wide distances. The hill, a modest eminence of some 240 feet, commands nevertheless from the flatness of the surrounding countryside vistas that range in clear weather from the Chilterns to the Surrey Hills, and up and down the winding Thames to Berkshire westward and eastward to St Pauls; and these, in the late eighteenth century, were the prerogative of the occupant of the house on the hill.

Though the small town of Chertsey lay some half a mile distant from the foot of the hill, the pleasures the district offered to Elizabeth were wholly rural. With neither theatre nor Assembly rooms to provide the local gentry with a venue for public entertainment, social occasions open to both sexes were private, and inevitably closed to a visiting Cyprian. The pastimes available to a lady excluded from local society must therefore be predominantly those to content the self-sufficient: walking, riding and perhaps gardening when the weather was favourable, reading, sewing and music-making when it was not.

When Elizabeth Armitstead first leased St Anne's Hill she was thirty-one years old, and of an age by which those capable of self-knowledge have normally attained to it. Whether she initially looked on this country home as a summer residence merely or already envisaged the possibility of ultimate retirement there, she would scarcely have assumed the liability of a second dwelling without having considered what her life there might be. The odds are that she was already inclining towards the pleasures of rusticity. That the gratification of any lover formed part of her intention is improbable, despite the *Morning Herald's* observation that: 'this seat is in the neighbourhood of *Windsor,* and a certain *heir apparent* frequently hunts and shoots near it'; in the summer of 1781 she had been trying to loosen the Prince's attachment, and the other lovers circling about her owned or had access to country houses compared with which St Anne's Hill was a cottage.

By the time Charles joined her at St Anne's in May, 1784, she had spent the better part of a year there, and had begun to use the place as her principal home. Considerations of cost may have affected her decision, for the upkeep of the Clarges Street establishment at its accustomed level was scarcely feasible without the earnings that had supported it, but already she preferred rural occupations to the gaieties of town. Her activities would have astonished the *Morning Herald.* She, whose observable pedestrian exercise had been an occasional descent from her phaeton to saunter the greensward of the Park, now rambled the woods and tramped the lanes of Surrey. Already perhaps she did so attended by the dog or dogs that soon would become inevitable walking companions, for even amid the agitations of the Westminster election Charles had written to her: 'Richard denies having given you the puppy, but I hope you called for it and took it with you to-day.' She discovered that riding was more than an uncomfortable means of self-display, and renewed the skills Lord Derby had imparted to range farther than her feet could carry her and deeper into the country than wheels could go.* In the evenings she sewed, read or practised her music. And, as her first spring at St Anne's advanced, she studied the birds that nested and the flowers that grew in her own grounds, and wished to know more about these things.

Charles, returning from London, flung himself delightedly into these pursuits, that became even more agreeable when shared. A great walker in his youth (he and Thomas Dickson, later Bishop of Down, had once as undergraduates with pockets to let walked from Oxford to Holland House in a day), he rejoiced to discover that his love was also an excellent pedestrian. He was eager to visit with her the scenes of beauty she had discovered in his absence. He was fascinated by the garden, and

---

*As an old woman she drove to Englefield Green in fruitless search of 'a beautiful vista there used to be a hundred years ago when I used to ride . . . in those days I used to go there on horseback.' Journal, 31st May, 1834.

soon was enthusiastically joining in plans for its improvement. Birdsong he loved, and how could a day more deliciously end than in twilight wanderings with Liz through the nightingale-haunted woods of St Anne's.

And if weather kept them indoors, there were books. Elizabeth's higher education now began under the guidance of one of the most widely read men of her time. Charles's appetite for reading had always been as voracious as his other appetites, and few even among academics of the period could have matched his knowledge of literature. The standard public-school grounding in Greek and Latin had been for him merely a foundation on which he had since constantly built, while in the then untaught living literatures he was deeply versed. Long before the Romantic Revival rendered them fashionable he read the plays of Elizabethans and Jacobeans other than Shakespeare. He read Chaucer in the original and Chaucer as rendered by Dryden, and he read Dryden's original work with such delight that he talked of wishing to edit it. He read Pope's 'Eloisa to Abelard', and then he read the letters of Heloise to Abelard and decided Pope had misrepresented her. He read Racine and Molière, he read Dante and Tasso and Ariosto; and having learned Italian he read Guicciardini too, for he applied himself to history as eagerly as to literature. All these and many more were now at Elizabeth's service.

Reading, when Charles was at St Anne's, was generally as mutual a pleasure as most others. Reading aloud – reading out, as Elizabeth called it – was still a common custom, and how could she more pleasantly become acquainted with the books he loved than by reading them with him. Sometimes it was Elizabeth who 'read out', but more frequently Charles read as she sewed. The hope he had expressed during the Westminster election, that she was not reading Herodotus, cannot have reflected any wish that she should continue unacquainted with the writer he described to her as the prince of authors; almost certainly his aim had been that she should not anticipate the mutual enjoyment he foresaw in their reading Herodotus together. This of course would have been in translation, or with Charles translating as he read, for, much as he delighted in classical literature, he did not expect Elizabeth to learn Greek or Latin. His enquiry as to her learning Italian may however have stemmed from a hope that she would master it sufficiently to read Ariosto, for this was the writer, in a living language not his own, who pleased him above all others. 'For God's sake learn Italian as soon as you can', he had once written to Fitzpatrick, 'to read Ariosto.'

The scene of these innocent pleasures was an upstairs drawing-room, chosen no doubt for its view, where Charles and Elizabeth now began to gather their books and their favourite pictures. Elizabeth's harpsichord too stood there, but this did not represent a shared pleasure. Disappointingly for her, the one art with which she was already somewhat acquainted, and in a modest way practised, was the only one to which Charles was wholly indifferent. Music gave him no enjoyment. Since she was no more prepared to sink her individuality in their union than he desirous that she should, she played and sang when she chose to whether he liked it or not. She later informed Samuel Rogers that Charles's aversion to music was the one fault she had to find with him, and that the best she could say for him was that he could read Homer while she played and sang to herself in the same room. The same room it had to be; Charles did not like to be separated from Elizabeth by as much as a door.

While Elizabeth loved to share with Charles the quiet life of St Anne's Hill, she may have had another motive for encouraging him to remain there; it was good for him. The determination once directed at professional success was now focused on his welfare. His health and his happiness were now her primary concerns, and though the latter might still be served by the way of life he had followed since boyhood, the former certainly would not. When the extent to which Charles's London life was damaging his constitution had been discerned even by an acquaintance like Wraxall, it is hardly possible that Elizabeth, loving and observing him more closely than any, should have been unaware of it. She herself seems to have had the regard to her own welfare advisable in those used to living on earnings that depend on continued health, and her gentle management of Charles suggests the application to him of her principles of healthy living. Exercise was good for him. A sensible diet was good for him, and unlimited wine was not. Gaming was bad for his health as well as his pocket, and his notorious abstentions from sleep were very bad for him. At Chertsey there were no gaming-rooms, control of the household gave control of diet, Charles loved to walk and ride with her, and there was no difficulty at all about getting him early to a bed she shared. Quietly and unobtrusively, the prostitute was setting about the reform of the rake.

His continued absence from London, however, perturbed the dispirited Foxites, gathering there to lick their wounds and ponder what courses might be open to so defeated a faction. Fox had attended Parliament (sitting as member for the pocket borough of Kirkwall) when it resumed at the end of May, to oppose the Westminster scrutiny, against which on 8th June he had made one of his most acclaimed speeches, but not long after, and though Parliament was still sitting, the lure of St. Anne's overcame him once more. 'Heard that Mr Fox had greatly offended his friends', wrote the former Maid of Honour Lady Mary Hamilton, 'by his *late* absence from the House of Commons, they wrote to remonstrate with him on the folly and impropriety of it; he sent for answer that he was very happy & quiet at St Anne's Hill with Mrs Armistead, that he thought he should stay sometime longer, & concluded his letter by saying that Mrs A. wondered that they did not come and see her.' The final observation probably distorts (Mary Hamilton, a courtier and a very proper young lady, disapproved of the couple at St Anne's Hill both politically and morally) a more graciously worded invitation. Elizabeth had no wish to keep Charles from his friends, so many of whom were hers too, and both were happy to welcome them at St Anne's. The house was small, but beds could speedily be re-organised to accommodate guests. 'If you come alone there is no doubt of room', Charles had written to Fitzpatrick the previous year, 'but even if Hare or Jack [Townshend] would come with you and you would let me know one day before I could manage it . . . The Hog is killed and one part or other of him will be good for several days to come.'

'The Hog is killed.' They were living simply now, and not only because they were both coming to appreciate plainness in diet. They were at this time very hard up. Charles's loss of office had brought all his creditors down upon him, and the very chair-carriers were dunning him for arrears of payment. 'Fox possessed no funds whatever', wrote Wraxall, 'and scarcely could raise money for his subsistence. His creditors had even become so numerous or importunate about this time, that his effects and books being seized at his lodgings, contiguous to Brookes's in St James's Street, he was reduced during a few days or weeks to take refuge at the house of a friend, Mr. Moore.' This may have been the reason why, this summer, he sometimes when in London used Elizabeth's house; Lady Mary Hamilton – a Clarges Street resident who seems to have kept interested watch on the door of her disreputable neighbour – more than once deduced, from seeing the Prince's carriage outside 'Mrs Armistead's' house, that Mr Fox was in London. Elizabeth herself came as far to the rescue of her beleaguered lover as her resources permitted, selling now, according to the *Morning Post,* the two settlements she had secured during her professional career. Thus she sealed her commitment to Charles by reducing herself, at the very nadir of his fortunes, to final economic dependence on him.

His career in ruins, his finances disastrous, but Elizabeth wholly his, Charles was happy as long as he could be at St Anne's. Hare at about this time compared him to Mark Antony, and Elizabeth to Cleopatra, holding her leader of men from the centre of power by the countervailing power of her allurements. It was a neat comparison (and would have been neater still had it taken in the cold young Octavian at Westminster), for Charles was enamoured not of a woman only but of her environment. 'He has given up all hope of change in Ministry,' wrote Lady Sarah Napier in September, '& comforts himself with Mrs Armisted, & all he seems to lament is the want of £2,000 for to buy the house at St Anne's Hill which he longs for.'

Somehow they managed, coming about over the next year well enough for the desire to be fulfilled, even if only by the incurring of a new debt. Elizabeth was the actual purchaser, the reason possibly being that her ownership would preclude any risk of distraint on the property for Charles's debts. On 8th September, 1785, her long unused surname was briefly disinterred when George, Duke of Marlborough (acting through his attorney), surrendered the copyhold messuage of St Anne's Hill (sic), with its buildings, pastures, woodlands and arable, and subject to its tenancies and occupations, for £2,000 'to the use and behoof of Elizabeth Bridget Cane of St Anne's Hill in the parish of Chertsey, spinster'; who at once surrendered it back to him on a loan of £2,000, at £100 a year interest.

St Anne's now her own, if mortgaged, Elizabeth set off for a destination which suggests that, however dear her home to her heart, its location was less than ideally suited to her constitution. Among the ailments for which the saline springs of Cheltenham, the still modest spa she now visited, were deemed beneficial was rheumatism, by which she was to be plagued in after years and which may already have begun to affect her. This, together with a liability to severe winter colds which now began to manifest itself, suggests that she might have done better to settle elsewhere than in a river valley. No such notion however would have been tolerable to her or to Charles. St Anne's was and was to remain their dear home, their paradise on earth, falling short of perfection only by such deficiencies as they might find pleasure in redressing. Most immediate, most delightful to improve, was the garden.

Even before Elizabeth purchased the property, they had set about improving it. Charles, whose genius for friendship ensured that he was seldom in want of any expert help he might need, numbered among the friends retained from his schooldays the amateur landscape gardener Uvedale Price, and Price was now levied upon both for plants and for information. 'What is the name of the particular Aliburnus you recommended to me?' wrote Charles to him. 'Will any trees or shrubs grow well under shade? Ought Rhododendrons to cost 10s a piece? do they require any particular soil? I want to know the same about Calme's and Azaleas? Was it not the *Canada* poplar you recommended to me?' Horticulture, Fox found, was an expensive pleasure; the man who had gambled away £130,000 now lamented: 'I hear of this plant costing 1s this 1s 6d and so on and in one little walk which is all that I have finished there appear to me to be thousands of plants. There are two nurserymen hereabouts both Scotchmen and my Gardener is a Scotchman too, so that it is not impossible but that I may be a little cheated into the Bargain! . . . there are great inconveniences in this perfect ignorance of mine, because they all know it and tell me what they please.'

Obviously help was needed at St Anne's and in due course Price visited the enthusiastic and ignorant horticulturalists and set them on the right track. Though Charles continued active in the garden – sallying forth girt in a green apron to prune his fruit trees –, the real beneficiary of Price's teaching was Elizabeth, who over the years was to render herself expert both in plant-growing and in garden design. She had of course more opportunity to practise her learning than Charles, for much as he delighted in St Anne's, he could not indefinitely so resist either his friends' entreaties or his own sense of duty as to remain perpetually a virtual absentee from Westminster.

Not even at St Anne's Hill could he be quite free from political worries, and in 1785 a substantial worry was pursuing him there in the person of the Prince aflame with his passion for Mrs Fitzherbert. This lovely widow, whom the Prince had first encountered early in 1784, had evoked in him an ardour chafed by the obduracy of her virtue into an obsessional determination to possess her, if by no other means, then by marriage. Such a marriage would have been both unlawful under the Royal Marriages Act and, Mrs Fitzherbert being a Roman Catholic, a bar under the Act of Settlement to the Prince's succession to the throne; these considerations proving insufficient to cool the Prince's ardour, the lady prudently went abroad to escape his pursuit. Absence had however its proverbial effect. The Prince grew frantic, declaiming his anguish to any friendly ear, and sometimes going to St Anne's to call upon the sympathies of Elizabeth and Charles. He cried by the hour, Elizabeth afterward told Lord Holland, and 'testified the sincerity and violence of his passion and his despair by the most extravagent expressions and actions, rolling on the floor, striking his forehead, tearing his hair, and swearing that he would abandon the country, forego the crown, sell his jewels and plate and scrape together a competence to fly with the object of his affections to America.'

They sympathised: how could they not. None knew better than they how a variety of attachments could precede a deep and exclusive devotion, and it was little more than two years since Charles had declared himself ready to abandon friends, country, everything, and live abroad in obscurity rather than part with Elizabeth. The lover in Charles could sympathise, but the politician, to whose hopes and prospects the Prince's succession was important, was alarmed. His alarm increased when towards the end of 1785, the lady returning from abroad, rumours of the Prince's intention to marry her were revived. On 10th December he wrote to the Prince a long and carefully considered letter, stressing the risks as well as the illegality of such a marriage, and wisely taking note of the lady's interests and the harm an ambiguous marital situation could do both to her and to any children who might be born of such a union. The Prince immediately replied: 'Make yourself easy, my dear friend: the world will soon be convinced that there not only is, but never was, any ground for these reports.' Charles was content. It was more than a year before he learned that, four days after writing that letter, the Prince had secretly married Mrs Fitzherbert.

Charles himself was happily adjusting to a largely marital way of life. While Parliament was sitting he spent most of his time in London pursuing much his former round, but solaced himself with brief visits to St Anne's. Elizabeth came often to stay with him at his house in South Street (she had given up the Clarges Street lease at about the time of the St Anne's purchase), for she had no intention of absenting herself wholly from the theatre, the Opera, or the best shops in the country. Her visits enabled her too to keep some check of Charles's less healthful courses; if she could not keep him from Brooks's or from the stag-parties at which he was apt to drink too much wine, she would probably reckon that the knowledge she was waiting in his bed would keep him from lingering there. She could ensure too that he spent some time in the fresh air, walking in the Park with her or driving in her vis-a-vis, the small open carriage in which she liked to take an airing; they were out in it together when William Ogilvie, second husband of Charles's aunt, the Duchess of Leinster,[*] encountered them, writing afterward to tell his wife that Mrs Armitstead was 'a pleasing, good-humoured-looking woman with good teeth and a bad complexion' – this last probably resulting from former use of the damaging cosmetics of the period.

Elizabeth's stays in London do not however appear to have been prolonged. The time Charles could spend with her there was limited, not only by the demands of the Commons but by his involvement in a social life in which she could no more join him at mixed than at all-male gatherings. When he was engaged to dine with the Duchess of Devonshire, with Mrs Crewe, with that less famous but scarcely less charming Whig hostess Mrs Bouverie or with any other of the many ladies who took pleasure in seeing him in their drawing-rooms, Elizabeth if in London must be left alone or go to places of public entertainment with another companion. Charles himself may have preferred on such occasions to think of her at Chertsey rather than visiting without him those haunts in which she was still the celebrated, and supposedly still purchaseable, 'Mrs. Armitstead'.

With the rising of Parliament in June there began the best period of the year, with the flowers out and the birds singing at St Anne's, and Charles free to enjoy with Elizabeth – and both of them happy to share with visiting friends – the rural pleasures of their dear home. Then when high summer was past some little holiday might be taken, perhaps

[*]As was then usual when a peeress by marriage remarried in widowhood a husband of lower rank than her first, the Duchess continued to use the title deriving from her first marriage; though for the last forty years of her life she was to modern thinking Lady Emily Ogilvie, to contemporaries she was the Duchess of Leinster to the end.

in Brighthelmstone, the Sussex fishing village that had caught the Prince's fancy, or in Cheltenham, the waters of which Elizabeth was finding beneficial; in August, 1786, Charles accompanied her there, and was reported by Hare to be entirely occupied in taming a young rabbit. After this, the longest separation of the year began, with Charles's departure for Newmarket and the subsequent shooting-parties at the mansions or lodges of friends and relations in East Anglia, with Lord Albemarle at Quidenham, the Duke of Bedford at Eldon, the Duke of Grafton at Euston – all these distant cousins by virtue of a common ancestor in Charles II –, and always with a stay at Thomas Coke's Holkham. No doubt because of the length of these separations, a high proportion of the letters from Charles to Elizabeth that survive were written from Newmarket or from one of those houses. From these letters it may be deduced that his dearest Liz did not approve of the Newmarket visits, no doubt for financial reasons (when, later, racegoing became permissible for ladies she enjoyed a day at the races, but as an added occasion for meeting friends and not from any interest in the sport), but approved the shooting. Letters from Newmarket are normally silent about the events there, whereas those from the shooting-parties enthusiastically recount the events of the day, and detail Charles's modest bags. Shooting in those days was a simple and unorganised affair, each sportsman setting out with his fowling-piece and his dogs to tramp for miles about the country in pursuit of game; this exercise in the fresh air was very good for Charles, and Elizabeth was pleased that he should be getting it. 'My Liz says she wishes she could shoot too, and so do I with all my heart, and when I have made a good shot I often think how I should like to turn round and see my dear Liz's lovely face smiling and encouraging me, and even when I do ill, I should like to hear her find fault with me and see her look contemptuously as she does when I am awkward at carving.'

The traffic of letters at these times was two-way, but none of Elizabeth's survives in the Fox and Holland House correspondence. The odds are that after Charles's death she destroyed her letters to him. Certainly it is improbable that he failed to preserve what so rejoiced him to receive. 'I am *so* happy my Love is pleased with my letters, to think that I please her makes me so very very happy. It is a nice thing to have letters the first thing in the morning, tho' here [Holkham] it is the next best time, because when I have done shooting and have perhaps three or four *dis** miles to walk home, I am thinking all the while, that as soon as I get to the house, I shall find a nice letter from my Love, & she will tell me she loves me and make me *so* happy and then I am never disappointed. Elizabeth herself had no opinion of her letters, once saying she did not think them worth the postage (then paid by the recipient), and certainly she was no Madame de Sevigné; the diary she later kept, and her surviving letters, are limited in vocabulary and flat in style. She had one epistolary gift only, clear in the letters she wrote in old age to a much-loved great-niece by marriage – a singular talent for suffusing her letters with the affection she felt for the addressee. To Charles it must have outweighed all deficiencies.

In November there would be a reunion at St Anne's before Parliament resumed and Charles began his London life again. At that time of the year, with Charles absent, the garden dormant, the weather damp and discouraging, Elizabeth was inclined to take a holiday on her own. In 1786 the two must have been feeling comparatively affluent, for she went to Paris, and was still there on 24th January, 1787, Charles's thirty-eighth birthday, when he sat down to write her a letter so comprehensive that the lost one it answers can almost be reconstructed from it.

'My dearest Liz, I went to the House of Cs just after I finished my letter, and upon the whole it was thought by others as well as myself that I should speak and not just let the thing go off quite silently which if I had not spoken it must have done. I spoke pretty strongly against french connections & France,' he had in fact been opposing Pitt's Anglo-French commercial treaty on the ground, among others, that the French were the natural enemies of the English, 'and Pitt made as bad a speech in answer as could be wished. There was no more debate and no division so that I was [in] time to go to dinner at Derby's where every body seemed to think I had done right. I know the French well enough to know that though they are very civil & such of them as hear me may say I speak well upon these subjects, yet they will make it the fashion some way or another to run me down, so that if you should hear me spoken of differently from what you wish, you must not mind it. It may be ridiculous Vanity in me to think that they will take any notice of me, but I know how attentive they are to these things, & how very adverse

*Dismal. Charles and Elizabeth's 'little language' reduced certain words to their first or principal syllables.

they were to me as a Minister, particularly on account of the friendship they thought I was cultivating with Prussia, but this is enough of *Pols*, so now to Liz's letter – I am very glad you saw Andromaque; I think upon the stage it is the best of all french tragedies, though Phedre, Athalie, Britannicus & Iphigenie all read as well if not better. I always thought Mlle. Vestris a good Actress, but not quite as good as you represent her. I used to think she had great propriety, but a little appearance of *study* which I do not like. I have always made one remark upon this play which is a very singular one and I think you will agree with me; I mean that in English Andromache appears to be much the principal part, but in French Hermione appears to be full as interesting; and yet it is a litteral [sic] translation. I dare say the dress at Paris is ridiculous enough by some specimens I have seen of it here. It appears to me particularly *ridic* for [illegible] as to the Women's dress I have not seen much of it. I suppose however you will grow to like it as one does all fashions, I dare say I shall like it upon Liz as I do everything else. Come home soon and be kind and good to old one, and it does not *sig* [signify] how you are drest. If you did but know the sort of longing I have to see you, you would not stay long; & the more I receive of your letters the more I long. I will if I can possibly go to St Anne's Saturday or Sunday if it is only to think of Liz in peace and quiet & to think over how happy I have been there. As you complain so much of cold it must certainly have been colder with you than here, for even I have never thought it very bad, & now it is very warm and much such winter weather as I like; it is very provoking to be shut up in Paris I allow, but that must not be a pretence for staying longer than you intended. I have not seen poor Mrs M. since I wrote, but I will go again. [This unidentifiable lady, apparently a friend of Elizabeth's, may possibly be Mrs. Marston.] It is indeed a miserable thing to lose [someone] one has so long lived with & death is the worst way but any way is bad enough – I dare say the assemblée de Notables is some scheme about money, and I wish to God they may be unwise enough to have recourse to some of their old tricks which would ruin their Credit, & be the only means of saving this Country, but I can hardly hope this. As to my sitting up I told you to-day was to begin the session, and I did go to bed reasonably early, but I was so much fatigued with speaking (not being in practice) that I did not get up very early, but it is now not two so that I shall have time for some walk before I go down to the House; about an hour hence

Liz will be drinking my good health. Thirty-eight years have I lived most of them very happy, and I do not know any thing at all serious that I have to reproach myself with; the remaining half of my life whether it is to be happy or otherwise depends entirely upon you, indeed it does. I never can be happy now I have known you but with you. It is not flattery but judgment in me. I have known many men and many women, and for many of them I have great friendship & esteem, but I never did know and never shall man or woman who deserved to be loved like Liz, & I am so convinced of this that having you for my Wife appears to me a full compensation for every disappointment.'

His wife she had become to his heart, but to the rest of the world she was still Mrs Armitstead, and to the law Elizabeth Cane, spinster. Their failure to give their union legal status appears to have been by Elizabeth's decision. For all Charles's insistence that he would love her always, she believed that one day he would wish to marry elsewhere, even if for prudential reasons only, and could not bear to think that a potentially unwanted legal tie to her should ever restrict his freedom. She herself may have paid some price in emotional insecurity for this decision, and also perhaps in a conflict between her situation and her religious beliefs, but Charles's good as she saw it came first.

Charles, unaware that any sacrifice was being made, was content with the position. He wholly, and rightly, trusted Elizabeth's commitment to him. No legal bond could strengthen a union that to him was absolute, and the sacramental aspect was irrelevant to one who, if not entirely agnostic, looked upon religious rituals as meaningless. One eventuality alone might have made him insist on marriage: the prospect of a child. It is improbable that he would in any circumstances have accepted bastardy for his child by the woman he adored, the more particularly as he was at this period heir presumptive to his father's title; his letter to the Prince about Mrs Fitzherbert had reflected careful thought concerning the problems caused by fertility in a dubious marital situation. But for him the question did not arise; Elizabeth did not conceive.* The defect almost certainly was in her, for Charles had

---

*Drinkwater in his 'C. J. Fox' recorded (p.287) that the Rev. E. V. R. Powys, Fox's great-grand-nephew, told him he remembered two old ladies at Chertsey who were the natural children of Fox and Mrs Armitstead. Mr Powys's annotations of Mrs Fox's Journal (entry for 9th June, 1823 and of a letter from Miss Marston (British Museum Add. MSS 52170) make it clear however that the ladies in question were Harriet Willoughby, Charles's daughter but not Elizabeth's, and Elizabeth Marston, who was no relation to either.

fathered two children.

In fact, of those Cyprians who ended their careers in marriage or in a stable union – such as Fanny Murray, Nancy Parsons, Harriet Powell as well as Elizabeth – not one is known to have borne a child. It is perhaps significant that all these were women of low birth, dependent during their careers on their earnings. In general, the few courtesans known to have borne children during their careers either did so within a temporarily stable union with a man who could be relied on to support the mother during pregnancy and the child when born (as with Charlotte Spencer and the daughter she bore to the Duke of Devonshire), or, like the well-connected Grace Dalrymple Eliot, had independent resources. For the necessarily self-supporting whore, sterility, whether congenital or induced by early venereal disease or abortion, was a professional advantage. A pregnancy carried to term, eliminating months of earning capacity and resulting in a second mouth to feed, could represent an irrecoverable setback. In the very month, January, 1781, when the *Morning Herald* had been issuing bulletins on the duel for the Prince between 'Mrs Armstead' and Mrs Robinson, the soberer *Morning Chronicle* had related the end of a woman who might once have rivalled them. 'On Sunday lately . . . died Mrs Elizabeth Wooley, one of the prettiest women to have figured in the circles of purchaseable beauty these many years past . . . A few years since, she was the chief toast among those who pledge the fair frail in their cups, and lived in all the splendour and expense attainable by the artfully complying fair . . . She has been on the decline for the past two years and . . . has moved in a very mortifying and humble state of prostitution. She now lies a corpse in her 25th year, and has left a young daughter without a shilling for her maintenance.' No reason is given for Mrs Wooley's decline, but the birth of her child could have been the accident that cast her down from the ladder she had ascended so high.

Childlessness in a stable and loving union was another matter. Both Elizabeth and Charles loved children, and her infertility was probably a severe disappointment to them. It may have been fortunate nonetheless, for both Charles's children proved defective. His son Henry Fox, apparently, born about 1780, was totally deaf – the effect perhaps of a defective gene deriving from Charles's Lennox inheritance, for the later consanguinous marriage of Charles's niece Caroline Fox and his first cousin William Napier, whose common blood was Lennox, produced two congenitally deaf children. Charles's daughter Harriet, known as Harriet Willoughby, had however all her senses, and that she lacked sense to a degree approaching weak-wittedness had not yet become evident. It was apparently she whom Charles first introduced to his 'wife', some time in 1787.* At this stage there was no question of bringing her to live at St Anne's for she lived with her mother, who apparently had married a Mr Harvey,** but they may have hoped to compensate with her occasional presence for the lack of any child of the house.

The real beneficiary of their frustrated parental feelings was however Lord Holland. No orphan was ever better furnished with father-substitutes than the youthful third baron, who, having lost a dull and stupid father before he was one year old, grew up the loved and cared-for nephew of three intelligent uncles two of whom – Lord Ossory and Fitzpatrick – were sonless while the third, Charles, had only his poor handicapped Harry. Holland was now at Eton, most conveniently placed for visits to an uncle at Chertsey, and Elizabeth loved having him there as much as Charles did. When Holland was at St Anne's she had two Foxes about the place, an old one and a young one, and 'old one' and 'young one' – pronounced old 'un and young 'un – became the pet-names in use among the three. Elizabeth's own designation was the Lady of the Hill, a dignity perhaps bestowed by Holland, in one of whose letters it first appears.

In April, 1787, the Prince's affairs again impinged on Charles's. In a debate on the debts of the heir apparent a Tory back-bencher raised the question of his marriage with a subject and a Catholic. Fox rose, confident in the assurance given him in December, 1785, and denied 'on direct authority' that such marriage had taken place. The outraged Mrs Fitzherbert (who indeed never forgave Fox) complained to the Prince, who assured her Fox had spoken without authority, and admitted the truth to Charles Grey. Grey naturally told Fox, whose turn it was to be outraged, both at the deceit practised on him and at his having been deluded by it into telling the House a lie. He broke with the Prince, who however refused to see himself as broken with; deleting from his

---

*Mrs Fox's Journal, 3rd August, 1831. 'Harriet's birthday, she is fifty and I have known her forty-four years.'
**Journal, 3rd September, 1830. 'Captain Harvey Harriet's Brother and his Daughter arrived.'

memory, as always, any action of his that had given offence, he continued to declare that Fox was his dearest friend. In the autumn he tried to arrange an encounter at Holkham, proposing himself for his usual annual visit there at a date to coincide with Fox's, whereupon Thomas Coke – vicariously offended by the offence to Charles – magnificently replied: 'Holkham is open to Strangers on Tuesdays.' Unabashed, the Prince descended on Holkham nonetheless, and what saved Charles from a confrontation that would have embarrassed him acutely was an illness of Elizabeth's. She had been so unwell in September – probably with one of the acute feverish colds that often smote her, and left troublesome after-effects – that Charles had hesitated over leaving her, but when she appeared almost recovered he set off as usual, only to learn soon after reaching Holkham that she had had a relapse. He left at once, and the same evening the unexpected and unwanted Prince arrived, to be entertained by an extremely uncordial host and to give at dinner repeated toasts to 'the best man in England – Mr Fox.'

Elizabeth soon recovered fully, and may have regretted that her illness had prevented a possible reconciliation with the Prince. She had a very soft spot still for Florizel, and perhaps could not enter quite into Charles's horror at his deceitfulness; it was not she after all who had been duped into lying to the House. She had yet to find out for herself that the Prince was, in Grey's words, 'the worst anchoring-ground in Europe.'

That winter, Charles began seriously to focus his attention on a public issue on which, more than most, he had Elizabeth's sympathetic interest. She never pretended to follow and understand all political matters that concerned her lover ('I know my Liz interests herself in some things in Politics', wrote Charles to her once, clearly accepting that in others she did not), but in the abolition of the slave trade, with its moral significance so clear to one Christian in belief if vague in doctrine, she did interest herself. A stray sheet of a letter from Charles, lacking its beginning and undated (but for 'Tuesday') may have been written about this time, for it shows him gathering information 'upon the Slave Trade, and have canvassed upon the subject with a very well informed person, who had an estate in the W. Indies and is convinced the plantations there can go on without Slaves as well or better than with them. In short I am very much inclined to undertake the business but I must both read and hear more before I engage. I should like very much to put an end to so vile a thing if possible, and so would Liz too.' This inclination brought him into unlikely conjunction with that pious Pittite William Wilberforce; yet all the two could in alliance achieve, on their first essay in the spring of 1788, was a small measure for the regulation of what they were resolved must be abolished.

To Elizabeth the summer of 1788 brought more personal cause for worry. Once again rumour was busy with a possible marriage, but not, this time, the Prince's; the marriage now being gossiped about was that of Charles. His friends, long convinced that only by marriage could he repair his shattered finances and sure that the step should not be much longer delayed, had found a fortune for him. The woman who went with it was the redhaired Henrietta Pulteney, heiress through her mother of the last Earl of Bath. Early in 1788 a campaign was launched to turn Miss Pulteney into Mrs Fox. 'All his friends aided a cause which, by rendering their chief independent in his fortune, would have healed the pecuniary wounds inflicted by his early indiscretion,' wrote Wraxall. 'Colonel Fitzpatrick, with friendly solicitude, usually kept a place for him near the lady [at the trial of Warren Hastings], and for some time the courtship assumed so auspicious an appearance that I remember Hare, when speculating on the probable issue of the marriage, said with inimitable humour that they would inevitably be duns with black manes and tails.' Anthony Storer too regarded the marriage as a settled thing, writing to William Eden. 'What do you think of Mr Fox going to be married, and to Miss Pulteney?'

The disregard by Fitzpatrick and Hare of Elizabeth's happiness was natural, and not only because to them Charles's was paramount. The union at St Anne's Hill was inevitably still seen by outsiders as temporary. Naturally Charles needed a mistress as long as he was a bachelor, and his domestication by his most recent love simply rendered him the better prepared for marriage. Naturally too his mistress would understand that he should, indeed must, marry, and be prepared for the ineluctable parting. So indeed she was.

The person who did not appreciate all these obvious facts was Charles, who did not even see himself as a bachelor. The most unsuspicious of men, he was perfectly willing to talk with any young lady pressed on his attention by Duchess Georgiana and his other friends, with no more thought of marrying her than of marrying Queen

Charlotte. Some time in the summer his friends' hopes were dashed, for, recorded Wraxall, 'the affair nevertheless terminated, from whatever cause, without success.' The cause may have been that Charles at last found out why his friends liked to see him talking with Miss Pulteney.

That discovery perhaps contributed to his decision to take Elizabeth abroad for a holiday. As soon as the election of 1788 (at which Lord John Townshend was returned with Fox for Westminster) had run its course, they set out together for a tour of the Continent – taking with them, indigent though they were, their own postchaise and a modest retinue of servants. The holiday was to be a complete break. English affairs were to be put quite out of mind; even newspapers were to be looked at for the racing results only; and Charles told his friends that he did not mean to send or wish to receive any letters. In consequence, little is known directly of the details of their jaunt, most information on it coming either from those whose tracks they crossed or from the letters that Charles exchanged some four years later with Holland, when his nephew was covering some of the same ground. These incidentally reveal that the irritation Elizabeth suffered from the attentions of vermin, so much more prevalent in Continental than in English inns, was aggravated by the discovery that her Angel was immune. Holland was not. 'She used to complain of the fleas sparing you,' he would write from Bilbao in 1792, 'they are not so kind to your nephew, for I am bit to death.' Charles replied: 'Mrs A . . . . . is not sorry you are bit by the fleas that you may sometimes pity her. She wishes you were bit by bed-bugs into the bargain, & I do not suppose she will wish in vain.'

About the middle of August they passed through Paris – their passage noted by the English ambassador there, Elizabeth's one-time lover the Duke of Dorset – to continue southward to Switzerland. There, they were delayed by Elizabeth's spraining her ankle, an injury from which apparently she had recovered by mid-September, when William Windham (who had been on their tracks for some days) caught them up at Bienne, to spend the 11th and 12th with them. On 13th September both parties left, separately, for Lausanne where – the presence of Fox at the Lion d'or there having been notified to the town's most famous English resident – 17th September was passed in the society of Edward Gibbon.

The two men had known each other previously, when Gibbon was a member of the Commons. He had never been a Foxite, but had declared himself independent of faction until, after in 1778 he had voted against Administration, North had bought his future votes with a sinecure worth £800 a year; whereupon Fox had written, in the flyleaf of a volume of 'The Decline and Fall of the Roman Empire' given him by Gibbon, 'The author, at Brookes's, said there was no salvation for this country till six heads of the principal persons of the Administration were laid on the table; eleven days after, this same gentleman accepted the place of Lord of Trade under those very same Ministers, and has acted with them ever since.' This observation became public two years later, on the sale of Fox's books after the seizure of his goods for debt (and sent up the price of that volume to three guineas), but, Gibbon wrote of Fox long after, 'Let him do what he will, I must love the dog.' He was delighted now to discover the dog in Lausanne, and a fortnight later wrote to tell Lord Sheffield all about it.

'The man of the people escaped from the tumult, the bloody tumult of the Westminster Election, to the lakes and mountains of Switzerland, and I was informed that he was arrived at the Lyon-d'or. I sent a compliment, he answered it in person we returned together to the Inn, brought away the fair Mrs Armstead, and settled at my house for the remainder of the day. I have eat and drunk and sat up all night with Fox in England, but it has never happened perhaps it can never happen again that I should enjoy him as I did that day, alone, (for his fair Companion was a cypher) from ten in the morning till ten at night . . . Our conversation never flagged a moment, and he seemed thoroughly pleased with the place and with his company. We had little politicks, though he gave me in a few words such a character of Pitt as one great man should give of another his rival; much of books, from my own on which he flattered me very pleasantly to Homer and the Arabian nights; much about the country, my garden which he understands far better than I do, and upon the whole he envies me and would do so if he were Minister. The next morning I gave him a guide to walk him about the town and country and invited some company to meet him at dinner. The following day he continued his journey to Bern à Zurich, and I have heard of him by various means. The people gaze on him as a prodigy but he shews little inclination to converse with them: the wit and beauty of his Companion are not sufficient to excuse the scandalous impropriety of shewing her to all Europe, and you will not easily conceive how he

Mrs A___st___d.

Sir. Matthew. Mite.

1) *Tête-a-Tête* engraving of Mrs. Armitstead and Sir Matthew Mite.
    The British Library. John Freeman Photographers.

The text within the image (rotated caption):

The Chinese House, the Rotunda; the Company in the Rotunda; Masquerade; La Maison Chinoise la Rotunde, &c. Masquin au Bal Masque.

2) The Rotunda and Chinese House at Ranelagh Gardens in 1751.
Museum of London.

3) Portrait of Elizabeth Armitstead by Sir Joshua Reynolds 1784. *The British Museum.*

4) Portrait of The Rt Hon C. J. Fox by Sir Joshua Reynolds. *The British Museum.*

General the Rt Honble Richard Fitzpatrick

Engraved for the Military Panorama,

by H.R. Cook, from the Drawing by W. Lane.

London, Publish'd by Martin & Co. 33, Orchard Str. Portman Sq.

5)   General the Rt Hon Richard Fitzpatrick, engraving by H.R. Cook from a drawing by W. Lane. *National Portrait Gallery.*

6) Charles James Fox 1749–1806. Painting by K.A. Hickel, *National Portrait Gallery.*

7)　Two vignettes from a commission by Samuel Rogers. *The British Museum.*

8). Mrs Fox's school. *Chertsey Council.*

has lost himself in the public opinion, which was already more favourable to his Rival. Will Fox never learn the importance of character.'

By her silence in his company, Elizabeth appears to have sensed and been constrained by Gibbon's disapproval. Though she could not have joined, at their level, in talk of books, gardening was a subject after her own heart and one of which she knew quite as much as Charles did; she would probably have been happy to join in talk of it had she felt at ease. She may also have been rendered already shy by evidences of disapprobation of her travelling with Charles, for their journey was not without unpleasant encounters. Elizabeth and Charles were always careful to avoid embarrassing those who might be offended by obligatory introductions to her (when, three years earlier, Charles had been playing with the idea of a holiday in Herefordshire he had told Uvedale Price that he would take Mrs Armitstead to see Foxley, the Prices' house in that county, only if the family were not there), and such considerations may have occasioned her remaining at the Lyon d'or when Charles went to call on Gibbon. But abroad it was not easy to avoid unplanned encounters with other travelling Britons, and the distasteful experience of meeting fellow-travellers who greeted Charles while cutting Elizabeth did befall them.

Neither irritations of this kind nor the delay in Switzerland were allowed to keep them from Italy, the aim of the whole journey, or from the pleasure Charles had promised himself of introducing Elizabeth to the works of art he most loved there. She proved delightfully responsive, by the evidence of his subsequent letters to Holland in Italy, which record her urgings as well as Charles's to see the pictures Charles had led her to admire. 'You were near losing all credit with the Lady of the Hill for speaking so coldly about the Correggio at Parma, but you recovered it a little by admiring so much that at the Caprera Palace, which was the first of the master she ever saw and which she was wild about.' 'I do not wonder at your admiring the Bologna school and Guercino particularly, but Mrs A. will never forgive you if you do not take particular notice of his picture of Christ in the Garden at Cento.'

The Bolognese school was the last they were to have the opportunity of admiring, for at Bologna, on 15th November, their holiday ended. A little earlier, an Englishman they encountered had told them that Lord Holland was very ill, and on the night of the 14th Charles had dreamed his nephew was dead; the next morning, an English banker arriving from Turin had told him: 'My Lord, I am sorry to inform your Lordship that you are now Lord Holland.' This was doubly grievous, smiting both the devoted uncle and the politician whose career could be satisfactorily pursued in the Commons only. A glimmer of hope remained, for the information proved to be based on a newspaper report and Charles well knew the unreliability of the Press, but even this was quenched by the arrival the same day of two Englishmen who told him that when they left Geneva an express message was on the road from England to him. At night the messenger arrived. Both Charles and Elizabeth were now so miserable and frightened that they could hardly brace themselves to receive the actual blow, and Jem Hare – son of 'the Hare with many friends', who was staying in Bologna and had visited them at their lodgings – undertook to go down and speak with the messenger. A few moments later they heard him racing up, and knew before he reached the door that bad news never came so eagerly. He burst in shouting: 'All is well.' Holland was alive: but there was more news than that. The King was ill, the King was mad, there was talk of a Regency, and the express messenger was from the Duke of Portland. Fox must return home at once.

For a little while Fox could grasp only the news that Holland lived, which had him crying with relief. At last however the force of Portland's message penetrated. He resolved on immediate departure; the unfortunate messenger was launched northward again, to book horses at the posting stations, and Charles and Elizabeth followed as soon as their gear was packed up. Travelling by day and night, they recrossed the Alps and descended to Lyons, where Charles found awaiting him further messages urging haste. Elizabeth was already exhausted by the speed of their travel, and they now agreed to part. Charles raced on northward in a hired carriage, while Elizabeth continued, at a more leisurely pace, to Paris, and there stopped.

There was no reason why she should hurry home. She enjoyed Paris, the weather was bitterly cold but was colder still in England, the season was that at which St Anne's was least attractive, while if she were to join Charles in London the session of Parliament, and the incessant consultations occasioned by such a crisis as Portland's letters had indicated, would ensure that she saw little of him. Indeed, his letters, bright with hopes of early office under the Prince as Regent, made the point. 'The sooner you come the better,' he wrote on 15th December, 'but I own I think this next fortnight will be such a scene of hurry that I should have little time to enjoy what I value most in the world, my dearest Liz's company. I take for granted you will want some money I will if I can send you some by next Post, but I have hardly a minute to myself either to get the money or to write, adieu my dearest Liz indeed indeed you are more than all the world to me.' This loving acceptance of her absence naturally did not move her to curtail it, and a letter of 24th December from Thomas Coutts to the Duchess of Devonshire – amusingly indicative of the extent to which even the wealthy and the noble sought to avoid customs duty – suggests that she still was not planning an early return. 'Lady Clermont gave Mrs Coutts two winter petticoats to carry to England for your Grace, but Mrs. Armistead having a woman going to London, and Mrs Coutts saying your Grace might want the petticoats this cold weather, I have taken it upon me to advise their being sent, as this person is going immediately and Mrs A. assured me they would be very safe.'

In mid-January, and still in Paris, she learned at last what Charles had been keeping from her. He was ill, had been ill ever since his return. In his race across Europe he had picked up some gastric infection. Its effects had been worsened by the speed and discomfort of a journey that had taken him eleven hundred miles in nine horse-drawn days – during which he had allowed himself only two sleeps in a bed, and of only two hours each time – with its later stages accomplished in an open and ill-sprung hired carriage jouncing over rough roads. On his arrival in London on 24th November, already sick and weakened, he had immediately been swept into a hurly-burly of consultations, negotiations, visits to the Prince, and plans of a Parliamentary campaign in which he was to lead the Whig forces in the Commons. His appearance there, when Parliament reassembled on 4th December, 'excited a great and general sensation', wrote Wraxall. 'I never saw Fox, either previously or subsequently, exhibit so broken and shattered an aspect. His body seemed to be emaciated, his countenance sallow and sickly, his eyes swollen, while his stockings hung upon his legs and he rather dragged himself along than walked up the floor to take his seat.' Illness may have contributed to certain tactical blunders he made in the manoeuvrings against Administration, the most serious being his hasty contention that the Prince was entitled as of right to monarchic power as Regent. This apparent dismissal of the rights of Parliament delighted Pitt, who, presenting himself as their standard-bearer, launched out on a brilliant delaying campaign of Parliamentary argument as to what powers might properly be accorded a Regent, and soon had reason to hope that deferment of their grant might obviate the need for it.

By late January, when Elizabeth reached London, reports of the King's improvement were growing in number, while Fox's state was such that rumours of his imminent death – seized on by the Pittites with, in Sir Gilbert Elliot's words, bloodthirsty eagerness – had begun to circulate. His illness had already virtually forced his withdrawal from Parliamentary activities; Elizabeth now put a check on private consultations, nursed him until he was fit enough to travel, and on 28th January carried him off to Bath. This one-time centre of extra-metropolitan fashion was already (in partial consequence, perhaps, of Wesley's frequent preachings there) declining into the dowdy respectability that was to characterise it in the nineteenth century, but its therapeutic virtues were still esteemed and in Charles's case proved rapidly effective. The 'Bath Chronicle', which on 29th January had recorded as if he were unaccompanied the arrival of the Right Hon. Charles James Fox, declared on 5th February: 'We have the best of authority for saying that Mr Fox's indisposition is not as alarming as had been apprehended; and that there is every reason to hope that a short retirement from public business, and the use of the Bath water, will restore him to his wonted health.'

While Fox recuperated at Bath, the King was gradually regaining command of such wits as he had formerly possessed. By the end of February, when Charles and Elizabeth returned to London (she to sit to Reynolds for the portrait of her in a black hat that later passed into the possession of the Powys family), public celebration of the royal recovery was already being planned by the Court and Administration. Charles, his hopes of office dashed, was nevertheless observed by Sheridan's sister Betsy to be in perfect health and spirits. His feelings may indeed have been mixed. Office was the object of the career he had pursued for twenty years and the door to the reforms he ardently desired, but its demands would inevitably curtail the enjoyment of that private life in which his personal happiness lay. Gibbon had been right in suspecting that to Fox public life was becoming a duty rather than a pleasure.

Charles and Elizabeth had been lovers now for six years, and their mutual devotion was unwaning. Year by year they were rooting themselves more firmly at St Anne's, where the placid way of life they had established changed only with the changes time must bring. Holland was growing up; in 1790 he left Eton for Oxford, where still he was not too far distant to join on occasion with his friends in the small pleasures that delighted Elizabeth and Charles. His contemporary George Canning, the clever fatherless youth whose education Fox and Sheridan were supervising, described from Oxford how he had 'met Mr Fox and his lady at places on the road betwixt here and London, & have paddled about with them and Lord Holland and other folks on the water, & dined by the side of clear streams at Clifden.' Holland was still the son of the house, whose visits could not be too frequent, whose birthdays were passed at St Anne's so that Elizabeth (who delighted in anniversaries) could honour them with a small dance or a firework display, but often now there were other children about the place. Other Etonians – Uvedale Price's son Bob, William Dickson's Coss – came as Holland had done to enjoy there outings and stays away from school. Though the legitimate sisters of boys of this class could not be let visit a house whose mistress notoriously was a man's – and had been many men's –, the marriage value of gentlemen's bastards was not high enough to be appreciably diminished thus' and St Andrew St John sometimes brought his illegitimate daughter to stay. Charles's own bastards, of course, came often, and at some time in the early 1790s Harriet Willoughby became a permanent resident at St Anne's.

But of the visiting children the one Elizabeth was to love best after Holland was no relation. He was Bob St John, a bastard child of the third Viscount Bolingbroke – Bully's son, whom she had known since he was a young boy and she his father's mistress. The third Viscount's promising career (promising at least in the partial eyes of Elizabeth) was shattered in 1789, when he ran away from his wife. Wife-desertion was not in itself ruinous to eighteenth-century noblemen – though it was more chic to elope, like Lord John Townshend in 1787, with another man's wife – but incest was; Lord Bolingbroke's inamorata had been his half-sister, Anne Beauclerk.* He had gone with her abroad and abroad he remained, but Bob apparently was brought up in England, and

---

*Betsy Sheridan's Journal, which gives the fullest contemporary account of this scandal, refers to the girl only as 'Miss Beauclerk'; Anne was, according to 'Burke's Peerage', the only one of Bolingbroke's half-sisters unmarried at the time.

Elizabeth had him at St Anne's as much as his unidentified guardians allowed. This was not as much as she wished, to judge from a letter of Charles's to Fitzpatrick a few years later ('Poor little Bob was taken away from us last Saturday sennight which has vexed Mrs A. very much'), but over the years he was about the place enough to leave his traces in the developing geography of the garden, where 'Bob's corner' and 'Bob's seat' were to appear among the landmarks.

Elizabeth was not, when Charles was in London or at shooting-parties, solitary or confined to juvenile society. She had adult friends of her own to entertain at St Anne's. Some came as house-guests: Charles, who liked to know her circumstances when they were apart as much as she did his, once wrote from Holkham: 'You said Company was to go on Monday & I concluded they were gone, & there they stayed till Saturday & Liz never told me till Wednesday's letter.' The unidentified company may have been friends retained from the days when Elizabeth had been 'a foolish giddy girl', or their children – the Marstons' two daughters used to stay at St Anne's –, or perhaps friends made on a visit to Cheltenham or Brighton. Her life-long friendship with Mr and Mrs Ludbey, of Chalfont St Peter in Buckinghamshire, may have originated in a holiday acquaintance.

She was not however dependent on imported visitors for company, for now the residents of Chertsey and its environs were beginning to visit St Anne's. Though the barrier between the 'respectable' and the 'unrespectable' woman was rising, it was by no means the impenetrable fence of high Victorianism, and might be tacitly traversed for purposes of social intercourse. The virtuous were more inclined to relax their morality where it might otherwise deny access to the hospitality of class superiors, and country-dwellers, with their limited social resources, tended to be more accommodating than townsfolk. (Thus in 1806 Lady Diana Beauclerk would write of her disgraced son Lord Bolingbroke and his initially bigamous second wife: 'G. and Lady B. are living at Lydiard [his country house in Wiltshire], the people round them are very civil and visit them – in this part of the world [Richmond] it is very different.') Both factors operated in Elizabeth's favour. Though there were in the vicinity of Chertsey or in carriage-calling distance a fair number of middle- or upper-class families, not one could boast so fascinating an assortment of guests – Members of Parliament, noblemen of every degree, occasionally even the Prince of Wales himself – as the lucky caller might encounter at St Anne's.

The first locals to venture an acquaintance with these reprehensible but alluring neighbours were apparently the Porters, owners of nearby Silverlands. Perhaps significantly, theirs was an all-male family, of a father – a Windsor brewer – and two sons, good-natured folk who over the years were to become regular and easy friends of both Elizabeth and Charles. To her pleasure, too, the younger son, William, liked music; later she taught him to sing, so that they could sing duets together. Another early acquaintance, perhaps inevitably in view of Elizabeth's rheumatism and her tendency to severe colds, was the local apothecary Mr Ives, to one of whose children Charles was to stand godfather. Indeed, professional acquaintance seldom stopped at that for Charles and Elizabeth; another man with whom and with whose family they began about this time to develop what became a life-long friendship was Stephen Rolleston, a London businessman who transacted some of Holland's affairs.

Women had initially, perhaps, been more cautious in venturing the acquaintanceship, but even among them the process of succumbing to St Anne's Hill may by now have begun. Certainly it would be well advanced by 1798, when a letter from Charles to Elizabeth greeting her news of a pleasant new arrival in the neighbourhood is expressed in terms that see nothing remarkable in the lady's visiting his Liz. Those who made the plunge found at once that there was nothing outward in her at which to cavil. Some respectable ladies may indeed have been a little disappointed on meeting – no doubt for the first and perhaps the only time in their lives – a famous Cyprian, to discover her indistinguishable in manners, appearance and conversation, from any other gentlewoman. The wife of Samuel Rogers' friend James Martin experienced such a surprise in reverse; she sat next Elizabeth at Warren Hastings' trial, conversed with her, thought her charming, and was astonished to learn afterward to whom she had been talking.

Chertsey friends tended to be, in Elizabeth's terminology, worthy rather than agreeable – that is, people whom she respected and liked (as indeed she liked most human beings, unless and until given reason not to) but did not find very stimulating. The most entertaining guests came when her need of them was least, that is, when Charles was at home. His old friends were now resigned to pursuing him into the country for their fill of the society that once had been on tap at Brooks's.

Fitzpatrick had accepted Charles's attachment to St Anne's so completely that when, in 1791, he decided to settle in the country himself, he bought a house at Sunning Hill seven miles away, from which he could easily ride or drive to Chertsey for the day. Through the summer, and when Charles was at home in the autumn, they came, by ones and twos or together, Spencer and Hare and St Andrew St John, and Burgoyne (who was staying at St Anne's only two days before his sudden death in 1792), and William Adam, once Charles's adversary in his only duel but ever since the coalition of 1783 his devoted friend, and sometimes John Townshend, despite his recent marriage to his divorced co-eloper. Another Benedick still occasionally to be met there was Charles's brother Henry, now Colonel Fox; Elizabeth had reckoned him a natural bachelor, but on his marriage in 1787 Charles had observed: 'I never thought him so unlikely to marry as you did, we are all of us of an affectionate breed.'

Now too a younger generation of Foxite Whigs was coming to take turns in the few guest bedchambers at St Anne's or to stay at 'the little Publick-House near by' (probably the Golden Grove at the foot of the hill, where, Charles once told Adam, 'there is I believe tolerable accommodation'), and to get their legs under the table at which there was always room, and to imbibe the wisdom of their Socrates. Foremost among them were the Earl of Lauderdale, Robert Adair, the Duke of Bedford, whom Fox almost certainly saw as the future leader of the party, and Charles Grey, who in the event was to attain that eminence. Elizabeth liked and welcomed them all: Adair, tall, clever, self-dramatising, whom she respected but found (as did most people not irritated into dislike by his dogmatising) slightly ludicrous; capable Lauderdale, of whom Charles once said, 'I wonder how the world went on when there was no Lauderdale to help it, or what will become of it when he leaves it'; Grey, who shared her taste for gardening, and who once on opening a political letter from Fox found inside it a violet inserted by 'Mrs A.' to show him how large they were growing at St Anne's; but almost certainly the dearest to her as to Charles was Francis, sixth Duke of Bedford. This awkward, intelligent, eager young man, with his practical concern for agricultural improvement and his ardent reformist principles, was a sport among Dukes, but a fitting head for the only magnate family to owe its rise to an ancestor's intellectual attainments and its Dukedom to another ancestor's martyrdom for his opposition to absolute monarchy. Orphaned as a small child and reared by his grandmother, attached in early manhood to the middle-aged but still fascinating Lady Maynard, who had been Nancy Parsons, Bedford liked and charmed older women, and Elizabeth was no exception. He it was who first moved in her what was to develop into an unvarying affection for the whole house of Russell.

A summer visitor of 1791, Anthony Storer, whom Charles had known since both were at Eton, sent William Eden a word-picture of Fox taking his ease at home. 'A few days ago I made a visit to St Anne's Hill and found our buff and blue chief lolling in the shade. Mrs Armstead was with him; a harper was playing soft music; books of botany lying about; and astronomy, in the shape of Sir Harry Englefield, assisted in the group . . . and thus, you see, like Solomon, he is to seek wisdom in the search of herbs and flowers.' (The harpist was probably Charles Meyer, son of a German musician settled in London, who taught Harriet, and then Elizabeth, to play the harp, and who made the transition so usual at St Anne's from provider of professional services into friend.) Storer, no politician, may not have realised to how great an extent St Anne's was for Fox becoming more than a country residence for the indulgence of *dolce far niente*. Increasingly it represented his refuge from the ever more troublous climate of the world beyond.

The enthusiasm with which he had welcomed the French Revolution – 'How much the greatest event it is that ever happened in the World', he had declared on hearing of the fall of the Bastille, 'and how much the best' – had been widely shared by his countrymen. Many of them had, like him, grounded their former hostility to France not merely on the frequency of warfare between the two countries but also on detestation of that absolutism of which France had been the nearest and most powerful exemplar. In 1789 all that, it seemed, was happily over, and France moving to join Britain and the United States in the small comity of enlightened nations that practised representative government. That widespread euphoria had begun to fail as reports crossed the Channel of conditions increasingly unlike those brought about by the English and American Revolutions. In 1790 Burke, alarmed by assaults on religious institutions that were plainly developing into an attack on religion, had moved into opposition to the principles of the revolution itself, and had repudiated on the floor of the House not only political association but a quarter-century's personal friendship with Fox. By 1791 signs were beginning to appear that this might not be the last severance of old ties that Fox would experience if he persisted in advocacy for the new regime in France.

Nor was there greater satisfaction to be found in affairs at home. As events in France provided more and more support for conservative claims that moves toward reconstruction could unloose avalanches of destruction, support for domestic reform began to weaken. As early as 1790, an attempt to secure the repeal of the Test Acts had failed; in April, 1791, a motion for the abolition of the Slave Trade was first watered down in the Commons and then rejected by the Lords; and in May a motion to repeal statutes declaring blasphemous the beliefs of the Unitarians was lost by 142 votes to 65.

The activity and stress associated with these unrewarded efforts, and worry over his increasing disagreements with party colleagues, were encouraging in Fox relapse into the bad habits of his youth. After the debate on the slave trade he wrote to Elizabeth: 'I never was so bad about writing to my Liz as I have been this time & yet there never was a time when I loved her so well or thought so much of her. It gives me the greatest delight you can conceive to find by your letters that you are so happy & your heart so light indeed it does my Liz and I am not so selfish as to grudge your happiness because you are without me. I have led a sad life getting up late always at the H of C or gaming and losing my money every night that I have played getting up late of course and finding people in my room so that I have had no morning time to myself & have gone out as soon as I could tho' generally very late to get rid of them, so that I have scarce ever had a moment to write. You have heard how poor a figure in numbers we made on the slave trade, but I spoke I believe very well and indeed it is the thing that has given me most pleasure since I saw Liz, for I think it a cause in which one ought to be an Enthusiast and in which one can not help being pleased with oneself for having done right.'

Elizabeth's heart was probably less light after reading that letter than before, and she cannot have been much cheered by another she received soon after from Stephen Rolleston. She had suggested to him that he go to the House to listen to the debate on the slave trade, and, though unable to get in, he faithfully notified to her the encomia he had heard on Charles's great speech. He continued, however: 'Mr Fox has had a sad life of it indeed since you left him and I think if he does not live more regularly when he returns from Newmarket, that it may seriously hurt him – for then he will probably have a good deal to occupy his attention and perhaps irritate his Feelings, upon which Occasion good Hours and domestic Comfort are highly requisite – and I see he cannot bear raking as well as he used to.'

As it happened, that Newmarket meeting witnessed the event that cured Charles of one mode at least of raking. It was at the meeting of 1791 that the Prince's jockey was accused of throwing a race, with the Prince, some covertly suggested, in the know. Elizabeth, learning of these events from letters in which Charles for once departed from his custom of not reporting to her the doings at Newmarket, was horrified, but she cannot have regretted the outcome. 'Instead of leaving it by degrees,' wrote Charles with a resolution he was to keep, 'I am determined to get rid of my horses as soon as *poss* and even if I can not do that I will send down the money for them and come down as seldom as *poss* . . . God bless my dearest Liz, and tho' I have lost my money I am quite sure she had rather I should lose much more than have such things said of me as [are] said here of so many people. I send you 100 gn. which I hope will do. Direct your next to Thetford. I think with *pleas* of shooting next week, but with disgust of the meeting here afterward where I fear I must be, but with most *pleas* of all of the week after when I shall be at dear home with my dearest Wife whom I love better than all the world.'

Such pleasure as he could hope for away from dear home, and above all at Westminster, continued to diminish in 1792. As English radicals, excited by the French Revolution and 'The Rights of Man', grew ever more enthusiastic for reform while events in France gave the cautious ever more reason to question its beneficence, corresponding fissures were widening among the Whigs. In April the enthusiastic younger members, led by Grey, founded an association called the Friends of the People to agitate for electoral reform. Portland repudiated their action, but Fox, though realist enough to see the injury done by events in France to the prospects of reform in England, could not bring himself to do so. The rift between him and his coeval associates, men who like himself had experienced the responsibilities of office, grew deeper when in the summer Pitt, alarmed by France's declaration of war on Austria and the consequent threat to the Low Countries, proposed through intermediaries a coalition with the Whigs. Portland was prepared to negotiate, but Fox, declaring himself so, refused even to contemplate serving under Pitt. In the autumn, news of the September massacres endorsed all the fears of those who had suspected that professions of benevolence towards humanity were compatible with extreme maleficence towards human beings. Opinion in the country and among the Whigs rapidly polarised; and at the Whig Club dinner on December 4th Fox ranged himself in the eyes of the public at large with those who ranked the professions above the performance, by declaring: 'I am, and I declare myself to be, an advocate for the *rights of the people.*' When Parliament opened on December 13th, it was plain that the coming session was likely to witness not only the crisis of peace or war, but also the crisis of the Whig party.

Elizabeth was at St Anne's. She did not care to be in London at times when the pressure of business would keep Charles from her, and normally he accepted this. Stress and worry always however intensified his need for her, and even before the session began he was wishing for her presence; a letter of 11th December, assuring her that there was little doubt that 'we [the Whigs] shall set out together', ended with the postscript: 'I went to bed earlier last night and will if I can continue to do so, but the sure way is for my Liz to come to town.' Two days later (and apparently just before a debate in which, opposing Pitt's proposals for the surveillance of aliens and for censorship, he was to muster only 50 votes against 290) he wrote again: 'I am afraid there will not appear as much Union as I had hoped, but still it will not be as bad as I feared. I am sure that no pains shall be wanting on my part for now that the danger of parting has been in my mind I find that my regard for the D of P and Ld F [Fitzwilliam, Fox's friend since both were at Eton and his political associate virtually throughout their adult life] is still greater than I knew myself. However that nor anything else shall hinder me from doing what is *right*. I am much obliged to my Liz for her nice gossiping letter of to-day. I have told the Cook to go back to-morrow. I will let you know by to-morrow or next day's post whether I shall be kept here or not. If I am I hope my Liz will come for even if I only see her at night or at break it is a great comfort to me.'

His Liz, possibly unwilling to disrupt her arrangements for the winter, made no promises; her next letter seems indeed to have been chiefly a plea to be told what happened in the debate. Charles – who could justly have pointed out that had she been in London she would have known – meekly replied: 'I am quite sorry to find from your letter to-day that you were impatient to hear the event of Thursday as you will have been disappointed at my not writing . . . Our division as you will have seen in the papers was miserable. I expected it bad but not quite as bad. It is a good thing and a great comfort to me that the danger of separation from those I regard is much lessened, but when I have said this I have no more good to say. War I think inevitable, and the rage against the French what they call Republicans is such that the Thing is at the moment quite Master of the country, and every effort one makes for the people of this country only renders one unpopular among them and if possible still more odious at Court, but it does not signify so long as one is satisfied one is doing right, and I am quite so – I am completely –

'I was interrupted as I was writing, and must finish my letter here at the H of Cs where I have not a moment's time so God bless my Liz. My voice is gone but will come again I dare say.'

That letter (perhaps that last pathetic remark) changed her resolve. In his next letter, of 18th December, Charles wrote: 'I expect you to-morrow to *din,* but it is doubtful if I can get from the House. I will if *poss* for I do long to see my Liz. My voice is recovered but I think I have hardly passed one pleasant hour since I left you.' Even when she reached London the next day, pressure of business allowed him scarcely more than the first comforting encounter. On 20th December he wrote from 'H of Cs past seven': 'I fear I may not be able to go home till late as I must see the D of P after he comes from the Play and that conversation may make it necessary for me to see others. It has been a most unpleasant day here . . . I am very unhappy indeed, for the worst of all is that if we break it must be with a quarrell and tho' I think he has acted very weakly & strangely I can not help loving the D of P, and if with him the D of D[evonshire] & Ld F are to go I never can have any comfort in Politics again. God bless my dearest Liz whose kindness to me makes up for all.'

Elizabeth continued in London until 30th December, a period in which the Whigs managed to maintain a shaky semblance of unity. With the guillotining of Louis XVI it tottered, and on 1st February, 1793, the French declaration of war on Great Britain gave it its quietus. While Portland and his associates determined that in a country at war the Government must be supported, Fox, still extenuating the conduct of the French Republic, pressed for further attempts at an accommodation. When on 18th February he moved for a continuance of negotiations, only forty-four Members followed him into the lobby.

Fox was in the wilderness now as never before. He was divided not from his former associates only, but from the mass of the articulate populace, as uncomprehending of his insistence on the indivisibility of liberty as he of fears that the implementation in Britain of reformist principles would be the prelude as in France to terrorist practices. Pilloried by the Press as a sans-culotte yearning to establish the guillotine in London, reviled as a traitor to his country, he held doggedly on his course. Hopelessly he opposed, supported only by his little band of devotees ('every man of them', said Thurlow, 'would be hanged for Fox'), the Aliens Bill, the Traitorous Correspondence Bill, the suspension of HABEAS CORPUS, and every retrenchment of liberty the Government deemed essential to the safety of a country believed to be threatened from within as well as without. Then in the summer of 1793 knowledge came that more were with him than the forty-four.

At St Anne's Hill, on 6th June, he opened the letter written the day before by Serjeant Adair to inform him that a contribution had been raised from well-wishers all over the country for the payment of his debts. If this moved him, more moving still was knowledge whence that subscription had come. The committee that organised it – which included Thomas Coke, Lord George Cavendish and Mr Crewe – might have been distinguished for fortune and rank, but many of the subscribers were not. Small shopkeepers, country clergymen, tenant farmers had contributed their shillings or guineas to the relief of a man who once had gambled away more money in an hour than some of them had to live on in a year. That relief was achieved; the funds accumulated proved sufficient not only to pay his debts but to yield an annuity sufficient for his future support.

For all the darkness of the political world Charles could not but be happy, not merely in the prospect of financial stability but in the knowledge how it had come about. To Holland, now abroad on as much of a Grand Tour as such troublous times allowed, he wrote: 'I may perhaps flatter myself, but I think it is the most honourable thing that has ever happened to any one . . . I need not tell you that Mrs A. is as happy as I am and she says she only wants to see the Young One to make her completely so.' They indulged themselves, that August, in a little tour of Hastings and Rye – which Charles declared, quite surpassed his expectations – and hopefully planned to join Holland in Italy in the spring of 1794.

There were domestic worries, of course: Elizabeth's health – she had two severe bouts of fever that autumn; the future of Harry, Charles's deaf-mute son, now in his teens; and, an unease never very far from Charles's mind as he grew older, Elizabeth's situation in the event of his own death. From his correspondence with William Adam, now a trustee of the fund for the payment of his debts, it appears that he was hoping something could be effected for her in the settlement of his affairs. Ideally he would have wished the still outstanding mortgage on St Anne's to be paid off, but as the house was hers and not his this was impossible, while the alternative he had contemplated, of paying off the mortgage on his own London house and settling it on her, was opposed by Elizabeth. She, he told Adam, 'did not like the thought of any part of the money being employed in any benefit to her. I did not think her reasons good but I could not persuade her.' He always had difficulty in discussing this problem with her because the initial premise was one she could not bear to contemplate.

But such concerns were incidental to the content of life at St Anne's. 'We have had a very pleasant Christmas,' wrote Charles to Holland at the end of the year, 'St John and his little girl for a few days & since only Harry & Harriet. The former is I think much improved and I think is in a way to improve much more . . . You will be sorry to hear that we have almost given up all thoughts of Italy next year. Every thing seems so troubled in most parts of the Continent and the animosities so violent that I think it wisest for a Man who takes as much part in Politics as I do to stay at home.' Indeed he could hardly have been happier in Italy, the following year, than he was at St Anne's whenever he could escape politics and be with Elizabeth there. 'Here I am', he wrote to Holland in April, 'passing a most comfortable week of holidays, the weather delicious, and the place looking beautiful beyond description, and the nightingales singing, and Mrs A. as happy as the day is long; all which circumstances enable me to bear public calamities with wonderful philosophy.' And in August: 'Here I am, perfectly happy. Idleness, fine weather, Ariosto, a little Spanish, and the constant company of a person whom I love, I think, more and more every day and every hour, make me as happy as I am capable of being.'

They had a new enterprise afoot, now, in the garden. Charles had a predilection for garden architecture which Elizabeth seems to have thought extravagent, but the establishment of his finances on a stable footing presumably overcame her objections, for now a temple was to rise on the south-western slope of the hill. Its dedication was to honour Holland's approaching majority, but wider affections moved them to name it the Temple of Friendship. A temple so named must obviously be dedicated in the company of friends and – the presence of the person celebrated being in the view of Charles and Elizabeth inessential to a celebration – invitations were sent out to a twenty-first birthday party for Holland. On 21st November, 1794, old friends, young friends, Chertsey friends congregated at St Anne's, and were led down the garden to gather outside the little building of brick banded with stone that honoured Holland and, in its naming, all of them. Late as was the season, the day was fair, and continued fine as the inscription over the entrance was unveiled to reveal that: 'In Memoriam Dies natalis Henrici Richardi Baronis de Holland Quo XXI annos aetatis attigit XI KAL DEC AD MCCXCIV Feliciter hic celebrati Haesce Aedes Amicitiae Ipsique sacres Carolus et Elizabetha Qui etsi non Parentes, paterno Eum amore diligunt Votivas Posituerunt.'* Opposite was to stand a pedestal surmounted by a vase and adorned by verses composed by Fitzpatrick (in English, for the convenience of those who, like Elizabetha, had no Latin) in honour of the occasion.

The ceremony over, the party returned to the house to eat, drink and dance; though Elizabeth had some of her servants taught to play musical instruments (or taught them herself), so that an impromptu dance was always possible at St Anne's, this occasion was doubtless attended by hired professionals. So comprehensive was the gaiety that even clumsy, unmusical Charles was coaxed once on to the floor. For as long as she lived, Elizabeth was to count this day one of the happiest of her life. 'How delighted my Angel was with my little Fete,' she wrote long after in her Journal: 'the dear General [Fitzpatrick] too;' 'the weather

---

*To commemorate the birthday of Henry Richard Lord Holland, who attained the age of 21 on 21 November 1794, which day was happily celebrated here, Charles and Elizabeth, who though not parents love him with parental love, built as they vowed this temple sacred to him and to friendship.

was fine and I was surrounded by dear happy faces full of love and affection.'

An element in her happiness may have been a renewal of her old friendship with Fitzpatrick, between whom and her there seems for years to have been a cloud. Once he had been closer to her than Charles, and Charles the conveyor of letters and messages between them; but the last such message seems to have been the 'Mrs Armitstead . . . desires me to give her love to you' on her return from Paris in 1782, a few weeks before her liaison with Charles began. No such messages had since appeared in Charles's letters to his friend, nor had his invitations to Fitzpatrick to St Anne's been expressed in the plural. But at some time after the dedication of the Temple of Friendship a new and more lasting tie seems to have been formed, like one between a brother- and sister-in-law who are also friends. A letter of 1796 from Charles to Fitzpatrick ends with 'Mrs A. desires her love', and thereafter such messages, requests from 'Mrs A.' for small services, and joint invitations are frequent. One letter, of 1802, indicates the ease that by then prevailed between Charles's love and his friend: 'Mrs A. is much better, and as she does not mind being in her nightcap before you we shall be very happy whenever you will come.' Their friendship was never again to slacken.

Holland, sent by 'the old one' an account of the festivities that had honoured his birthday, responded from Italy with a poem to Elizabeth. It was not (in the view of his uncle, touched but nothing if not critical) a very good poem; but the sentiments were beyond cavil. The final stanzas in particular must have held out hope to two people who were beginning to feel it was time Holland came home:

> 'Grant me with one whose tender breast
> Burns with a mutual fire
> To rural seats and scenes of rest
> Unruffled to retire.

> 'Ye Gods how far such golden schemes
> All Poets' flights outdo.
> Nor are they wild – behold my dreams –
> But paint St Anne's and you.'

In fact, though they may not yet have suspected it, love was both keeping Holland away and ensuring that such domestic serenity would never be his. Earlier that year he had encountered the beautiful, restless, domineering Lady Webster, who for three years off and on had been dragging round Europe an increasing family and an increasingly depressed husband, and in Florence she now had him in thrall.

Charles wanted him home for political as well as personal reasons. Holland's coming of age entitled him to take his seat in the Lords (where his arrival would increase by 50% the representation of the Foxites), and it also stressed, to a man who had begun his own career at twenty, that it was time for Holland to start on his. Naturally Charles desired his nephew to follow his own course. Two years earlier he had written to Holland: 'The truth is that all men when they are no longer young must look forward to something they expect to last beyond themselves. My friends whom I love best are all about my own age, & consequently one supposes they will go off the stage about the same time as oneself. Poor Harry tho' an excellent Boy from his misfortune is not what one can look forward to with much satisfaction. So when I have a mind to build castles and to look forward to distant times with pride & pleasure I must think of you & only you.'

The times were inauspicious for any buff and blue aspirant to political success, but Holland was young enough to found himself on his uncle's principles and await a change of climate. For himself, well on in his forties, Charles was increasingly weary of politics, and it was only his sense of duty that when Parliament was sitting dragged him to Westminster for the dreary routine of motions and amendments supported by his devoted handful only and voted down with the aid of those who once had been his colleagues and allies. The conflict in him of duty and inclination emerges clearly in a letter to Holland, quaintly commencing with evidence of a distinctly unusual mode of measuring the passage of time: 'Mrs A. tells me it is a long time since I wrote to you. I thought not, but yet I recollect that when I wrote last I was in the 9th book of the Odyssey, which I have since finished and read 18 books of the Iliad, so that it must be a good while since.' After a happy discursus on Homer, Virgil, Milton and Ariosto, he turned to politics and, having brought Holland up to date, continued: 'I wish I could be persuaded it was right to quit public business, for I should like it to a degree that I can not express, but I can not yet think that it is not a duty to persevere . . . I am so sure that secession is the measure a shabby fellow would take in our circumstances that I think it can scarcely be right for us. But as for wishes no man ever wished any thing more. I am perfectly happy in the country, I have quite resources enough to employ my mind, and the great resource of all, literature, I am fonder of every day, and then the Lady of the Hill is one continual source of happiness to me. I believe few Men indeed were so happy in that respect as I.'

His wants now were modest indeed; the simple routine of St Anne's, good weather, and Elizabeth's society. They all were met on 7th May, 1795, a day on which nothing happened, a perfectly ordinary day except that it was extra-ordinarily perfect. Prose was insufficient to celebrate it, and Charles burst into song:

> 'The seventh of May
> Is the happiest day
> That ever I spent in my life.
> The sun it did shine,
> The birds sang divine,
> And I was all day with my Wife.'

Of that ultimate source of joy he wrote to Holland in June: 'You were never more right than in what you say of my happiness derived from her. I declare I think my affection for her increases every day. She is a comfort to me in every misfortune and makes me enjoy doubly every pleasant circumstance of life. There is to me a charm and a delight in her society which time does not in the least wear off, and for real goodness of heart if she ever had an equal she certainly never had a superior.' Before many weeks had passed from the writing of that letter, the happiness it hymned was under threat. The agency was a member or members of the Coutts family.

Thomas Coutts was banker to the King, the Government and Pitt. He believed however in taking precautions against a change of monarch and so of Government, was not without Whiggish sympathies, and furthermore was interested in advancing his family into that high society in which the Whig grandees stood highest. In 1787 he had written to Fox, then personally unknown to him, to offer financial accommodation, declaring at the same time that though he dealt in money, acquiring it was not his object in life. His letter continued: 'My family consists of a wife and three daughters with whom I live in the greatest comfort and happiness and I would hardly wish to alter *any* of them from what they are, only that one of them distresses me by her unfortunate state of health – but I have hopes that she will mend, and as to fortune they will have enough – I wou'd wish they had more good connexions in case I shou'd die – but these they must find themselves. As to me my principal ambition is to acquire the friendship and acquaintance of men eminent for benevolent minds great talents and respectable characters.'

The possessor of a benevolent mind and great talents – if not perhaps of a respectable character – to whom he addressed himself was naturally delighted by, and eagerly took up, the offer of financial help. If he considered at all the rather gratuitous reference to the Misses Coutts, it must have been to reflect that girls with such prospects of dower could only be assets to a parent interested in social advancement. He facilitated Coutts's acquaintance with his friends – including the Duchess of Devonshire, from whom the banker was to derive financial loss as well as social gain – and set about the gargantuan task of recording for Coutts a total of debt he himself could no longer grasp. In the course of one of the resulting letters to the banker he wrote: 'There are circumstances which it is difficult to mention with delicacy; but I wish you to understand that when I speak of my circumstances I do not (like Mr Hastings) wish to distinguish persons very intimately connected with me from myself; and when I say that I have paid all my debts I mean all those for which I can be considered responsible, in short all those of the person you saw at Cheltenham as well as my own.' The reference to Hastings concerned the nabob's recent self-dissociation from gifts received by his wife, and the terms of this statement would have indicated to any thoughtful reader that Fox saw himself as a married man.

All the world knew however that he was not, and in 1795 two of the three Misses Coutts were also still unmarried. Now, it would appear (unless the whole intention existed only in the imaginations of Elizabeth and William Adam), one or more of the Coutts family saw in Fox – forty-six years old, impoverished, politically ruined, but still the most loved and sought-after member of Whig society – a possible husband for the twenty-two-year-old second daughter, Fanny. She was her father's favourite, the daughter whose ill-health in girlhood had caused him such concern, and it is not impossible that it was she herself who saw a desirable husband in Charles. Apparently one of those girls who are attracted by much older men, she was eventually to marry – entirely, her father insisted, by her own wish – the first Marquess of Bute, who was five years Charles's senior.

Charles was an unsuspicious as ever that anyone might look on him, who saw himself as a married man of many years' standing, as a potential husband. He had by now long been on friendly terms with the Coutts family, and when in London and not otherwise engaged was quite content to accept invitations to their house in the Strand and listen to Mrs Coutts extolling the charms and virtues of her daughters. He was mildly surprised by the suggestion that a lock of his hair would make an acceptable gift to Fanny, but could not imagine refusing anything so trivial. Elizabeth, when she learned of the request, saw it in a very different light.

She clearly had never been quite convinced that Charles's attachment to her could be lifelong; she believed that eventually he would leave her to marry, if only for reasons of family, connection or fortune. Now the prospect had materialised. Connections Fanny Coutts had none, but this was of little importance to Charles, belonging as he did by birth and friendship in the heart of the political aristocracy, whereas the dowry Fanny could bring would make him a wealthy man, and she, young and doubtless fertile, could bear him children. The time had come for Elizabeth to step aside, and this, she now told Charles, she was ready to do.

The offer, it may reasonably be surmised, was made in a state of considerable agitation, to the extent perhaps that he found it impossible to reason with her at the time. The considered response he promised her was made by letter.

'I have put off writing to my Liz till this hour that I may not write in a hurry. Indeed my dearest Liz I have considered the question as much as it is possible to consider one where every thing is on one side & next to nothing on the other. I love you more than life itself indeed I do, & I can not figure to myself any possible idea of happiness without you, and being sure of this is it possible that I can think of any trifling advantage of fortune or connection as weighing a feather in the scale against the whole comfort and happiness of my Life? Even if you did not love me I could not endure the thought of belonging to any other woman, but my Liz does love me and will make me happy by living always with me, and if so & she is happy herself every wish of my heart is satisfied. Indeed my dearest Wife you are too suspicious. I assure you upon my honour that neither by word or look did I ever give the least reason to Miss C even to think that I thought her pretty nor till Mr C asked me for the hair had I the least suspicion that there was any notion about me of the sort you suppose, nor indeed am I now clear about it. I do assure you my dearest Liz I tell you upon this occasion the whole truth as exactly as I should to Ld. Rob or Fitz if I talked to them upon this subject. Mr Adam's conversation with Mrs C arose as I understood it in this manner. She was speaking of me very highly as she always does, and saying that it would have been better for me as a politician if I had led a different sort of life, if I had been married and led a domestic life; and this led Adam to say that I did lead a domestic a life as any man and that from what he had seen of us he was sure I considered you exactly as my Wife and that my life was in fact that of a married man though very scrupulous and *straitlaced* people (that was his word) might see it in a different light. That is what he told me, but my Liz what *sigs* what was said? I never can be happy without you and you have promised to be ruled in this instance by my determination. That is fixed and if you love me I shall be happy if not I shall be miserable, but still with my Liz, for never can I give my consent to part with her. Do repeat to me my dearest Love that you love me tenderly dearly and fondly it is such a *comf* to me to hear it and read it; and it is true, my dearest Liz, is it not? I will call at Coutts' soon, and will not give the hair, tho' I own in this I act against my own judgment to conform with your wish. I am much afraid that after having been asked for it & having said of course that I would give it, my not doing so will give Mr C an idea that I consider his request as of more importance than it becomes me to do, and possibly that I put an interpretation upon it which may make him ashamed of having made it. These are points upon which People are apt enough to be delicate & even touchy; but my Liz's opinion shall be my rule of conduct on this & on every other occasion – In your Sunday's letter you say that if I can be sure of always loving Liz, & being entirely hers, you will be the happiest woman in the World. Do pray my dear Angel repeat and confirm that sentiment & I shall be the happiest of Men. To think that I contribute to your happiness is a reflection so pleasing that while I enjoy it, it gives a zest to every other satisfaction in life, and makes me almost indifferent to every other unpleasant event. Indeed my Liz if I were to consider for a year I could think no otherwise than I do, & therefore pray let me understand that every thing is fixed, for till you say so directly an uneasy feel will hang about me, tho' it ought not as you say you love me & leave the matter to my decision. God bless my dearest mistress friend & *wife*, and make her love old Kins,* and believe (what is true) that he is & always will be entirely *hers*, yes every bit of him.'

So Fanny Coutts did not get the lock of hair, or the husband she may have been hoping for. Charles however had been given more to think about than the termination of that embarrassment. Now, perhaps for the first time, he realised that the absence of a legal tie between himself and Elizabeth was seen by her as being for his sake, and that in protecting what she deemed to be his interests she was inflicting distress upon herself. Understanding at last that her happiness, and his that depended on hers, would be securer if they were married, he resolved that married they must be.

Elizabeth's arguments were overborne, as inevitably they would have been at any time when he had made up his mind to marry her. He disposed even of her secondary objection, to being known to be his wife. Her reasons for this nowhere appear – possibly she suggested distaste for the scoffing of the Press – but may perhaps be surmised from what happened when eventually the marriage was made public, to be ascribed by most of Charles's friends to her importuning and his weakness. The thought of her appearing to have degraded him in the eyes of friends would have been unpleasing, and she may have feared too that the question their marriage would pose, of her social recognition, would strain Charles's relations with his female and married male friends. But Charles, having carried the main point, was not to be defeated on a minor one. If Elizabeth wished their marriage not to be known, let it be unknown; they could be married secretly.

This might have seemed impossible for a man so famous, but once he had set his mind to the matter Charles could find his way over or past any obstacle. A wedding in Chertsey or London was out of the question, but his enormous range of friendship still in its comprehensivity embraced every sort of person, of every rank, ability or professional qualification, who might help him at need. In Huntingdonshire lived a modest country parson, John Pery, incumbent

* 'Kins', of unknown origin, was Charles's pet name for himself, used solely to Elizabeth or in their private journal. Her name for him, Carlo or Carl, was less private, being sometimes used to Holland or before other people such as the painter Opie, who (Farington Journal) misheard it as 'Car'.

of the parish of Wyton, whom Charles long had known (possibly through St Andrew St John, whose family was connected with that of Barnard, in whose gift the living was), and who would tie the knot in a location no one would dream of as the venue for the wedding of Charles James Fox. Pery was pleased to help, and to comply with the wish for secrecy.

At the beginning of September Elizabeth journeyed north, accompanied by her maid Mary Dassonville, who was to be admitted to the secret, to stay with Pery at Wyton Rectory. Charles meanwhile, having secured a licence, set off to East Anglia for his usual round of shooting-parties, to be cut short this year, his hosts understood, so that he could escort Mrs Armitstead home from a stay with friends. In the pleasant rectory at Wyton, overlooking the church in which she was to become her Angel's lawful wife, Elizabeth passed in unaccustomed idleness the weeks necessary to establish a residential qualification. Severed from her household duties, her garden, her neighbours and her harp, and without the social or therapeutic activities that occupied her during her holidays, she had little to do but think, and think about her marriage. She met Pery's clerk, Jeremiah Bradshaw, who was to witness the wedding and give her away, and was worried by an impression that he was a gossip likely to talk about a ceremony so unusual. In the end her qualms attacked her all over again, and on 23rd September, with less than a week to go to the date of the wedding, she wrote to Charles proposing its cancellation.

He was not to be thrown at the last fence. Lovingly he wrote back: 'My dearest Liz, I have received your Wednesday's letter, kind as usual yet full of doubts, that indeed indeed are wholly unfounded. I do assure you I have long ago given the subject all possible consideration and am for many reasons convinced that by following our plan we are doing for the best. In case of any thing happening to me I am sure your having been my legal Wife will make your situation less uncomfortable and though this is a case that my dear Liz can not bear to think of yet according to the course of nature and of accidents it is a very probable one. There are besides other reasons which you yourself allowed to be good after having very seriously considered the subject, and though perhaps you do not think so yet I am convinced the opinion you then formed was right. On the other hand what possible reason can there be against it? I know myself, I know my attachment to you. I know you and all those qualities that belong to you and make me love and adore you more and more every day, and I will answer for it that on my side, aye and I believe on your side too, we may go year after year for the flitch at Dunmow. I can easily conceive what you say that you had rather see me married to another then have to think that I repented being married to you and wished myself free; but indeed indeed my dearest Angel you never never shall have cause for such a thought. So on Monday morning you must say love and obey, and be Mrs. Fox – I do not much like what you say of the Clerk but I understood his presence was necessary even if there had been another Person to give you away, otherwise I would have spoken to St John. If he is such a gossiping Person as you describe perhaps Mr Pery had better get the Clergyman who does duty for him or some other acquaintance to give you away; but my notion is that *he must* know of the register. After all if it should get about there is no great harm, indeed after the first talk it would be pleasanter that it should be known than not, and what *sig* a few additional paragraphs in the Newspaper. However as we shall manage it I do not think it will be known, and I do not intend at present to tell it to any body except perhaps my Brother, and so now good-bye till Monday morning at the hour of eight. I have no coat but a blue one. God bless my dearest Liz.'

And so on Monday, 28th September, 1795, a day of glowing sunshine, Elizabeth with Mary Dassonville at her side walked from the Rectory garden through the gate into the churchyard, and so to the church where Charles in his blue coat awaited her, and said love and obey and became Mrs Fox; and was told as Charles kissed her after the ceremony: 'Nothing now can part us, dearest Liz, but death.'

CHAPTER FIVE

The Most Able and Tranquil Felicity

The measures for secrecy succeeded. Mr Bradshaw did not gossip about the eccentric ceremony at which he had given away a stranger bride, and Elizabeth returned south with Charles still Mrs Armitstead to the world at large. When therefore they paused at Wolmer in Hertfordshire, where Charles wished to confer briefly with Samuel Whitbread, she waited for him, with the delicacy they always observed in avoiding potential embarrassment to his friends, in the carriage outside; Mrs Whitbread however learned that she was there, and in goodhearted defiance of convention invited her in to join them at breakfast. Warmed by this small act of kindness, which Elizabeth never forgot, husband and wife returned to St. Anne's Hill to the now licensed enjoyment of that 'able and tranquil felicity' that Charles had extolled so many years ago as the consequence of marriage for love. Experience of lawful marriage would serve only to confirm, for them both, the justice of that declaration.

Though the hopeless struggle in Parliament grew ever more wearisome, the happiness that rendered that duty more repellent by contrast gave him strength to endure it. There were private griefs, of course, and private rubs. A great grief was the decline of Charles's son Harry, possibly in consequence of an unidentified illness he suffered in 1795, into imbecility. There was no joy now, for him or for his father, in having him at St Anne's, which moreover was too small to house the separate establishment he needed; Charles had set up for him in his infancy (possibly when his handicap first became apparent) a small trust fund, and the income it yielded enabled him to be boarded and cared for at a house in Parsons Green. Harry's degeneration was the sadder in that his father and stepmother must by now have been beginning to fear that his half-sister's childishness was not a feature merely of her years. At the time of the marriage Harriet was fourteen, an age at which a normal girl might have been developing into a companion for an affectionate stepmother. Over the next few years Charles and Elizabeth came evidently to accept that this could not be hoped for, for in 1798, in a letter welcoming Elizabeth's news of a congenial neighbour, Charles remarked: 'Harriet is no resource.' Possibly in the hope that more formalised education would effect an improvement, Harriet was sent to school.

A rub was Holland's continued absence. Their disappointment in this was implied in a letter Elizabeth had written him in August (the earliest of hers to survive), enclosed in one from Charles: 'My Dear, Scarce of Days I have neglected a long time thanking you for the very pretty ring you were so kind [as] to send me in hopes you would by returning to England give me the opportunity of thanking you in person but your return is I fear so far off that the safest way is to thank you now which I do from the bottom of my heart as it makes me really happy any proof of your kindness to me and it makes my old one happy which I know you like to do – He is nice and well indeed I think he is better in health and spirits than I ever knew him to be – It is very long since he had a letter from you and I hope you will find time to let him hear from you a little oftener.'

Holland wrote, but he still did not return, and they apparently gave up hope of persuading him home. The next joint letter, written from Charles's London house in South Street on 18th February, 1796, shows that Elizabeth at least was now thinking of turning his continued stay in Italy to account. After Charles had discoursed depressedly on the little prospect of peace with France, Elizabeth took over and wrote: 'If you get to Venice before you return to England which it will be a pity not to do I shall be greatly obliged to you and so will the full of days [presumably another nickname for Charles] if you will have your Bust done for us by a Man who is there of the name of Canova as I understand he is one of the best sculptors that has been for ages – I hope it will not now be a long time before we see you it is what all your friends long for and none more than my old man and I – He does nothing now but read Greek all day and I suppose soon he will know it better than Dr Parr. God bless you my dear Lord Holland pray write soon and often you are grown very idle for it is very seldom that we hear from you.'

Charles then took over again with: 'If you have not named your Chaplain I wish you would appoint a Mr Taylor of Kensington to whom I understand that it would be some advantage. Pray mind what the Lady of the Hill says about the bust and if you get done for me by the same Canova a copy of the bust upon Ariosto's tomb at Ferrara I should like it very much, that is provided that it would not cost a great deal.' Holland disappointingly replied that Canova was undoubtedly very good, but very expensive, very spoilt and anyhow in Rome, and he said nothing about returning. In June however he did so, to replace one rub by another and a permanent one. With him he brought the pregnant – by him – Lady Webster, to be made, as soon as her husband could be prevailed upon to divorce her, Lady Holland.

The prospect of Holland's union with a divorcee cannot have gladdened an uncle, particularly one who hoped to see his nephew make a name for himself in politics. Even the permissive society of the 1770s and 1780s had looked somewhat askance at women who deserted their children for lovers, and now the moral climate was growing colder. The issue in 1787 of a Royal Proclamation against vice and immorality had been made by Wilberforce occasion for founding the society that was later named the Society for the Suppression of Vice and Immorality, which, given a powerful impetus by the French Revolution – seen by many as the fruit of aristocratic licence – , was steadily gaining ground. A recent and unpleasant manifestation of its effectiveness had been a proposal to legislate against the remarriage of divorcees to their co-respondents. Charles may have had this in mind when he wrote to Holland soon after his nephew's return, urging a temporary separation. He commended this, rather than the blatancy of open cohabitation, as being in the lady's interest, particularly should her husband refuse her a divorce. He may however have hoped that a temporary separation would become a permanent one; especially if he had by then met the lady.

Lady Webster, soon to become and later to become famous as Lady Holland, was a beautiful termagant whose considerable intelligence was veined with an impenetrable stupidity. This possibly derived from a solipsism that, rendering her incapable of apprehending the effect of her conduct on other people, was worsened by the tolerance of her bedmates. She herself seems, from her later Napoleonomania, to have hankered inwardly for masterfulness in the male (her scene-making with Holland, vividly reported by Lady Bessborough, suggests efforts to provoke him to violent response), and indeed she would probably have been much improved by a husband who beat her. Unfortunately she attracted submissive men only. Her first husband Sir Geoffrey Webster and her previous lover Thomas Pelham had been reeds in the varying gale of her whims, Holland now was another, and their tacit acceptance of her misbehaviour confirmed her in it. Lady Holland had her virtues. She was an excellent mistress to her servants (resembling in this that other solipsist, the Prince, whose servants declared him the kindest of masters), and could be notably kind to social inferiors, but this was little comfort to the equals to whom her rebarbative traits were lavishly displayed. No woman could have been a less welcome in-law to that affectionate breed the Foxes, who now must endure her or be severed from their head and hope. None found the endurance a greater strain than Charles.

He must quickly have perceived that Lady Holland herself as well as the circumstances of the marriage would do Holland's career no good. (Indeed, though Lady Holland was in time to become the most famous political hostess in English history, her loudly professed admiration for and goodwill toward England's greatest enemy, and her boasts when Holland was in office of her admission to official secrets, would have injured the career of an abler and more ambitious man). Her most immediately repellent feature to Charles was probably, however, her manifest dislike of the woman he loved. This of course reflected no personal acquaintance with 'Mrs Armitstead', and probably stemmed from a subconscious fear that, Holland's union being like his uncle's unconventional, Charles's liaison equated her in the world's eye with an ex-prostitute. In fact, the delicacy with which Charles and Elizabeth avoided embarrassing his friends was extended to Lady Holland no less than to the chastest of his friends' wives, and Elizabeth was taken to see Holland House – the family mansion in Kensington which Holland was now restoring – only when the Hollands were absent in Scotland. No corresponding delicacy, however, was shown in return. The wives of Charles's friends accepted that those who did not meet Mrs Armitstead could not visit St Anne's, but in 1798 Holland, whose subservience to his wife could make him the instrument of her discourtesy, wrote to Charles: 'If it is not inconvenient to you Lady Holland would like to walk round St Anne's on Wednesday in her way to town as she is very anxious to see it particularly the seats. If I hear nothing from you I shall probably see you on that day & if it is fine Lady H. will walk in the grounds.'

From her Journal it appears that, by an odd psychological quirk, Lady Holland justified her dislike by attributing to Elizabeth some of her own unadmitted faults. It was Mrs Armitstead's extravagance that had ruined Mr Fox, declared the woman who travelled with retinues of servants astonishing to those of higher rank than she, while the brevity of Fox's visits to London was ascribed to the tight rein Mrs Armitstead kept on him by the wife who would not let Holland visit Holkham at all because she as a divorcee was not invited there. It is fair to say that Charles and Elizabeth did enjoy playing at the roles of complaisantly henpecked husband and managing wife; Elizabeth's wedding gift to her Angel had been a seal engraved with a hand holding an ear. At Holland House their play was reality.

But the vexations of Holland's marriage, the worries over Charles's children, were troubles on the periphery the central serenity of St Anne's was inviolate. In 1797 the plenitude of felicity was attained. That summer, after more than two years' fruitless struggle against the erosion of liberties that the Government deemed necessary to national safety, the Foxites agreed that they could with honour secede from Parliament. Now at last Charles could with an untroubled conscience give himself up to his personal life. In fifteen years he and Elizabeth had never had enough of each other's society, nor he enough of their dear home. 'I should not care,' he had told Samuel Rogers a year previously, 'if I was condemned never to stir a mile beyond St Anne's Hill for the rest of my life.' Now he need not.

Now in the world's eyes he gave himself up to indulging to the full his unique capacity for idleness. But 'how manifold are his activities whom the world deems idle,' he quoted once of himself, and in his retirement he found new employments to delight him. With the stabilising of his financial affairs he had reverted to the traditional eighteenth-century attitude towards property, that it was to be extended and improved, and now when opportunity offered he was augmenting their little estate (which legally had become his on his marriage, the secrecy of which had precluded a settlement on Elizabeth); in 1797 or 1798 he leased the small adjacent property of Fan Grove. With land came concern with the use of land. Agricultural improvement had for decades been an interest of some of the wealthiest and most intelligent of the magnate landlords, two of Charles's best friends, Coke of Holkham and the Duke of Bedford, being in the van of the movement. Now, on a Trianon scale if without Trianon architecture, Charles followed suit. Friends, acquaintances, people encountered casually, from Coke to an agricultural labourer met sheltering under a tree from the rain, were consulted for their views on stock and crops. The Chertsey farmers stopped in the lane past St Anne's to talk across the pales about the corn and the weather. Advice was supplied, sometimes good, sometimes not ('Dear Lauderdale . . . you persuaded me last year to sow a greater proportion of rye grass with the clover than is usual here – The consequence has been that the rye has got quite the better and I shall have but little clover.'): gifts were received with pleasure ('Dear Price, I have just time to tell you that your magnificent Present has just arrived . . . . We have not had time to give the animals due examination yet but both Mrs A. and myself are full of admiration for the beautiful *faces* of the sheep and especially the Ewe that is si bien coiffée'): and Charles was as happily intent on his little plot as Coke or Bedford on their thousands of acres.

Elizabeth was and continued deeply interested in the farm, but her activities too were manifold. To start with, she had the household to manage. The St Anne's establishment was to small to justify employing a house keeper, and the running of so hospitable a house required time, thought and competence in its mistress. She had her own livestock, for there was always at least one dog about the house and often a litter, for she bred from her pets. She kept songbirds too (which delighted Charles, for the sole music to please this unmusical creature was birdsong, and he often wondered that the ancient poets made so little mention of it), and liked to think that they knew her, and welcomed her back after an absence. Her own music was kept up; Charles had written to Holland in Italy: 'If you do [go to Venice again] pray see Sig. Gazzaniga, a composer, and give him Mrs A's compliments and mine, and desire him to send her some new airs, easy and pretty'; and she had recently learned to play the harp. She had and practised other accomplishments, at least in Mr Bingley's sense of the word. She painted a table to present to Holland on the reoccupation of Holland House (Holland loyally declared it the prettiest he had ever seen; Lady Holland's opinion was not recorded), and a letter of Charles's from Holkham shows her engaged upon another piece of decoration: 'My Love is very good-humoured about the Harp [Harriet's harp lessons] more than I should be, but it gives her more time for drawing dear skreen which I shall be very fond of because it was the occasion of my Ange's saying such a kind thing about the temple of her Happiness.'

Various and satisfying as were her activities within doors, her chief active pleasure was in the gardens and grounds. Though Charles too loved and worked in them, an entry in her later Journal suggests that hers was the designing hand in their improvements; when a visitor admired the beauty of the St Anne's gardens: 'I thought how pleased Angel would have been had he been with us, all the little things I had done in the grounds which he used to praise so much Ld. Fortescue admires also.' Already she was becoming an expert, whose advice Holland sought on the restoration of the long neglected garden at Holland House, to be told: 'I am quite delighted at the little commission you have given me, and I will look in all my books for the prettiest things that grow.'

Her own grounds were now showing the effect of the loving improvements which over the years would make her demesne one of the loveliest, for its size, in England. Before the house a sweep of lawn, shaded here and there with well-spaced cedars, led on the eye to the distances beyond the hill. From the lawn the wanderer might by flower-fringed walks be enticed into or through the planted gardens, or if shade were desired follow winding paths into the woodland, now carefully thinned and planted with decorative trees and shrubs and cut through here and there by vistas opening out over the Thames or to the hazy Chilterns. Where beauty and shelter most pleasingly joined there were seats, and here and there small summerhouses afforded the settings in which Charles and Elizabeth could pass a sunny morning with his books and her needlework. Charles, his appetite for architectural follies whetted by the Temple of Friendship, hankered for more – a Temple of the Muses, perhaps – but Elizabeth deemed this extravagant. Her concept of garden building was practical. A greenhouse was approved, and great successes she achieved there with camellias and with oranges, and the needs of pleasant sociability were saluted by the incorporation of a tearoom, so that in fine but cool weather tea and coffee could still be enjoyed in the garden. Practical regard both to her flowers and her housekeeping doubtless underlay too a request put through Charles to Fitzpatrick in 1797; 'Mrs A. would be obliged to you if you would buy her a glass Bee Hive at Dalmahoy's in Piccadilly.' At St Anne's practicality went hand in hand with beauty and even the production of fruit and vegetables was blended, in anticipation of a much later fashion, with pleasure to the eyes; a visitor enquiring after the kitchen garden as he was led through shrubs and flowers was told: 'You are now in the midst of it.'

The Cyprian had vanished, to all but unkind remembrance, in the country gentlewoman, and little of her remained to outward view. Elizabeth was well up in her forties now, growing stout, her beauty on the wane. But to Charles she still was lovely; and, inconveniently, to another person.

The year that saw the wedding of Charles and Elizabeth had witnessed also that of the Prince of Wales. Temporarily seduced from Mrs Fitzherbert by the attractions of Lady Jersey, overwhelmed by debt and conscious that the only hope of Parliamentary succour lay in a marriage acceptable to his father, he had resigned himself to open if bigamous matrimony; abjuring any interest in the bride with the words: 'One damned German frow is as good as another.' Fate proved him wrong; the ceremony over, he found himself tied for life to a sluttish hoyden of dubious mental balance. Recoiling from his marital catastrophe and tired of Lady Jersey, the Prince began that quest for the happier past that was eventually to bring about his reunion with Mrs Fitzherbert. That past however had held pleasures unconnected with her, and one of these was apt to come to his mind when he called on Fox. Calling and finding Fox out now opened, it seems, pleasing possibilities to him. These being denied, he took measures the full flavour of which can be appreciated only when it is remembered that the Prince was still declaring Mr Fox to be his dearest friend. Their nature emerges from a letter Charles wrote to Elizabeth from Holkham, undated but probably written in October or November of 1798 when, having suffered one of the bouts of illness that often assailed her in early autumn, she was contemplating a recuperative stay at Brighton. 'I hope the Prince will not be at Brighthelmstone as he is so troublesome to my Liz, & talks in the style you told me. I am not afraid of my Angel's doing anything wrong, I know her too well for that if I did not, Good God, how *mis* I should be; but I collected from what you said that his way of persuading you was to tell you inventions about me, and though I should think Liz knows him too well to believe him, yet I have observed that the next time I have seen my Liz after the P has been with her she has had one of those *coldish* looks that make Kins so *mis*.'

Elizabeth did go to Brighton in the late autumn of 1798, but, whether for reasons of economy or to render herself inconspicuous to the Prince, took a very modest lodging. Samuel Rogers met her there in November and wrote to a friend: 'Here is Mrs Armstead (Fox is pheasant-shooting in Norfolk) who lives in a small cabin with a man and a maid and who is reading 'Emily Montagu' for the third time.' Frances Brooke's novel was then nearly thirty years old, and virtually devoid of the melodrama that characterised most popular novels of the period, but it retained a readership. Part of its charm lay in its setting, chiefly in Canada, but much as Elizabeth enjoyed books about distant countries, there was more than that to please her in 'Emily Montagu'. The heroine, having initially refused the hero on the ground that marriage with her will injure his interests, eventually yields, to settle with him on a small income in a modest country home, which with its garden they set about improving. The last volume is virtually a celebration of quiet marital happiness, and it is easy to imagine Elizabeth translating Mrs Brooke's account of her fictional couple into a picture of herself and Charles at St Anne's Hill.

Their way of life there was a simple one. To the inhabitants of the fashionable world it might have seemed quiet to dullness, but Charles and Elizabeth had had their fill of Vanity Fair and St Anne's was their Delectable Mountain. They rose before eight – in summer between six and seven – and breakfasted some two hours later. The weather being propitious, a stroll in the garden followed, after which the morning would be passed with Elizabeth at her harp while Charles read in Greek or Latin, or in reading together either history or poetry. One winter, Charles told Rogers, he read nine epics aloud to her 'if I could call Lucretius one, which he is not; Iliad, Odyssey, Apollonius Rhodius, Eneid, Tasso, Ariosto, Milton's Paradise Lost and Regained, Fairy Queen.' At half-past two in summer, at four in winter, they dined; even the later hour was already unfashionable in its earliness, but they liked a long evening. Their fare was described by John Trotter, later Charles's secretary, as 'frugal but plentiful,'* the oxymoron probably suggested by the plainness of the cooking. Charles's contours – and, increasingly

*Memoirs of the Latter Years of the Right Honourable Charles James Fox.' Though this book displeased the family intensely, Fitzpatrick approved the accuracy of 'his description of the private and domestic life of St. Anne's Hill.'

130

Elizabeth's – were not those of asceticism. Indeed it is clear from his letters, and, later, her journal, that they enjoyed and took an interest in their food, but not in haut cuisine; they would have agreed with Elizabeth Bennet in preferring a plain dish to a ragout. Charles's references are almost always to roast meats, of which he especially preferred pork. 'Pork is excellent in all its shapes,' he once told Rogers, and one letter to Elizabeth from London, whither he had evidently taken a joint from St Anne's, informed her: 'I think the leg of pork was the most *squiz* I ever tasted, and so did the company, for I do not believe there was an ounce left on it.' Elizabeth too approved a good roast, and was also observant of excellence in fruit and vegetables, which now on their tables was usually of their own growing.

After dinner was the time for walking, if the weather allowed, until the hour for tea or coffee, followed by the second reading period of the day. This was assigned to novel reading; when Fanny Burney's *Camilla* came out in 1798, and Charles in his eagerness started to read it at the 'wrong' time of day, Elizabeth confiscated the book. 'A light supper of fruit, pastry, or something very trifling finished the day,' wrote Trotter, 'and at half-past ten the family were gone to rest.'

As the day was patterned, so was the year, the returning cycle of expected seasonal pleasures punctuated with the anniversaries that Elizabeth loved to celebrate. The first of these, lightening the dull days of mid-winter, was 24th January, Charles's birthday, for which she delighted in thinking up small surprises. Fitzpatrick sometimes came to pass that day with them, and Holland if Lady Holland could be induced to let him go. Now the days were beginning to lengthen, and soon the beasts on their small farm would be dropping their young, to be visited, admired and named. About the garden the first shoots of spring began to appear, the birds grew active, and as the sun increased in strength Charles and Elizabeth would conceal themselves to watch the work of nest-building. Their ears were stretched for the first mating-song; the first blackbird's, the first thrush's song were worthy of note, but as April advanced there was the eagerest listening of all, for the first nightingale. In London Parliament was in session and noble mansions were opening for the season, but Charles went thither rarely, reluctantly and briefly. Once, dragged up for a debate on an alleged overture for peace from France, he found on reaching Holland House that it had been postponed because Pitt was ill. 'He . . . sat silent and overcome,' wrote Holland, 'as if the intelligence of some great calamity had reached his ears. I saw tears steal down his cheeks, so vexed was he at being detained from his garden, his books and his cheerful life in the country.' Least bearable of all was such detention at the start of the summer, when everywhere St. Anne's was burgeoning with delight for all the senses.

May 7th went by, with its memory of how in 1795 Charles had declared it 'the happiest day that ever I spent in my life.' Now the beloved garden was at its peak of beauty and now if the weather were fair it might be enjoyed from dawn to darkness. The house need be entered for breakfast and dinner only. Daylight hours were passed among the flowers and trees, and at dusk lamps were lit along the verandah, and on the lawn and under the cedars good talk went on into the scented night.

For as the high midsummer pomps came on the flow of visiting friends grew to a flood, the little house overflowed with guests and the table was crowded to its limit. The hospitality of St. Anne's was simple, no greater diversion being offered than a visit to the haymaking, country walks, or strolls up to Fan Grove or down to the farmhouse for tea (for tea at the home farm was becoming a popular entertainment for country-house visitors), or perhaps a boating excursion on the Thames. The fascination of Charles's talk, however, was no less than ever it had been, and Elizabeth, quietly attentive to everyone's needs and comfort, was a perfect hostess. 'The assiduous care, and excellent management, of Mrs Fox, rendered his rural mansion the abode of peace, elegance and order . . . Nor were Mrs Fox's captivating manners conducive in a faint manner to the harmonizing of everything around,' wrote Trotter floridly; 'the watchful and refined attentions she paid to her guests anticipated everything they could desire, and charmed away every feeling of embarrassment, which diffidence, in the presence of so exalted a character, might be apt to occasion.' Lord John Russell, close in adult life to many who remembered the golden days of St. Anne's, put it more simply: 'She was kind to his friends.'

11th July was the summer's climax, the day that Charles declared the happiest day of the year, Elizabeth's birthday. With its passing the blossom-time of midsummer was over, the flowers began to fade, the foliage to grow dusty, and they would contemplate a little holiday together, a tour perhaps of Kent or Sussex. They would however be at home if possible for the next 'happiest day of the year', the anniversary that could not be openly celebrated, 28th September, when if they could contrive it they dined quietly and alone together. There followed now their annual separation, for though there was a little rough shooting to be had in the woodlands at home, the sport it offered could not compare with that available in East Anglia, and Elizabeth had no wish for Charles to give up the amusement he enjoyed so much. Off he went therefore to Holkham or to Eldon, and again the letters would speed to and fro between Chertsey and Norfolk, Elizabeth's now vanished but their constancy and nature apparent from those of Charles. 'My angel, what happiness it is to love [one] another so . . . How I do feel all my love's warm expressions about it [their wedding anniversary] go to heart and make it jump and swell! Yes I am quite sure we could never have been quite happy if we had not known each other, & I believe my Liz doats on me just as she says, but the only dispute is which doats most, and that I never will give up.' 'O! Lord how I do love her! but the more the better because she deserves it all and does not think it too much nor is tired or teazed with it, and though it does cause me to be sure some terrible anxieties [she had been ill during his absence] yet it makes me I verily believe the happiest Man in the world when I think that my Liz is well and happy and pays me back all my love.'

After the shooting-parties, one more separation followed. Lord Robert Spencer had in 1797 settled at Woolbeding in Sussex, where in winter he held house-parties of his friends. Charles would usually visit him there in November or December, while Elizabeth took a little holiday at Brighton or Bognor, and then they would return together to St. Anne's and the quiet enjoyments of winter; reading by the fire, or planning next year's embellishments to the garden, or playing at battledore and counting the number of strokes – often into the thousands – for which they could keep the shuttlecock in the air. Christmas would be quietly kept, for the day was seen as one for the servants – the family, as they tended in their oldfashioned way to call them – to have their own celebration; above stairs any company would usually be family in the modern sense of the word, including perhaps Fitzpatrick, who qualified as family by his indirect brother-in-lawhood to Charles, and who as early as 1785 had at this season been told 'come if you can eat good Turkey Chine & minced Pyes.' Their own festivity would be held on Twelfth Night, when neighbours would be invited in for a small party, with a 'twelfth cake', music and dancing, and with it another happy year would be completed and the cycle of felicity begin anew. On 24th January, 1799, his fiftieth birthday, Charles gave Elizabeth some lines he had written to celebrate the day.

> 'Of years I have now half a century past
> Yet not one of the fifty so blest as the last.
> How it chances my troubles thus daily should cease,
> And Happiness still with my years should increase,
> This defiance of Nature's more general laws
> You alone can explain who alone are the cause.'

Superlative idler though he was (one summer visitor discovered him recumbent in the garden, trying, he said, to make the birds believe him dead). Charles did not positively mean to indulge in idleness mitigated by farm-management only for the rest of his days. He had long been playing with the notion of writing an account of the reign of James II, and this was converted into a positive project by Elizabeth's saying that she wished they could afford to build on another room. The little house must have felt smaller than ever since, in 1798, Charles had disposed of his London house and, while selling the furniture, brought down from it most of the books and pictures kept there. To move was unthinkable and the only solution would be to extend; but how to find the money? The production of a book, Charles decided, might raise the necessary funds, and 'it will ever be a great comfort to me,' Elizabeth told Holland years later, 'to reflect that had it not been for me this dear History would in all probability never have been written.'

She had, she was to find, rather more to do than suggest the desirability of raising money. Charles so enjoyed his *dolce far niente* that a fair amount of her teasing was sometimes needed to get him even to answer his letters ('my passion for writing letters,' he once told Fitzpatrick when catching up with a backlog, 'is partly owing to a desire of contradicting Mrs A's calumnious accusation of Idleness'), and how much more was required to get him down to the serious business of research and writing. There were so many distractions. Immediately, there was the overmastering allure of the great Faddle affair, into which Elizabeth, no doubt to her subsequent regret, initially urged him.

Faddle was a stout and elderly dog, the property, it would appear, of Fitzpatrick. Faddle, at some time in the late summer or early autumn of

1798, was mated – or possibly mated himself – with a bitch called Flora. The union proved fruitful but, so soon after it as to suggest *post hoc ergo propter hoc,* Faddle died. This erotic tragedy seemed to Fitzpatrick, and to Uvedale Price, with whom he was staying at the time, worthy of celebration. Together they set about composing epitaphs for Faddle in every language at their command, deriving so much amusement from their efforts as to suggest joining others in the pleasure. Lord Ossory was invited to participate and did, after which the invitation was extended to Charles. At first he was not interested and proposed passing on the suggestion to Holland, but Elizabeth cried shame on him and he decided to try his hand. Soon an uncontrollable addiction to epitaph-writing had him in its grip. At one point he tried to shake it off, declaring to Fitzpatrick:

'And now no more my brains I'll addle
 With making verses about Faddle:'

but 'the itch of versifying' was strong upon him and soon he was at it again. Epitaphs flew to and fro between Surrey and Herefordshire; Price's neighbours Payne Knight and Sir Edward Winnington were drawn in; and just when enthusiasm might have begun to wane, the whole entertainment was given fresh impetus. One of Faddle's posthumous progeny, a half-grown pup, was observed playing with a little bitch. Soon afterwards, the poor little fellow grew emaciated and died, and soon after that the bitch was found to be in pup. The fate of the Faddles had struck again, and 'as to the enmity of Venus,' declared Charles, 'Phaedra herself had no more right to complain of it with respect to her race, than the Faddles.' The epitaph-makers flew to their pens anew. The Faddles were lamented in Greek and Latin, in French and Italian. Old Mr Meyer, Charles Meyer's father, was applied to for an epitaph in German and obligingly provided two, though – since the elegists knew neither the language nor its literature – they could not yield the pleasure afforded by the rest, of round-robin literary criticism.

For this of course was the amusement; both to compose your epitaph acccording to the rules of the language used and its prosody, and to apply these rules to the productions of the other participants. The incessant letters about Faddle were burdened at least as much with criticisms as with epitaphs. 'Your Latin epitaph is very well tho' there is something equivocal in the expression *praecipium vitae* placed as it is.' 'I do not like Omens; it is like Jack Cade calling the man's death a warning

to him' 'I do not recall that the Italians ever wrote couplets of that sort.'
Price, to whom the last comment was directed, owned as he shifted to
French and Italian: 'The two last languages I certainly understand much
better than either greek or latin, but the rules of versification in them
not so well.' It is an unconsciously wry comment on eighteenth-century
upper-class education, which nevertheless must be given credit for the
development of mental resources that kept a bunch of middle-aged ex-
rakes happily and innocently occupied for months on end.

The women of course were virtually unable to join in. Neither Lady
Caroline Price nor Elizabeth had any turn for versifying, and the former
was as incapable as the latter of even understanding the Greek and Latin
verses. 'Lady Caroline, who was very angry at your sending nothing
but Greek epitaphs, was delighted to have some english from you,'
Price told Fox, and Elizabeth too read such productions as were in
English with amused interest, copying those she liked best for her
commonplace book.

All this was great fun, and so was the reading of Chaucer, with
Charles comparing his handling of the Griselda story with Boccaccio's
and his manner of writing with Ariosto's, but it was not advancing the
History. Bracing himself, Charles began to tackle the necessary research
with Lauderdale's help, the after-dinner reading period was given up to
relevant historical works, and through the summer of 1799, against the
competing temptations of natural and literary beauties, the assembly
and consideration of material went on.

His pleasures however delayed its progress by more than their own
attractions; two, that summer, led to accidents. The first was trivial;
boating with Elizabeth, he fell in at one of the deeper reaches. His
immediate concern on surfacing being for her alarm, he swam at once to
a stretch within his depth, stood up, and called: 'You see, I am safe.'
This accident was followed on 1st September by a more serious one; he
was shooting in the home woodland with William Porter when his gun
exploded in his hand. Porter took him at once to the nearest farm, from
which, his first thought again Elizabeth's ease of mind, he wrote: 'My
dearest Liz, I have hurt my left hand a good deal by the Gun bursting,
but I am very well otherwise, only would not go home directly lest you
should be frightened by my hand bloody.' In fact the damage appeared
serious. Ives, the local apothecary sent for at once, bandaged the hand
but advised immediate consultation of a London surgeon, and husband

and wife set off as soon as horses could be brought up from Chertsey. In the carriage Charles, 'in dreadful pain and his hand all bloody,' as Elizabeth noted on the letter sent her from the farm, composed a poem to distract himself and comfort his anxious love.

> 'How can I at aught repine
> While my dearest Liz is mine?
> Can I feel or pain or woe
> When my Lizzy loves me so?
> Where's the sorrow that thy smile
> Knows not sweetly to beguile?
> Sense of Pain and Danger flies
> From the looks of those dear Eyes,
> Looks of Kindness, looks of love
> That lift my mortal thoughts above,
> While I view that heavenly face,
> While I feel that dear embrace,
> While I hear that soothing voice,
> Tho' maimed or crippled Life's my choice.
> Without thee all the Fates can give
> Has nought would make me wish to live.
> No, could they foil the power of Time
> And restore youth's boasted prime
> Add to boot Fame, Power and Wealth,
> Undisturb'd and certain Health,
> Without thee 'twould nought avail,
> The source of every joy would fail;
> But loved by thee, by thee caress'd,
> In pain & sickness I am blest.'

Happily, he was not to be crippled; though the surgeon consulted feared initially that amputation might be necessary, the hand eventually healed without the loss even of a finger.

The year was drawing now towards its close, most of the material needed for the earlier chapters of the History had been assembled, and still no start had been made. Once Charles had recovered from his hand injury, Elizabeth resumed her constructive teasing, and, as she told Holland in a letter written when he was arranging posthumous publication nine years later: 'The History was begun on the 19 of Decr 1799, but literally only a few words as I had made a point that it should be begun before that year was out. It will ever be a great comfort to me to reflect that had it not been for me this dear History would in all probability never have been written and the world have never known half the beauties of the great and good mind that is now no more. It was on my saying that I longed to have a new Room that made him resolve to write it. Ah my dearest Young One when I reflect on the many very many happy hours and weeks this dear history has been the cause of my passing in this dear room you will not wonder at or blame me for being so fond of it or so jealous that any body should even touch the original. When I have the book in my hand or on the Table near me I see again all that dear expression that used to beam in his angelic eyes when he had written anything he liked or that he thought gave me pleasure to read.'

Later, she described Fox's way of work when he had at last got down to the task of writing: 'He never wrote any thing at breakfast but if it was fine we always went in the garden for a little while and if it was bad we generally lounged with some book before he came up to this dear room. I was always in the room with him when he wrote for he did not like my being even in the next. Alas, alas, my dearest Young One what happiness mine was to live with such a man and to know that there was not a thought or wish in that angelic mind that I did not partake [of]. He used to write while I was either at work or Harping without there was any left uncopied, and then I used to sit at one Table copying while he wrote at the other and then I used to read out to him what I had done while he looked over his own writing which he used to tear and put in the paper basket when he had read.'

The History still advanced but slowly; in May, 1800, Charles admitted to Fitzpatrick that he still had not completed even the introductory chapter. Elizabeth herself had briefly distracted him in January by asking for a poem on his birthday, to be rewarded with:

> 'Some verses Bess says she must have for this morn
> Because 'tis the day on which Darling was born,
> Let her make them herself then for I in the year
> Some others can find more deservedly dear.
> Ah, the Gift of this Day's in comparison small
> While that which first gave me her Love gave me All.'

Research and writing history had charm by comparison with politics only; compared with virtually any other mental or physical activity that might engage Charles, they lacked appeal. To Grey, with whom he had engaged in an epistolary argument concerning the justification for describing the nightingale's song as merry, he ended a letter – that called Chaucer and Theocritus in support of his case while admitting the contrary evidence of Sophocles – with the remark: 'I am afraid I like these researches as much better than those that relate to Shaftesbury, Sunderland etc, as I do those better than attending the House of Commons.'

Early in 1801 the question of resuming House of Commons attendance again forced itself upon him. Pitt resigned, his sticking-point of principle having been reached when the King refused consent to the Catholic emancipation to which Pitt felt himself committed as a condition of the union of the British and Irish Parliaments; and hard on his resignation came reports that the King was again mentally ill. The ghost of the Regency and its opening up of office to the Foxites rose to cast a shadow in which Fox deliberated unhappily between his wishes and the claims of duty, while Elizabeth, as always when he was uncertain in such matters, begged him to send for Fitzpatrick. Obediently he wrote, on 2nd April, to Foxley where again Fitzpatrick was staying with the Prices, asking that if his friend thought there was any truth in the rumour he should come to St. Anne's.

Fitzpatrick evidently thought there was none, for he stayed where he was. Elizabeth and Holland meanwhile convinced themselves, the one that Addington's Administration would not survive anyhow, the other that a good push from the Foxites would overturn it. In deference to his Angel, Charles wrote again to Fitzpatrick on 18th April telling him that: 'Mrs A. says a few days will produce a Crash, and that therefore the sooner you come the better.' The next day he informed Holland (who had gone so far as to set unrequested about finding a London house for his uncle): 'Never did a letter arrive in worse time, my dear young one, than yours this morning; a sweet westerly wind, a beautiful sun, all the thorns and elms just budding, and the nightingales just beginning to sing, though the blackbirds and thrushes would have been quite sufficient without the return of these seceders to have refuted any arguments in your letter. Seriously speaking I cannot conceive what you mean by everybody agreeing that something may *now* be done; I beg at least not to be included among the holders of that opinion, for as it appears to me there never was a moment when all exertion on our part was more certain to be useless if not worse. Pray therefore put a stop to any trouble or expense (as soon as possible) you or any one else have been at or are incurring about a house.'

His judgment proved right; the Administration survived. Again he could with a clear conscience yield to the never-weakening magnetism of his home. 'This place never was so beautiful as it is just now (ask Unkle Dick),' he wrote to his niece Caroline in May, 'and there never was a time when I felt so much disinclination to leave it.' About harvest-time he informed Uvedale Price: 'We certainly are very eager just now about farming and Bob [the Price's son, now at Eton and often a visitor to St. Anne's] has been reaping with me a piece (a small one as you may guess) of Wheat this morning. But I do not think Farming will be in the way of history. Idleness and idle reading more likely.'

Public affairs however were soon to intervene again, and more happily, for that autumn Addington commenced the cautious negotiations with France that would lead, the following spring, to the Treaty of Amiens. For these Fox could have nothing but welcome. An associated source of contentment was the stimulus given to rapprochement with old friends, such as Fitzwilliam, whose estrangement from him had been so largely an effect of his attitude to the war. Joy at the imminence of peace (formally achieved by the signature of the Treaty on 25th March, 1802) was sadly cut across by the death on 2nd March of Francis, Duke of Bedford. To Fox this was not merely a personal but a public loss, of the man he had both loved and seen as the leader of the next generation of Whigs. Encouraged to move the writ for a by-election at Tavistock (vacated by Lord John Russell's succession to his brother's dukedom) as a means of paying public tribute to his friend, he feared at first that he might be overcome by tears while speaking. Accepting the risk, he set about preparing his speech with an anxious care never – since he normally spoke impromptu – directed to his major Parliamentary orations; with the ironic result that, though he did not break down, it was reckoned one of his poorest performances. Fitzpatrick devoted himself, in sad earnest now, to the production of the finest elegy he could compose, and in melancholy sequel to the fun of three years back it was passed to and fro in draft among those who had so lightheartedly elegised the Faddles. Even Elizabeth, normally hesitant in criticising literary efforts, looked over the draft with Charles and ventured her ideas as to possible improvements. She herself, lacking creative outlet for her sorrow, could do no more than collect for her commonplace book such eulogies as she could gather of her friend. The sixth Duke was to become himself a much loved friend, but years afterwards it would give her pleasure to discern in the faces of his children some likeness to their 'dear late uncle.'

Despite all the distractions of public joy and private grief the History had been progressing, and was now advanced to a point at which the author felt he could make little further progress without the consultation of French sources which peace had rendered possible. That summer, therefore, their travel plans were for a tour of the Low Countries and a visit to Paris for the sake of Charles's research. First, the Westminster election must be got through: for with the ending of the war the main ground of the Foxites' secession had been removed, and Fox after some deliberation had concluded that he must hold his seat. That over, the preparations began. John Trotter – a nephew of Charles's old friend the Bishop of Down – was summoned to join them in the capacity of secretary. Harriet, though now approaching her twenty-first birthday, was dispatched to a school in Chelsea for the term of their absence; the coach was put in order, clothes and books were packed up, and a new journal-book was acquired for the recording of their travels.

At some time in the quiet years of retirement (not later than 1799, for a letter from Fitzpatrick to Holland indicates that diary-keeping was going on at the time the History was begun) they had started to keep a journal. Of the volumes before 1806, other than those of the 1802 tour, nothing survives but a couple of odd pages and the fragment of another among the Holland House papers, recording such important events as 'We saw a Butterfly and a Bee' (evidently deemed worthy of note because the month was February), and 'Devonia calved a bull calf.' These stray leaves appear to have been written both by Charles and by Elizabeth – whose handwritings were or had become remarkably similar. Such an entry as 'We played at shuttlecock for the 1st time this year and kept it up 1407 and only left off because Liz was tired,' was presumably his, while 'Went a shoping with Miss St John' is unmistakably Elizabeth not merely in activity but in idiom and spelling – she habitually failed to double a p after a short vowel. The 1802 tour journal, however, would be kept entirely by Charles.

Before he formally began it – on 29th July, the first night of their journey, which was passed with Lord Thanet (cohabitant with a mistress he later married) at his house near Maidstone – one other preparation for their tour had been made. In letters to friends, who could be relied on to spread the news, Charles had announced his marriage. This action had been decided on in the light of their knowledge that in Paris they would meet many other English visitors, and their memory of the small hurts occasioned by such encounters, with compatriots who greeted Charles while cutting Elizabeth, on their last tour abroad. Anyone who slighted her now must do so knowing that the offence was to Mrs Fox. The announcement itself, seven years after the event, was not entirely without embarrassment; why not at the time? The reason for secrecy then, if as seems probable it was fear of an ungenerous response in Charles's friends, was hardly susceptible of tactful presentation to the friends in question. Charles took a robust line, either stating merely that they had been married several years, as he did to Fitzpatrick and Lauderdale, or frankly saying, as in his letter to his niece Caroline, that 'a Secret which need never have been one is now divulged.' Elizabeth was (in the light of Charles's letter to her just before the marriage) rather disingenuous; writing to Harriet from Calais to notify her of the party's safe arrival there, she signed herself 'E. Fox', and added in a postscript, 'this is long has been my name* but till now Mr F had reasons for not wishing it to be known but has them no longer.'

Almost as soon as they had reached the inn at Calais the municipal officers of the town came to call upon Fox, thus giving the first warning that if he had imagined he could travel with the inconspicuousness of a private person, he was mistaken. His support for the Revolution and his ceaseless advocacy of peace were well known in France, and what the English saw as his dangerous Francophilia naturally produced a very different impression there. Of all Englishmen living he was in France the most admired and most welcome and – rather to the dismay of one who hated to be lionised – the French meant to show their feelings. After a visit to Cassel (where Farmer Fox enquired about cattle prices, to compare them with those prevailing in Surrey) the party came to Lille, where the authorities had had time to prepare for their distinguished visitor. A public dinner in Mr Fox's honour had been

---

*The insertion of a couple of commas – a punctuation mark generally scorned by Elizabeth – makes sense of this.

organised, a separate reception was given for Mrs Fox by the wife of the mayor, a ceremonial visit was arranged to the theatre, where the applause was less for the play than for the embarrassed visitor, and, wrote Charles in the journal, 'a painter sent a very bad picture of Kins which he had done he said from seeing him at the Comédie & the Mayor sent some bad verses.' It was a relief to get off to the Low Countries for a rapid tour that took in Ghent, Antwerp, Breda, Utrecht, Amsterdam, Leyden, the Hague, Rotterdam and Brussels in less than a fortnight, the journeys wiled away with the reading of 'Joseph Andrews' and the halts largely occupied with picture-viewing – though in Amsterdam they 'went to the great Church to hear Organ, very wonderful indeed and even to Kins delightful.' In mid-August they turned away from these enjoyments and travelled south-west ('Tom Jones' now succeeding to 'Joseph Andrews') to Paris, already crowded with English visitors. There, in a suite at the Hotel de Richelieu, Elizabeth on the evening of their arrival received Holland, Fitzpatrick and Lord Robert Spencer, for the first time as Mrs Fox.

Charles had decided to indulge himself with a small holiday before tackling the archives, and the first few days were given up to pleasure – including the theatre, at which he had again the embarrassment of being publicly applauded – and society. Here it rapidly became plain that, however unwelcome to him personally might be the determination of the French to honour him, nothing could more favour his wishes for his beloved wife. Indeed, the Foxes, though innocent of ulterior motive, could have chosen no time or circumstance for the announcement of their marriage that would have advanced Elizabeth more rapidly. Respectability was now, by the First Consul's decree, the order of the day, but his respectability required merely that persons living together be married to each other. By the same decree, pasts (such as Madame Bonaparte's) were to be forgotten. Mrs Fox was no less respectable than any other lady in Paris, and as she was the wife of a man the French wished to please, she was to be honoured. It did please him. After a great reception given by Talleyrand and his wife – another ex-courtesan, whom Talleyrand had married in compliance solely with Bonaparte's requirements –, he noted in the journal: 'Profusion of civility to us both which Kins liked.'

Aided by Trotter, Adair and St Andrew St John, he began his work in the archives on 23rd August, but as he spent there only the hours from eleven until three, ample time remained for enjoyment. One great pleasure was viewing the paintings in the Louvre. Thither they went repeatedly, often meeting there the banker-poet Samuel Rogers, their former slight acquaintanceship with whom now developed into friendship, and the painter John Opie with his charming wife Amelia. Amelia Opie wrote to Thomas Coke after one of these encounters: 'Mrs Fox looks like a clever woman, and I am told that she is, but I have seen too little of her to form any correct judgment of her abilities – all I know is that she is a very agreeable woman and has a very prepossessing manner.'

The Opies and the Foxes were together in the Louvre on the day when Bonaparte, as 'First Consul for Life' opened the Senate. As they were admiring Raphael's 'Transfiguration' the returning procession went by, and the two women ran to the window to see it, Mrs Fox remarking that for a republican Bonaparte seemed very fond of state and show. Fox had kept away from the window. He was already perhaps beginning to wonder just how true a republican Bonaparte was.

His doubts were not relieved by his audience with the First Consul on 12th September. Bonaparte was seen to be speaking to him at length, but when the audience was over and Elizabeth asked what he had said, Charles replied only 'Oh, he was very civil,' and asked her where they had left off in the novel they were reading. Later that evening, in private, he told her what had been said; Fitzpatrick who was with them, recorded it in his own Paris journal. 'It was very flattering to him personally on the score of his distinguished talents. The chief feature of this Speech was an idea he expressed of the World's being divided into two nations, the Eastern and the Western, that the laws manners customs and religions of each should be held sacred supported by all Governments and that whoever attempted to disturb any of them should be considered an instigator of civil war.' It was not a concept to gladden a lover of liberty.

There were other, more pleasing, occurrences. Koscuisko called upon them; they met, and were charmed by the beauty of, Madame Recamier; they visited La Fayette at La Grange, where Charles planted an ivy that twenty-seven years later Amelia Opie found 'green and flourishing, like his memory.' And on 28th September they could celebrate without concealment the anniversary of that 'day of happiness, day of joy, Liz nor Kins will never repent.'

The aristocratic Englishwomen now in Paris in large numbers were observing without enthusiasm the elevation of the former Mrs Armitstead to the heights of Parisian society. Their disapproval stemmed less from her obscurity of birth (which in England seems never to have been an issue in the question of receiving her) than from her past notoriety. By no means all these ladies had been beneficiaries of late eighteenth-century permissiveness. Many had gone virgin to the beds of husbands not necessarily of their choice, to remain thereafter faithful wives. Of these chaste matrons many could remember the great Cyprian flaunting herself in the Park or at the Opera in the company of some of the most attractive men in London. Now they beheld her fêted by the best society in Paris. Resentment is human in those who cannot both eat their cake and have it for those who contrive to do both, and no-one had eaten more of the cake of licence than she who now, it appeared, was enjoying also the cake of social acceptability.

Irritation was not confined to the always virtuous. Lady Holland was exasperated, her resentment probably edged by realisation that the ex-harlot was in England likely to share such social footing as was available to her divorced self. For her the non-recognition now under debate by many of the Englishwomen in Paris was not possible. Holland had been pleased to learn of the marriage (as was his uncle General Fox, who, arriving in Paris in September with his family, at once took his wife and daughters to meet Charles's wife), and she was expected to acknowledge the relationship. She did so, but how stupidly visible an unwillingness appears from a letter Robert Adair sent to Lady Melbourne. 'I find since Lady Holland's departure [the Hollands were setting out for a prolonged tour of Spain] that she is not supposed to have behaved by any means kindly to Mrs Fox. I am so very blind a person that I should not most probably have found it out in a thousand years, but I hear it from foreigners & women who have no sort of interest in telling fibs about her. The grand object of jealousy, I fancy, was the presentation to Madame B[onaparte] *on the same day.* This Her Ladyship did not much like, & whether Mrs. Fox's dress really was not ready, or whether she gave the point up I cannot tell, but it did not take place as it had been projected & Lady Holland alone was presented. I take it, however, that she left Paris in great dudgeon, for she fully expected that, after the ceremonial was over, she would have been asked to the private parties. In this she was disappointed, & perhaps Mrs F. has it all visited upon her.'

The odds are that Elizabeth did give the point up, for it seems unlikely that French milliners would have failed to complete in time a dress required for the presentation to the wife of the First Consul of the wife of a celebrated English visitor. If she did deceive, the deception succeeded where it mattered; Charles wrote in the journal: 'Sad disappointment, Wife's Gown did not come in time for her to be presented.' (The presentation was only postponed, and took place on 10th October at St Cloud, when Mme. Bonaparte held her first court there.) The effect on Lady Holland was also successful, insofar as she wrote to Caroline: 'I am truly pleased at your intention of meeting your new aunt. For his sake you will like and esteem her. She is always occupied in attending to his comforts, and that absorbs a thousand little blemishes. To us the *declaration* will be productive of much real enjoyment, as it will bring us all together without restraint. Her manners and conversation are as correct as possible. The only ridicule she has arises from his ardent love and her short memory which dispose her to forget the half-century and upward which has rolled over her head; but her temper and disposition are as good as any Fox of you all.' The two women had in fact parted on good enough terms for them to correspond occasionally while the Hollands were in Spain.

The Foxes left Paris on 12th November' Hare wrote to the Duchess of Devonshire that he thought it as well, 'as the Duchess of Gordon and Ly C. Greville, and some other English ladies lately arrived, are caballing against her.' The travel journal closes on 17th November, when they reached 'dear dear home where we arrived about six, very very glad to be here and happy *so* happy that my Liz bore all the fatigues of the journey so well.'

Fox's friends and kindred at home had had more than three months in which to consider what attitude to take to his marriage. For his female relatives the matter had never really been in doubt. His niece Caroline and her aunt Marianne, the General's wife, might agree by letter that: 'it is truly to be wished that he would have married some amiable woman whose society we could have cultivated,' but for neither of them was there any question of avoiding the society of the woman he had married; and there was compensation in the prospect of enjoying more of his.

Similar considerations may have affected his aunts, the Duchess of

Leinster, Lady Louisa Conolly and Lady Sarah Napier, whose
recognition brought in its train – since though the second was childless
the other two had more than made up the deficiency – a host of new
family acquaintance. The Duchess, married at sixteen to her first
husband, had borne him nineteen children; after which the Duke it was
that died, whereupon the Duchess had married her sons' tutor, William
Ogilvie, and borne three more to him. Most of these had survived to
grow up, had by now married, and were adding to the throng of the
Duchess's descendants. Lady Sarah, who had started her family (beyond
a daughter by the lover for whom she left her first husband) only on her
late second marriage, could not compete, but she had borne Colonel
Napier eight children. Elizabeth already knew some of the male issue of
Charles's Lennox aunts (she had certainly known the tragic Lord
Edward Fitzgerald, for years later on meeting his daughter, she traced a
likeness to 'her poor father'), but now her acquaintance widened to
embrace the female Fitzgeralds, Ogilvies and Napiers, a host in
themselves.

Charles's friends too were moved by the awareness that recognising
his wife would mean seeing more of him. There were other
considerations to sway them in her favour. Chief among these was
simply love for Charles, whom few could bear to hurt by cutting his
wife. His political associates also hoped that her acceptance into society
might lessen his inconvenient unwillingness to visit London (as indeed
it did, not because he loved St. Anne's the less but because it gave him
such pleasure to see his wife received by his friends). Moreover, among
his female intimates of his own rank and generation, not many were
well placed for casting stones at Elizabeth. Among the great Whig
ladies who had been young in the days of his youth, few had neither
been divorced nor borne while married a child not the husband's; the
beautiful Mrs Crewe, vainly lusted after by Charles long ago, was an
exception, but she had always been a Burkean rather than a Foxite, and
had had no dealings with Fox since 1793. The moral tone of high Whig
society was indeed such as could scarcely be lowered by Mrs Fox's entry
in it, to judge from a letter written some years later by the rigidly
virtuous Lady Spencer: 'When one considers the frequent admission of
the Dowr. Ly. Jersey, Ly. Holland, Ly. Hamilton, Mrs Fox, your poor
cousin [Lady John Townshend], Mrs Bouvery, Mr Fawkener and others
into all companys, we must acknowledge there is great merit in the

uniform steadiness that is able to exclude them all.' Lady Spencer could have added to the list of those uniform steadiness would have excluded the addressee of the letter, her daughter Lady Bessborough, and her other, by then dead, daughter the Duchess of Devonshire.

The admission of Mrs Fox into their company reasonably caused more heartburning to the genuinely respectable. Some, like Coke of Holkham – whose morality appears to have excluded even visiting Fox at St. Anne's – did observe the uniform steadiness desired by Lady Spencer. Lord Fitzwilliam, though he had been a visitor to St. Anne's (and though, Lady Sarah Napier reported, he said of the marriage that 'all things considered he was glad of it, for that it would be much *less* disadvantage to Charles to be seen with his *wife* than his mistress'), preferred his own wife not to visit Mrs Fox. Many however were as willing to receive her, and let their wives do so, as the Duke of Bedford, and probably for similar reasons; in a letter he wrote to William Adam after Fox's death, the Duke said: 'It is impossible to conceal from ourselves that from Mrs F.'s former unfortunate life, Fox's marriage with her was a severe blow to public morals, yet our affection and attachment to him induced us to overlook what nothing else ought to have suffered us to countenance, and we gave her our support and protection.' Countenance was shown her, too, by Lord Albemarle – like Bedford a very distant cousin to Fox – and his wife, both of whom were to become dear to her, while William Dickson, Bishop of Down, ensured a fittingly Christian welcome in his family.

Of the Foxite politicians, most were understandably prepared to have their wives meet Mrs Fox. Samuel Whitbread and his wife, who once had entertained at Wolmer her whom they supposed still Mrs Armitstead, were ready to greet her. Lord and Lady King, whose seat at Ockham made them almost-neighbours at St. Anne's, welcomed her there. William Plumer, who had entered the Commons in the days there of Charles's father and who long had been a supporter of the son, opened hospitable doors; and Grey made her known to a wife in whom she was to find a shared interest in gardening.

To Chertsey neighbours the announcement of the marriage probably gave unqualified satisfaction. St. Anne's Hill could now be openly recognised as socially the most important house in the vicinity, and its mistress given the place which Chertsey was increasingly to see as hers, that of first lady of their neighbourhood. It may have been partly the thronging of neighbours to greet the returning Foxes and felicitate them on their marriage that caused the 'great deal of company' that crowded the house in December and early January, and interfered sadly with work on the History.

One January visitor was not local. This was Samuel Rogers, of whom Fox wrote to Fitzpatrick: 'I like him very well but he is too complaisant (a fault on the right side) to have so much critical conversation with him as I should like.' The accusation would have surprised Rogers's friends of later days, among whom he became notable for his soft-voiced acerbity. To the Foxes, however, his sole distasteful observation was a result of sheer thoughtlessness. 'Most unfortunately,' he recalled much later, 'one morning during breakfast at St. Anne's Hill, I repeated and praised Goldsmith's song "When lovely woman stoops to folly," etc., quite forgetting that it must necessarily hurt the feelings of Mrs Fox. She seemed a good deal discomposed by it. Fox merely remarked, 'Some people write damned nonsense.''

Rogers's apparent complaisance may partly have reflected the natural diffidence of a youngish man in argument with an older and very eminent one, but it may have stemmed also from mental distraction occasioned by his determination to memorise as much as he could of Mr Fox's conversation. Rogers had the habit of noting down (often in direct quotation) all he could remember of the remarks of the men who most interested him; the resulting notebooks – published, long after, as his Recollections – come nearer than any other record to capturing the range and liveliness of Fox's talk.

His notes of that visit began with a description, itself the most detailed to survive, of St. Anne's Hill:'A small low white house on the brow of a hill, commanding a semi-circular sweep, rich and woody . . . In the hall books and statues. The library on the first floor – small and unadorned – the books on open shelves.' This was clearly the Book Room, the heart of the house. 'In the eating room a portrait of Lord Holland sitting, carefully painted by Reynolds; and of Lady Holland sitting, by Ramsey. Several good old pictures. In the garden a handsome architectural greenhouse, and a temple . . . containing busts of Charles J. Fox, Lord Holland, and a son of Lord Bolingbroke [presumably Bob St. John], all by Nollekens. The garden laid out in open and shrubbery walks, trees breaking the prospect everywhere . . . There is a terrace-walk, thickly planted, to a neat farm-house; in which there is a tea-room, the chimney-piece relieved with a Fox. The drawing-room prettily furnished with pink silk in pannels, inclosed with an ebony bead, and a frame of blue silk.

'Had just read Euripides. Alcestis his favourite. Hercules's resolution, 'I must do some great thing. I have used them ill'. Heraclides, 'And these men wore Greek habits!' – he repeated these instances twice . . .

'The Greek historians were all true; the Romans liars, particularly Livy, who never scrupled to tell a story as he pleased . . . .

'Ministers wish for peace but have not the courage to be peaceable . . . .

    'Read Homer more than once a year . . . .

    'A distant prospect indispensable for a house.

'Vanburgh almost as great a genius as ever lived. Sir John Brute – 'and this woman will get a husband!' Confederacy from the French; with so much the air of an original! Who would have thought it

'Very candid – Retracts instantly – Continually putting wood on the fire – His Trojan, his Venus, his Mosaics from Tivoli – His attachment to particular books – his commonplace book – they keep a journal at home and abroad . . .

'Dryden exquisite – no man reasons like him in verse – his defence of transubstantiation – his verses to Congreve admirable but in general deficient in feeling and tenderness . . .

'I write with difficulty. Perhaps with the greater ease a man speaks, with the greater difficulty he writes. I believe so . . .

'Temple in gardens – wished for a temple to the Muses – wished any body would let him build one . . .

'After all Burke was a damned wrong-headed fellow through life – always jealous and contradictory . . .

'Ghosts – No man, however theoretically an unbeliever, but practically a believer more or less . . .

'When he said he carved ill and she confirmed it – ''Yes my dear, I thought you would agree with me''.

'Speaking of the new room projecting – ''Then you'll be always in the new drawing-room – you'll never play again where I am – never in the poor back [clearly a mishearing of book] room. . . .''

'No dark ages – Hildebrand's as dark as any, yet his *writing* is good. Eloisa's letters, what good latin! . . .

'All serves to convince me that women must have a great influence in Society, do what you will! Certainly no man of his birth and generation had done more to accord it to them.'

Towards the end of January the Foxes went to enjoy together the hospitality of Lord Robert Spencer at Woolbeding, and in February to London, where he had leased a house in (rather inappropriately in view of its connection with her 'unfortunate past') Clarges Street. Thence her entry into Whig society really began. Some even of the people well disposed towards her had feared that – particuarly after her reception in France – she would damage her chances of acceptance by presuming too far on them. Hare had written from Paris the year before, reported Lady Bessborough, 'that Mrs Fox is so well receiv'd that her head must be better than he thinks it is not to be turn'd, and he fears it will induce her to do a thousand absurd things in England and expose herself to mortification.' Her head was however considerably better than Hare had supposed, while the allurements of the society he and his friends represented were perhaps less than he had imagined to one whose personal life was so happy. Elizabeth was content to meet only those who signified willingness to meet her, and accepted the unwillingness of those who would not as philosophically as she would have accepted quarantine after contact with an infectious disease. Received for Charles's sake, she often came to be welcome in her own right, prevailing not by wit, which she had never had, nor by beauty, which she had outlived, but by sheer sweetness of disposition. 'Goodnatured' is the term most constantly used of her; her niece by marriage, Caroline Fox, was only one of those to employ it.

Caroline had settled with her half-aunt Elizabeth Vernon, who was only four years her senior, at Little Holland House, a former farmhouse on the Holland House estate. Accompanied by the other Mrs Fox, the General's wife, she went to call on her 'new aunt' as soon as the household had settled in at Clarges Street, and wrote afterwards to tell Holland: 'I think she looks very good-natured, but has less grace in her manner than I expected. She was very much struck with my likeness to you and my Uncle. I see he is quite delighted with his nephew Harry and no wonder, he is such an eager frank open-hearted little fellow.*

*This Harry was the General's son, who was to be left in England to pursue his education under his Uncle Charles's supervision while the rest of the family went to the Mediterranean, whither General Fox had been posted.

Mrs Fox says she expects to hear him say 'I say my Uncle' [a catchphrase of Holland's that had become a family joke] and seems quite happy there should be another coming to replace you at St. Anne's.' A subsequent letter shows that she had noted Mrs Fox's attempts to moderate her uncle's drinking at stag-parties. 'My Uncle Ch. dined the day before yesterday at Ld. Moira's with the Prince. I saw him last night . . . he did not seem the better for that princely dinner, & has another in prospect at Carlton House to-day, but had promised Mrs F. to be very good and behave better than at the last.'

Most of Fox's friends were amazed and delighted by his well-being. 'Fox seems in the highest spirits,' wrote Grey to his wife, 'and is in the best looks. He is like a young man in the prime of life who has just married a girl of sixteen. Is it not a fine thing to grow young at fifty?' And Creevey: 'You would be perfectly astonished at the vigour of body, the energy of mind, the innocent playfulness and happiness of Fox. The contrast between him and his old associates is the most marvellous thing I ever saw – they having all the air of shattered debauchees, of passing gaming, drinking, sleepless nights, whereas the old leader of the gang might really pass for the pattern and the effect of domestic good order.' So indeed he now was.

The public world however once more presented omens to grieve the statesman. Bonaparte – now the Emperor Napoleon – appeared to be using the peace as an opportunity of extending both France's military might and her control over nominally independent states. To Fox, however dismayed he might be at the transformation of a republic into an empire, peace with England was so obviously in Napoleon's interest that he could not believe the new Emperor could desire anything else. History would endorse his judgment of where Napoleon's interest lay; his error was in relying on Napoleon's recognition of it. Napoleon was indeed beyond the understanding of Charles Fox, who could not really believe that any man (save possibly one born to kingship, and so badly brought up) could desire either war or the domination of a hemisphere. To Britons who did not find this incredible, it seemed better to make ready for battle with the serpent before it grew large enough to swallow Britain. On 18th May the war was renewed. On 23rd May, in the Commons debate on the issue, Fox pleaded for a reopening of negotiations in what was generally reckoned one of the greatest speeches of his life, but in vain. In June he and Elizabeth departed from

Clarges Street to savour again their own peace at home.

The months of high summer were always those in which especially St. Anne's attracted visitors. These were in 1803 more numerous than ever, for ladies who had long heard of without seeing the charms of Mr Fox's country home could now take advantage of his marriage, and their own recognition of his wife, to visit the place. Except for those who lived near enough to come and go within the day, the usual pattern – in a house too small for house-parties – was a two-day visit, the guest or guests arriving in time for dinner and leaving after breakfast on the second day following. One such visit was that of the Duchess of Leinster, with an unidentified grandson, in August: she wrote afterwards to Caroline Fox to tell her about it. 'I took him [her 'boy'] with me to St. Anne's where he was most kindly received and you would have been pleased I am sure to see your Dr Uncle playing at Cricket with him, but there is nothing like him except your Dear Brother. I passed two of the pleasantest days with him and Mrs Fox that I have known for years, the lovely Weather, the Beautiful place, their comfort in one another, their extreme kindness to me and my Dear Child all gladden'd my heart and gave feelings that I almost despaired would ever revive there again, she is a most obliging good natured woman and her conversation was particularly pleasant to me as it was all about him giving me a sort of History of those years I had lost sight of him. You may say it required some delicacy and management to do this well, her own being so interwoven with it, & I assure you she shew'd no want of either.'

Autumn came, and with it the season for their own travelling; no longer always separately now that houses once closed to Elizabeth were opening. Shooting seems to have become less of an addiction with Fox after his accident in 1799. He may also have been affected by the criticisms of Gilbert Wakefield, the classical scholar and radical with whom he long had corresponded, who had taken that occasion of pointing out that killing for sport was cruel; the great polemicist had been obliged to admit that there was something to be said for that view. This year, sport was anyhow less important than taking advantage of the invitations that now extended to Mrs Fox. After a fortnight at Woolbeding in September they went to Southill to visit the Whitbreads, and to Woburn, where Elizabeth was at last able to see the Temple of Fame created by the Duke of Bedford, with a bust of Charles for centrepiece and busts of the principal Foxites round about it. There followed a second visit to Woolbeding, where Charles always felt, and Elizabeth was beginning to feel, comfortably at ease. Woolbeding may also have afforded an opportunity of increasing her intimacy with the lady usually to be met at Lord Robert's house-parties, the one among the Whig ladies in whom Elizabeth was to find a friend of her own, Harriet Bouverie.

Mrs Bouverie, wife of a Whig back-bencher, was one of the beautiful women in whose drawing-rooms, ever since the 1770s, the Foxites had met to talk over politics, to consider tactics, or just to gossip. For as long a time she had been the mistress of Lord Robert – who was generally reckoned the father of Mrs Bouverie's youngest daughter Diana (known as 'the tell-tale Bouverie' from her likeness to the Spencers), and who would posthumously confirm suspicion by bequeathing Woolbeding to Diana. The Bouveries, comparatively poor, had never been able to match the splendid hospitality of Devonshire House or Crewe House, but still 'the Bous' was a house that Foxites liked to drop into after dinner for a comfortable chat over tea or coffee about Addington's mismanagement or Pitt's very uncertain adjustment to retirement. Elizabeth was soon to acquire this pleasant London habit.

The autumn house-parties had naturally had their quota of political talk, into which – doubt of Administration's capacities not being confined to the Foxites – discussion of a possible conjunction between Pitt and Fox was obtruding itself. Fox, though wondering whether this might afford an opportunity for advancing such dear objectives as the emancipation of the Catholics, was no keener on office in itself than he had been for years. Lady Bessborough, on whom he called during a brief visit to London at the end of December, could get little from him 'except his dread of leaving St. Anne's and mixing in Politicks.' Pitt in any case proved unwilling at this stage to overturn Addington, and Fox happily put politics out of his mind and, back at home again, settled down to his History. 'Monmouth would have been dead yesterday,' he had written to Fitzpatrick on 5th December, 'if the fine weather had not saved him; and though I have a terrible number of letters to write to-day, so that I dare not quite say I will not dine before his head be off, I have hopes.' They were not fulfilled, for it was on 1st January, 1804, that he wrote declaring: 'Yesterday, and not before, died James, Duke of Monmouth. It will be as well if the historian has not made as bungling a piece of work with him as the hangman.'

Not long after, the question of political coalition reappeared in a new form. Lord Grenville and his brother Thomas, leaders of a group long in support of Pitt, were sufficiently despairing of Addington and disappointed by Pitt's current unwillingness to act to propose a direct association with Fox. He as so often was uncertain what to do, and Elizabeth as usual wanted Fitzpatrick's advice: 'Mrs F. says I should say nothing but *come, come, come,* and she would say it down on her knees. You know she thinks there is no adviser but you.' The whole issue was complicated yet further by a recurrence of the King's illness, raising yet again thoughts of a Regency. But the King recovered; Pitt at last decided to oppose Addington, who resigned in April; Pitt came back into office and the King declared, as obstinately as ever, that he would not have Fox in the Administration.

That summer Charles began to be troubled by a frequent pain in his side. Ailment was unusual for him. Elizabeth was still a victim of rheumatism, and prey to every cold and influenza germ at large, but Charles seems to have enjoyed perfect health for more than ten years. One particularly vigorous influenza germ had in 1801 managed to give him 'one day some feverishness with a cold,' leaving a feeling of weakness, but, he told Lauderdale, 'I found drinking some more wine than usual set me quite right or nearly so.' He would not anyway have contemplated calling in a physician, then or now, for (understandably in view of the then state of therapeutic science) he had little confidence in the profession.

Spa waters and hot springs were another matter, however, and in July he set out with Elizabeth on a tour designed to combine healing with pleasure. First they went to Cheltenham, where they met the Bishop of Down, also driven there by ill-health, and his family. From Cheltenham (where the Pittite MP Hugh Hunt had observed and been impressed by their inseparability and their visible happiness in each other's company) they moved on, as did the Dicksons, to Bristol Hot Wells, now eclipsing Bath as a fashionable spa. There they found Lady Sarah Napier and her husband – also in quest of health –, and, in Lady Sarah's words, 'a *train* of Foxes and Lennoxes.' It was virtually a family reunion that took place at the Hot Wells, and when Charles and Elizabeth diversified their stay with a brief visit to Torbay, it was to meet Fitzpatrick there.

Their journeying crossed his again when they finished their travels in the west with a purely social stay in Foxley with the Prices. This they greatly enjoyed, much approving Lady Caroline's housekeeping; Elizabeth declared she would welcome any kitchenmaid trained by Lady Caroline, while Charles – in a letter to Fitzpatrick, who stayed on a few days after them – asked for 'a receit to make the good cutlets with the Onion sauce.' As however the same letter mentions that he had a painful boil in his side, and as Elizabeth suffered a severe attack of rheumatism a few weeks later, it does not seem that the therapeutic aims of their holiday had been achieved.

That western holiday was probably the tour on which Charles took Elizabeth to Winterslow, the family estate the mansion on which had burned down in his brother's time, and to see the family vault at nearby Farley. Five years later she would revisit it alone: 'the last home of all those once so gay alas what were my feelings at being so near the remains of all those once so dear to him who was my soul's delight and who used to talk with delight of our ashes being mixed there together.' They had occasion, that autumn of 1804, to reflect on mortality. The illnesses from which Colonel Napier and the Bishop of Down had sought relief were beyond remedy; both died that October.

The resumption of Parliament took the Foxes back to London, and Fox to the Opposition front bench he seemed destined to occupy while George III reigned. In February the old question of slave trade abolition, so dear to his heart, was moved again. The abolitionists lost as usual, but by a lesser margin than on previous divisions. The Grenvilles, still interested in political accommodation with Fox, renewed negotiations, no longer dealing with him through emissaries but face to face, and were fascinated by the man they now came to know personally for the first time. The diversions that rendered London tolerable were pursued; Charles and Elizabeth visited the theatre to see the current rage, 'The Boy', Master Betty; there were pleasant evenings gossiping with friends over coffee in Mrs Bouverie's drawing-room – or Mrs Fox's; Charles developed a passion for chess and challenged any visitor who could play. As always when a period of weeks had to be spent in the 'odious place', they refreshed themselves with frequent brief visits to St. Anne's, and at the end of June, 1805, without waiting for Parliament to rise, they returned there to take up the old happy pattern of summer.

It was a cold summer, and prolific in gnats, but no damps could chill their happiness or the warmth of their hospitality. Friends came and went, friends long acquainted with St. Anne's, friends admiring its beauties for the first time. Parties strolled up the long walk to take tea at the farm, down to the Greenhouse to admire Elizabeth's camellias. Charles hung over the palings at the foot of the garden to discuss with passing farmers the progress of his crops. Politics tiresomely intruded; a letter to Grey, enclosing some anemone pulsatilla seeds Elizabeth wanted sent to Mrs Grey ('it should be put in light bog earth as soon as possible'), reported a visit from Lord Grenville, with whom, at Stowe, Charles spent a week in July. But the politically motivated were few among those who came to share the pleasures of dear home. Visiting children tumbled about the lawns, aristocratic little Russells and Keppels, middle-class little Rollestons; and, most welcome of all, two little Foxes, for the Hollands with their small sons had at last returned from their long Peninsular tour. Harry Fox, now an Etonian, came and went as his cousin and namesake had done. Lady Bessborough came with her lord, her daughter Caroline and Caroline's new-made husband William Lamb, and with them, self-invited, that habitué of St. Anne's, the Prince of Wales – who, Charles informed Samuel Rogers, drank three wine glasses of liqueur in succession. The crops ripened, the harvest was taken in, and the latest in the long tale of happy summers at St. Anne's drew to its close.

On 21st July Charles had made a new will. His occasion for doing so was probably no more than that a legacy of five hundred guineas bequeathed but not yet paid him, together with the grant to him by the Duke of Bedford of an annuity of £500 for the life of Harriet Willoughby, represented additions to his small assets so relatively substantial as to justify arranging for their disposition. The annuity was assigned to Elizabeth for her lifetime and then to Harriet, while the legacy was to be divided between his nephew Harry and 'Robert Stephen a young man living with Lord Viscount Bolingbroke in America.' The first name and the identification by reference to Bolingbroke suggest that this youth was Bob St. John, 'Stephen' being either a second Christian name or a name used as surname by the bastard who had no legal right to that of St. John.* Elizabeth was to be his

*This supposition is reinforced by an entry in Mrs Fox's journal for 24th May, 1811: 'Went to Sir A. Piggott's early and he went with me to the office to receive the Legacy left by Mr (she left a gap for the name, which evidently she had forgotten) which I placed at Mr Coutts to be laid out in the Funds for Harry and Bob.' Journal references to 'Bob' without surname appear always to refer to Bob St. John.

residuary legatee and executrix. 'Only I wish her to make presents in my name of any books pictures or marbles she thinks fit as remembrances of me to the following friends Lord Holland   General Fox   General Fitzpatrick   Lord Robert Spencer   Lord John Townshend   Miss Fox and Mrs. Bouverie. There are many others whom I love and value to the greatest degree but those are my oldest connections.'

Towards the end of August they visited London briefly, staying at Holland House, where they met Lord Minto; he recorded the purpose of the visit, to buy china, 'cheap china, I mean, for they are great economists.' (He noted too that 'Ly. H. does not admire [Mrs Fox], and would willingly indulge herself now and then with a fling at her.) The autumn brought a visit to Goodwood, and at the end of November they went to Woolbeding for the winter stay with Lord Robert that had become part of their annual cycle; Charles, still chess-mad, was delighted to find there a worthy opponent in Diana Bouverie. December saw them at home again, and there it was that they first heard reports (which Charles was inclined to discount) that Pitt, said for some time to have been in poor health, was seriously ill.

The usual quiet Christmas at home was followed by the usual little festivity on Twelfth Night, with a small dance at which, as Elizabeth wrote years later, her Angel 'enjoyed seeing his old wife jump about.' Ten days later he went up to London to attend the state funeral of Nelson at St. Paul's. Holland, who accompanied him, observed that the length of the ceremony and the coldness of the cathedral exhausted his uncle as he had never before known fatigue to do. Charles returned to St. Anne's, but the reports of Pitt's illness grew too authoritative to be scouted, and on 16th January he went back, with Elizabeth, to London to keep in touch with his supporters and allies.

They were distressed to learn that some Foxites were positively glad of Pitt's illness. Lady Elizabeth Foster recorded how, when on 20th January she called with the Duchess of Devonshire to welcome the Foxes back to town and they arrived just as the previous caller was departing, 'Mrs Fox said, "That was a mild, gentle little creature who went out, yet she had been rejoicing at this good news – as she calls it – of Pitt being so ill." "Oh, no," said Fox, "shocking." "It is impossible," the Duchess and I said, "to be glad." "Quite," said Fox, "How can one rejoice in the death of any man? Death is a thing without remedy. Besides, it is a poor way of getting rid of one's enemy. A fair, good discussion that turns him out is well – but death – no!''

'Fox then expressed the view that the news would ''render every debate flat and uninteresting. I hate going to the House. I think I shall pair off with Pitt.''

Pitt died on 23rd January, 1806. The next day was Fox's fifty-seventh birthday. They celebrated it with a little ball and supper for their friends, and in the journal volume she had started a week earlier (the first to survive after the 1802 travel volumes) Elizabeth wrote: 'This is the day of all the year that is to me most dear. It brought into the world him that makes me the happiest of women and God Almighty keep him to me in health.'

CHAPTER SIX

Stable Yard and Chiswick House

The long exclusion from office was over. Without Pitt, his Administration could not carry on. Addington – now Lord Sidmouth – could not form another, and Grenville declared that without Fox neither could he. The King yielded to necessity. Grenville drew up his Administration, the 'Ministry of all the Talents', with Fox in the office that had always by preference been his, Secretary of State for Foreign Affairs, Lord Robert Spencer at the Home Department, Fitzwilliam as Lord President of the Council, Grey (now Lord Howick) as First Lord of the Admiralty, Sheridan as Treasurer of the Navy and Fitzpatrick as Secretary at War. On February 3rd Elizabeth wrote: 'Ld. G. saw the K who accepted the new Ministry which God Almighty grant may prove a fortunate one for the country and for my angel Husband.' On 13th February, having offered himself for re-election as then was requisite on the taking of office, he was triumphantly returned; Duchess Georgiana, who had hoped to see the parade but arrived too late, wrote to her son: 'They say, dr soul, he looked like Bacchus, for the chair was done round with laurels.' Soon, most un-Bacchus-like, he was immersed in business.

Private life was at an end. Fox's days were passed between his office and the Commons. The house in Stable Yard which the Duke of Bedford had lent the Foxes on Charles's taking office swarmed day and night with colleagues, Foxites, place-seekers in search of the Secretary of State or the channel to his ear which his wife represented. Their old-fashioned early dinners were impossible now; when Charles did contrive to get away from the office or the House for a hurried meal at home, it might be eight or nine o'clock, and once they did not rise from dinner until midnight. Impossible too were relaxed post-prandial readings, for his return home was normally burdened with official papers on which, with his secretary, Sir Francis Vincent, he would work far into the night. Not paperwork alone excluded – though early rising had become from a pleasure a necessity – their St. Anne's practice of going early to bed. If work, official dinners and the business of the House did not keep Charles up late, night visitors could do so, among them the Prince, to whom night and day were still indifferent and who was inclined to call after dinner and stay till the small hours. By April it would be matter for record when they got to bed before midnight. Elizabeth, precluded maintenance of the regime with which she so long had conserved her Angel's health, could only worry and hope for the best. In January he had suffered a severe cold, and in mid-February another, but in mid-March she could observe more happily: 'Thank God he seems nice and well and not the worse for all the fatigue he has.'

The Secretary's wife had her business too. Social intercourse, for so many years a matter of pleasure alone, now became a constant duty. 'He . . . is occupied so as to leave it to *her* to do the civil things,' wrote Lady Sarah Napier: 'I believe she succeeds.' Another letter, from Lady Elizabeth Foster to her son Augustus, serving with the British mission in Washington, gives a glimpse of Elizabeth succeeding in the civil things: 'Mrs Fox is happy, but has the most perfect good sense as well as good nature in her new situation. One of her first ideas was to ask me about you. I shan't forget that.'

Mrs Fox's task was no light one. Besides the constant entertainment at Stable Yard of unpredictable numbers of guests, besides appearing, poised and sociable, at the functions Mrs Secretary Fox was expected to grace, she must be always alert to handle, with discretion as well as affability, the social exigencies that derived from Fox's office. A major part of her duty was to govern access to him at home in such a way as to spare him all avoidable drain on his energy while ensuring him such society as would afford happy relaxation in his few moments of leisure. This was not easy. The house in Stable Yard was besieged with callers, many of them place-seekers – for themselves, for relatives, for protegés – anxious for a share in the fruits of office. Fox had always found this distribution of minor places one of the most distasteful aspects of office and now, with the Foxites having their first prospect for more than two decades of a share in the loaves and fishes, the pressures were worse than he had ever known them; 'the degree to which I am distressed is incredible, everybody must have something and nobody points out the means,' he wrote to Georgiana. Elizabeth as far as she could took the brunt of these importunities, her chief aim the tactful discouragement of those refusal of whom was necessary, but with the burden always of judging whether exclusion even from access to Charles would be too harsh a measure. Lady Elizabeth Foster recorded with approval her tactful handling of one difficult problem, that of Robert Adair.

Adair, always interested in foreign affairs, had confidently expected that, in the event of Fox's return to office, the appointment of secretary to the Minister would be his. Sadly, he had the year before ruined his chance of it by marrying a Frenchwoman widely suspected (and, by her own admission to the Duchess of Devonshire, justly) of being a Bonapartist agent. It was thus impossible – above all for Fox, whose resolution in the national defence was still doubted by many – to appoint Mrs Adair's husband to any post in the Foreign Office. While guessing the cause of his disappointment, Adair, always inclined to make the most of his emotions, took it very badly and rushed about town declaring that it was all the fault of his marriage, that he would separate from his wife, that he would blow his brains out. Duchess Georgiana, made an audience of such lamentations, sent him to Stable Yard, where Elizabeth received him with the utmost kindness, assured him of Fox's affection, and arranged a small private dinner with Charles for him. The question of his occupation was later resolved by sending him – without his wife – on a mission to Vienna – a happy solution, for diplomacy proved to be his metier and the rest of his long career was passed in it.

Such small intimate dinners as that at which Adair was comforted ('Darling Mr Adair and Mr Trotter dined with us,' wrote Elizabeth, her scorn of commas implying an unfelt devotion to Adair) were seldom possible now. What little time Fox had to spare after the hours at his desk and in the House tended to be consumed by ceremonial functions – the Speaker's dinner, a Mansion House banquet, the formal entertainment of foreign Ministers – or in working meals with his colleagues. The year was lifting towards spring, but at St. Anne's the woodlands budded unseen by those who loved them. The Secretary of State and his wife had small time to enjoy even such freshness as London allowed. An open carriage was substituted for the closed one in which Elizabeth used to pick Charles up at the office or take him down to the House, these brief journeys now being often the only time they had alone together except in bed. His health was giving new cause for anxiety. His legs had begun to swell so that walking became painful, and to spare him effort they got a wheelchair for use when the swelling was troublesome. At the end of March a burden of sorrow was added to that of fatigue; the Duchess of Devonshire, his constant and cherished friend since her girlhood, died. 'A better heart no-one ever had,' wrote Elizabeth sadly. Charles worked on. He was beginning to sense now that his health might not indefinitely support the burden of office, and to think of an ultimate retirement in which Holland might take over the Foreign Office. First however came the completion of two tasks he was resolved to see through himself, the attainment of peace with France and the abolition of the slave trade.

The Easter recess afffforded them a few happy days at *'dear dear home'*. Fitzpatrick joined them there, as did Trotter, and Lord and Lady Albemarle came with their always welcome children. One of these – George, afterward 6th Earl of Albemarle – recorded in his memoirs many years later a child's-eye view of the great statesman. After the mid-day meal – the children's dinner –, when Mr Fox was wheeled in to take a bowl of soup with them, he became 'the exclusive property of us children, and we all adjourned to the garden for our game of trap-ball. All was now noise and merriment. Our host, the youngest among us, laughed, chaffed and chatted the whole time. As he could not walk, he of course had the innings, we the bowling and fagging-out; with what glee would he send the ball into the bushes to add to his score, and how shamelessly would he wrangle with us when we fairly bowled him out.' Elizabeth watched happily, reflecting that if Charles were denied the walking she thought so necessary for health this wheelchair exercise at least might be good for him. Less than a week however could be allowed for such pleasures, and on 14th April they were back at Stable Yard.

The first pressures arising from the coming into office of a new Administration were beginning to ease. The congratulatory calls had been paid, the main distribution of places had been effected, the initiatory functions were over and the demands on their evening time at least had lessened somewhat. Early in May they managed another brief visit to St. Anne's, arriving on the 3rd to leave again on the 5th. Charles was well enough to walk in the grounds for a long time: 'darling had a little pain in his side but was not tired.' Elizabeth was now however keeping a continuously anxious eye on his health. The next day, after their return to London, she noted: 'Carl dined in the City at a dinner given by the East Indian directors, came home about 11 quite well.' Official banquets were happily less frequent now, and quiet friendly little dinners were sometimes possible again. One day Lord Ossory and his daughters and Mr Rolleston and his dined, with Samuel Rogers and his sister and Caroline Fox, Caroline and Miss Rolleston sang and played, and it was a very pleasant party; five days later they had another happy evening with the Bouveries, Lord Robert, Fitzpatrick and Sir Francis Vincent. Elizabeth managed an occasional visit to the Opera. Much of her daytime was passed in paying calls, not least on those who had no claim on the attention of the Secretary of State's wife but who by right of friendship, kinship or former kindness were entitled to whatever she could spare of her time. 'To me she is most attentively good-natured,' wrote Lady Sarah, '& I feel very much obliged by it because *now* I am of no earthly use to her.'

Elizabeth was still however conscious that unofficial but real duties attached to her position, and one of these was entertaining on a grand scale. Fox as a bachelor Secretary of State had discharged that duty himself as far as he could, but now he had a wife, and the fact that her past rendered her place in society equivocal in many eyes did not in her own absolve her from the obligation to take it up. She determined to give a ball and supper.

May 19th was chosen as the date, and the Duke lent Bedford House for the occasion. The Prince of Wales's upholsterers, Marsh and Tatham, were commissioned to undertake special temporary decorations of the State apartments there, and the invitations were sent out. Even Mrs Fox's friends feared that she might now be pressing her luck too far. 'One can't bear to think of any mortifications to her,' wrote Lady Elizabeth Foster, 'both for her own sake and Charles Fox's.' Elizabeth herself probably felt apprehensive, for on the night of May 18th she did not get to sleep until six in the morning, but in her journal she would admit only to being frightened lest she be unable to get through the fatigue of the night ahead. In the morning she inspected the apartments, now hung with plate glass, and the gardens, then dined with the Bouveries, went home to dress, and at nine was back at Bedford House to supervise the lighting-up of the rooms. At half-past nine the confounding of the pessimists began.

That evening social apotheosis reached its climax. At the head of the Bedford House staircase, elegant in yellow crape and silver, stood the ex-Cyprian of unknown origin, Mrs Secretary of State Fox receiving her guests. They came; friends and relatives who could be relied on, members of Government and Foxites who could be expected, but acquaintances also, the non-political, Grenvillites, even Tories; the Duchess of Leinster was naturally there, but so was the Duchess of Gordon who once had 'caballed against' Mrs Fox in Paris. They came with their grown-up sons, bringing daughters who were out, and watched complaisantly their children taking the floor as guests of her whose marriage had outraged public morality. Mrs Fox, increasingly footsore, stood smiling and greeting the still arriving guests. 'At 12' she recorded 'very full indeed in the whole I fancy about 400 there were 240 sat down to supper and between forty and fifty sat down afterwards everything seemed to give satisfaction.' Her own satisfaction was completed the next day, when she observed, 'my angel was not at all tired.' A week later, however, he developed another bad cold. His legs were swelling again and he was troubled by pains in his thighs, which they attributed to rheumatism.

He continued to work, and on June 10th had part of his reward when the resolution he moved for the abolition of the slave trade was carried by 114 votes to 15 and the foundation laid for the Act of 1807 that rendered the trade illegal. It was a beautiful day; that evening they spent quietly in the garden at Stable Yard with Trotter and his sister, and Bedford's very young sons Lord William and Lord John Russell. Two days later Mrs Fox went, escorted by the Russells' elder brother Lord Tavistock, to a masked ball at Lansdowne House at which Fox was to have joined her, found him not there and, returning to Stable Yard, 'found Carl in bed he was kept at the House till 12 and was too tired to get to Lansdowne House.'

His colleagues were growing concerned for him. Through Howick he was given to understand that should he wish to withdraw from the demanding post he held to one of dignity without burden, this would be arranged, and that the path was also open, should he choose to take it, to honourable semi-retirement in the Lords. 'Mrs Fox was in the room when this suggestion was made,' recorded Holland in his 'Memoirs of the Whig Party'. 'At the mention of the Peerage he looked at her significantly, with a reference to his secret but early determination never to be created a Peer; and, after a short pause, he said: "no, not yet, I think not yet." On the same evening, as I sat by his bedside, he said to me: "If this continues (and though I don't fear any immediate danger, I begin to see it is a longer and more serious business than I apprehended) I must have more quiet than with my place I ought to have, and put the plan I spoke to you about, sooner in execution than I intended. But don't think me selfish, young one. The Slave Trade and Peace are two such glorious things, I can't give them up, even to you. If I can manage them, I will then retire.'' '

The way to abolition of the slave trade had been paved, but peace was another matter. 'Ministers want peace but have not the courage to be peaceable,' Fox had told Rogers four years earlier. Now, in the changed perspective of office, he was beginning to realise that the making of true peace required, besides courage, pacific intentions in both parties. Napoleon certainly saw as in his interest the making of peace with Britain, and almost as soon as Fox took office had sent over as messenger of his readiness to negotiate the dissolute Lord Yarmouth (caught in France on the renewal of war in 1803), but the interest that moved him was in freedom to extend his hegemony in Europe without further interference from Britain. Indeed, rightly confident that his separate negotiations with Russia and Prussia would shortly leave Britain without an ally among powers of the first rank, he expected a payment for the making of peace; control of Sicily. Fox had been prepared to treat on the basis that each side should retain its existing position of control, but a concession of this order (quite apart from the distastefulness to his principles of transferring a population regardless of the people's wishes) was something he could not contemplate. He was to be disappointed even in his hopes that the French – the soi-disant standard-bearers of liberty – would join the British in abolishing the slave trade.

On June 14th, in the evening, the Foxes went down again to St. Anne's. There, the next day, they enjoyed 'a nice lounge', and in the evening drank tea at Fan Grove. No more than a brief visit could be indulged in, and on June 16th, at four in the afternoon, St. Anne's was left behind. The next day Fox attended the Commons again, Elizabeth driving down there with him, and on the 19th she recorded again; 'Carl at House.' It was the last such entry. On 21st June they were engaged to dine with Lord Ossory. Charles was looking so ill that Elizabeth tried to persuade him not to go, 'but he said I am not well my Liz but it will be a pleasant dinner and if I were to stay at home people will think me worse than I am.' It was indeed a pleasant dinner, but on the morrow he was too tired to leave his dressing-room, and in the days following the effort of transacting business even at home grew increasingly too much for him.

The swelling in his legs, now recognised as dropsical, increased, and the pain worsened. Elizabeth, masking with resolute calm her inward dread, read aloud to him – Caroline Fox and Trotter, and in the evenings Holland, taking turns with her –, dealt with enquiries, passed through callers she thought would please and cheer him. This last task was rendered more difficult by Lady Holland, 'whom he *will not* see', wrote Mrs Creevey, 'but she plants herself in one of the rooms below stairs, under pretence of waiting for Lord Holland, and so prevents his admitting any other woman.'

She was fortunately absent when on June 29th Lady Bessborough visited him, to be appalled by his looks. 'his face and hands are dreadfully drawn and emaciated, his complexion sallow beyond measure, his bosom sunk – and then, all at once, a body and legs so enormous that it looks like the things with which they dress up Falstaff. I fear he is very ill; but his Countenance was delightful, beaming with kindness and benevolence. He kiss'd my hand repeatedly, saying: "This is very, very good of you; I take it very kindly, for I long'd to see you, but thought you would dislike coming."* I assur'd him I would always come with pleasure to him, though I had been nowhere else. I cannot tell you the sort of gentle, suffering, patient expression there was in his countenance. Ld. Holland told he look'd well; he smil'd and said: "I shall end with being the handsomest Man in England, for every body who comes in compliments me on my improv'd looks, and so much improvement must end in beauty." "

His illness was now public knowledge, and from all over the country there poured in allegedly infallible cures for dropsy, then thought a disease in itself rather than a symptom. Some, including exterior application of a decoction of snails and colewort, were even attempted, in desperation, by his physicians. In fact, greater medical knowledge than was available in 1806 would probably not have saved him, for both his symptoms and the findings of the autopsy subsequently performed upon his body, when 'the liver was found greatly diseased and what is termed scirrhous,'** suggest that what ailed him was cirrhosis of the liver, now as then fatal.

In July Elizabeth's journal entries shrank to brief occasional bulletins.

*She was still in deep distress over the death of her sister, the Duchess of Devonshire.
**Trotter, op.cit.

'6   I have thought him worse though Vaughan and Moseley [his physicians] assured me there was no danger but I thought yesterday the worst day.'

'12   all the days so much alike that I did not think it necessary to say anything about them till yesterday when I thought him a great deal better indeed.'

'19   Some days better and some worse but very bad and low the day before yesterday but thank God pretty well yesterday and seems better still.'

'24   Much the same as for some days passed though he had a badish night owing to the hardness of the Poultice.

'25   Much the same.'

'26   A good deal better.

'27   the same though no appetite but in good spirits and seems to get stronger.'

'28   a good night seemed very well when he first woke but afterwards very heavy to sleep.'

After that entry the journal was closed. Almost two months had passed when she opened it again. She drew a line below that last entry, and began to write:

'Went on much the same some days better some worse (on the 7th he was tapped which he bore very well and seemed relieved by it) till about the 15 or 16 when he appeared to get much better and continued so much so that we settled to go to St. Anne's but the physicians were afraid it would be too far for him to go in one day and as the Duke of Devonshire had kindly offered us Chiswick we went there on the 27th. He bore the going there very well and the next day was so much improved that I flattered myself he had quite got rid of the disorder and that a very few days would enable us to get to our dear little home. But alas the dreadful disorder increased so very rapidly that on Sunday the 31st of August he was obliged to be tapped again and thirteen quarts of water brought away. It lowered him very much but in a day or two he seemed to get better and recovered a little appetite went out airing on the Friday in a garden chair and on Saturday and Sunday in the carriage with me. He was very cheerful and talked a great deal to me kept my hand in his all the time we were out made me kiss him several times and admired the Thames that we saw in the road back from Kew Bridge and made me repeat from Cooper's Hill Thames the most loved etc. . . * I thought he seemed very heavy to sleep all the afternoon but in the evening and the night he had Mr Trotter to read to him. He got some sleep in the night but not much and on Monday the 8th of Septr soon after ten when Mr Trotter was reading to him Johnson's Life of Dryden the fatal symptoms came on which left no ground for reasonable hope afterwards. Oh my God and I am here to write this but I must not repine for by his great goodness to me in giving me strength to go through my last sad duty in the way I knew my angel Husband would like best which was by staying by him and giving him everything he wanted. [sic] On Tuesday Ld. Rt Spencer came to Chiswick and brought Mr J. Bouverie with him he read prayers for Miss Fox Harriet and I. He missed me out of the room and asked Dr Vaughan if I had gone to get a little rest. He had asked Dr V that afternoon what he thought of his case and his answer was that the symptoms were not as good as was expected. I saw him the moment after and could see no change in his dear countenance except that he seemed to look at me with a greater degree of tenderness. Harry Fox came in the course of the day Wednesday and he was pleased to see him – I forgot to mention that he talked with Ld. Holland after he had spoke with Dr Vaughan. He saw and shook hands with General Fitzpatrick. Mr J. Bouverie read prayers by the bedside on Wednesday morn: there were in the room besides Harriet and I the General Ld Robert Mr Trotter Miss Fox Mr Hawkins [the surgeon] Harry Fox and Conway [Fox's valet] and Dr Vaughan – he put his dear hands together and kept his eyes fixed on me. Mr Pitcairn saw him on Wednesday night and said he thought all over. On Thursday morning he seemed to be a great deal better and I could not but flatter myself with hope. He walked as far as the Drawing-room with Mr Trotter and talked to him very cheerfully of different Books. He continued pretty well all Thursday till between nine and ten when he got very restless getting out of bed every instant. Friday he was very weak and every moment we expected to be the last. I was so low and weak I could not as I had hitherto done hide my feelings and when he

---

*By Sir John Denham.
'Thames, the most lov'd of all the Oceans sons
By his old Sire, to his embraces runs,
Hasting to pay his tribute to the Sea,
Like mortal life to meet Eternity   '

felt that I was almost in hysterics he looked up and said oh fie Liz is this your promise. We had agreed some years ago that whichever was likely to die first the other should stay by all the time and to try and look gay and cheerful but my God who could do it. I did I believe more than most people could have done and I shall never forget the goodness of the Almighty in enabling me to do it – It was dreadful all night and all Friday from the extreme restlessness but thank God he had no pain. Friday evening Ld Fitzwilliam came but it was thought best not to mention to him for fear it might disturb him. He had very little sleep and continued getting out of bed every moment almost as soon as he was in he said he wanted to get up again. I had sent to St. Anne's Hill for a comfortable sick chair that I knew he liked and he was much pleased with it though he did not say so but we found that he sat up longer at a time than he had before alone and he looked up at me with a sweet smile and said I like this Chair Liz – Oh Father of mercys help me to go on – Saturday morn: he seemed rather quieter. I think it was about 12 or one o clock that he bid Ld H good-bye. He had hold of my hands bid me kiss him looked at me with a heavenly smile said 'I die happy but pity you.'

'From this time his voice was less intelligible and he said something that I could not understand and when he saw that I was unhappy he made an effort and said it don't signify my dearest dearest Liz – those were his last words. He remained very quiet with his dear eyes fixed on me. I was seated on the bed and he had my hand between his two but as he grew weaker he took away his left hand and made a sign to me to leave my hand upon his right hand which I continued to do. Dr Moseley sitting on the right hand side of the bed Miss Fox Mr Trotter Mr. Hawkins and Conway at the foot all out of sight except Mr Trotter. About three his dear eyes lost all motion but seemed quite fixed still on me and lay as quiet as a lamb only breathing rather hard. I still stayed with him and till Mr Hawkins saw the last moment was at hand had me carried out of the room.

'Merciful Father let me adore thy great goodness to me oh make me worthy of it and of my dear departed angel's affection for me. Give me strength I beseech thee to bear with fortitude and resignation the calamity it has pleased thee to inflict me with. Oh grant great God that it may enable me to make myself more worthy of thee by teaching me humility and kindness to all mankind and purity of thought so that I may not be quite unfit to appear before thy Mercys seat when it may please thee to call me from this world.'

'Indeed if one had not known it before,' wrote Holland to the Prince of his uncle's death, 'his last hours would have convinced us that the ruling passion of his heart was affection and tenderness for her. She has the consolation of knowing that he died with that sentiment & the comforting reflection that her society formed the happiness of his life for years & that her care prolonged it.'

CHAPTER SEVEN

The Widow of the Late Illustrious Statesman

From Chiswick House the word rolled out, to London, to England, to the world: Fox was dead. The great upholder of the indivisibility of principle from politics was gone, and the voice silenced that had declared the one true end of government to be the happiness of the governed. In England, soon in France, then across the Atlantic, the lamentations arose.

'Not one great people only raise his urn,' wrote the young Byron,
'All Europe's far-extended regions mourn . . .
Fox! o'er whose corse a mourning world must weep.'
The world indeed had suffered loss, and many who had known but the name and reputation saddened as for personal bereavement, knowing mankind the poorer by his death.

Those who had known the man were stricken at once by a community's loss and by their own. Few had experienced Fox's friendship but had felt their lives enriched thereby, and to some it had given their existence a significance, even to themselves, beyond anything their own achievements could yield: Lauderdale, who was to declare, 'Charles Fox was not only the most extraordinary man I have ever seen, but also the best man'; Townshend, for whom the friendship of Fox was the only distinction he desired might be remembered after his death; Fitzpatrick, who ensured that record by asking that it form part of his epitaph; Adair, who looked back all his life to the effulgence Fox's friendship had cast over his youth. 'To so many of his particular friends it must be misery,' wrote Caroline St. Jules: 'He was their world.' Her father, the phlegmatic Duke of Devonshire, sat that evening in his accustomed silence, shedding unaccustomed tears; Fitzwilliam fainted at the news; the Prince sobbed uncontrollably for hours.

His family, that had lost the statesman, the friend and the kinsman, were taking thought in their grief for a sorrow greater than theirs and, measuring by the intensity of their pain the anguish of her who had been closest of all, found time in their mourning to grieve for Elizabeth Fox. 'Oh dear, how I do feel for her, knowing what she feels and must endure for such a length of time,' wrote Lady Louisa Conolly to Caroline, and the other Mrs Fox, the General's wife: 'What one must feel for poor Mrs Fox is beyond all expression.' At her side Holland and Caroline closed about her in support, finding perhaps some assuagement for their own grief in striving to protect and comfort her in hers. Fox had had little to bequeath her in worldly goods, but in family he left her a valuable, and valued, legacy.

The brother and sister remained at her side in Chiswick House. Holland wrote the necessary letters to friends and kindred, set about the dreary business of funeral arrangements, and negotiated with a sympathetic Grenville for a pension for the widow. Caroline shielded her in the first agony of loss from the pressures of the outside world, receiving and answering notes of condolence, seeing callers who could not be sent away unmet by the family, and watching with respect no less than compassion as Elizabeth compelled herself to face a world without Charles. To her uncle Lord Ossory Caroline wrote: 'Mrs Fox's patient fortitude, her gentle piety, endear her to me every minute, and loving her as I do for his sake, still I must do so for her own, for she deserves it.'

From her initial collapse and from the sheer physical exhaustion that must have contributed to it (in the ten days before Fox's death she had not undressed, and had rested in brief snatches only on a bed a few feet from where he lay) she dragged herself into activity. Her first thought was the fulfilment of his wishes. The will of which she was executrix had named a few friends only, out of the many he loved and valued, to receive remembrances of him, but either he had asked or she herself thought it right to spread his memorial gifts more widely. She set herself to the task of listing possible recipients, only to be overwhelmed by its immensity; for who could number the friends of Fox. She tried. She made out a list and, certain of its inadequacy, sent it by Caroline to Fitzpatrick (who had returned to his office) with a request that he should add to it such names as she might have overlooked and he thought should be included; at the same time she invited him to choose his own gift. The reply was as unhelpful as it was affectionate. 'I return you Mrs Fox's list, to which I have not used the authority she gave me of adding any names, I am afraid they would become too numerous if half or even a quarter of those truly and tenderly attached, & who would consequently feel gratified at receiving a memorial so dear to them, were to be included. I am rather inclined to think that according to the terms of the Will Mrs Fox should herself make the selection of the presents, & I am sure I shall feel more satisfaction in what she destines for me in considering it as connecting her in a bequest I shall so dearly prize.'

As her strength increased, so did her longing for home. On 20th September, one week after Fox's death, she left Chiswick House, with Harriet, for St. Anne's. Fitzpatrick went ahead, so that a friend should be awaiting her there; Caroline accompanied them, and the next day sent a bulletin to Holland: 'Our arrival here was not more dreadful than I expected. The Gen'l met us at the door & aided by his arm she hurried upstairs to the dear Book Room which he used to call his Paradise & there was a good deal agitated for some time but by degrees grew more tranquil, dined with us below & allowed herself to be sent to in the evening. I am afraid she did not get much sleep in the night but towards morning a little from fatigue, & since breakfast we have taken two melancholy walks.' In her journal Mrs Fox had written the night before: 'Oh my God give me fortitude to bear up and behave worthy of his love and friendship.'

In London the body of Charles James Fox lay at Stable Yard, while preparations were made for the public funeral of a statesman. Holland's arrangements for the private funeral at Farley which had been his uncle's wish were halted by the dismayed protestations of friends and colleagues, that so great a man must be entombed in the place and with the honour his fame demanded. Fox must lie in Westminster Abbey. Holland yielded, as did Mrs Fox, sadly appreciative of the feeling behind the demand and as yet uncomprehending the threat to their dream of lying together after death. On 10th October, the anniversary of Fox's first election for Westminster, the great procession set out to the tolling of all the bells in Westminster, through crowded streets to the Abbey. A gallery had been erected there for the family, but its only occupants were Lady Holland, glorying in her conspicuousness, and her sons. The woman Charles had adored and been adored by sat with Harriet, Caroline and Elizabeth Marston at the home he had loved so much, and afterward wrote in her journal: 'My Angel carried to his last worldly home – as far as such a ceremony can give satisfaction they tell me this was attended by so many proofs from all ranks of people of love and esteem for his Memory and deep felt regret for his loss that I cannot but feel grateful that so much goodness was not thrown quite away upon an ungrateful world.'

On 14th October Caroline left, and on the 17th Mrs Fox went briefly back to London to give up the lease of Stable Yard and to prove Fox's will. Then she returned to St. Anne's. In that dear home she could continue. Grenville had arranged the grant to her of a pension of £1,200 a year (Harriet receiving a lesser, independent, pension), the trustees being Holland, General Fox, and William Adam. It was sufficient to maintain her in St. Anne's, and there, where every sight and every action brought her angel to her mind, she began to push herself through the motions of life again.

She was not left to do so in a solitude relieved only by Harriet and the visits of Chertsey neighbours. Friends were anxious to offer what comfort and support they could. Elizabeth Marston, probably Mrs Fox's closest intimate outside the family circle, had gone to St. Anne's, no doubt by invitation, within a fortnight of the widow's return, and had stayed there till the funeral was over. Mr and Mrs Ludbey, old and good friends, spent a few days with her at the end of October; John Pery, the clergyman who had married her, came with his wife a few days later; Mrs Dickson, the bishop's widow, came with her daughters to offer what consolation she could. Friends from London made the journey to Chertsey for a morning call, or to dine and stay overnight. Holland came, both to share in grief and to discuss necessary business, his visits always welcome, his companion less so: 'Oh my sweet niece what a misfortune it is such a heart as his should be thrown away upon such a woman as she is,' wrote Mrs Fox to Caroline in healthy exasperation. Nor was she too sunk in sorrow to be incapable of anxiety over Fitzpatrick, who was so seriously ill that autumn that at the end of November she made a special visit to London to see him; but by 27th December he was fit enough to call on her and she wrote: 'The Gen'l seemed a great deal better God Almighty keep him so.'*

The dreadful year came to an end. Mrs Bouverie and Di brought companionship to St. Anne's over the New Year, returning to London on 2nd January. Winter wore away to spring, and still each re-encounter with friends not seen since Charles's death, each first

*This, like all quotations in this chapter for which no source is otherwise indicated, is from Mrs Fox's Journal.

revisiting of a place last visited with him, was a stab of pain. After dining with the Bouveries on a short visit to London in March, she wrote: 'it was dreadful going into that house where I had been so often with him,' and meetings with Lady Sarah Napier and the Duchess of Leinster were anguish relieved only by their affectionate kindness.

In April she went on a short visit to the Beauclerks* at St Leonards near Horsham, and though it was pleasant there she wrote on returning to St. Anne's: 'I do not feel in spirits to enjoy any place but this, here I feel as if he was still with me.' But he was not, and with each resumption of a once-shared pleasure her loss smote her anew. 'I began to work in the garden alas how different from former times when he whose presence made every thing delightful used to stand by to help and encourage me.' The History was brought out again, for Holland sensibly thought Mrs Fox should benefit from any profit publication might yield. 'I had hard work at first to get the better of my feelings to be able to read it but thank God after a little struggle I was able to go on.' (Published in 1808, praised by Fox's friends, condemned by critics, it brought Mrs Fox £4,500.) Gradually she was bringing herself to terms with widowhood.

She was aided by trust in God and by feeling for others. Faith in one gave her hope of reunion with Charles, sense of duty to the others required her to mask her misery. Religion had always, perhaps, been a silent area between Elizabeth and the free-thinking Charles (her anxiety that prayers be said at his deathbed having probably reflected her fear lest he lose salvation) and after his death – reconciled, she was now certain, with God – she began the observance of belief that in his lifetime might have stressed the silence. At first this was a matter of having prayers and the lesson for the day read at home on Sunday. In 1807, however, measures for the restoration of the parish church found in her a ready supporter and contributor, and in due course she became a regular attender of the services there; on the chancel wall she had set a plaque: 'To the Memory of the best of Husband, and the most excellent of men, CHARLES JAMES FOX, Who died September 13th 1806 Aged 57 And is buried in Westminster Abbey His most affectionate Widow places this Tablet.'

---

*Charles Beauclerk was a nephew of Lord Robert Spencer and his wife Emily ('Mimi') a daughter of the Duchess of Leinster by her second marriage. Mrs Fox later stood godmother to one of their daughters.

Below were the lines Fitzpatrick had written of him:
> 'A Patriot's even Course he Steer'd,
> Mid Faction's wildest Storms unmoved,
> By all who mark'd his Mind revered,
> By all who knew his Heart beloved.'

On 1st January, 1809, she recorded: 'I took the Sacraments for the first time in my life. May the Almighty make me worthy of his goodness to me.' Her faith was uncomplicated and undoctrinal, a trust in a loving God who had given her her happiness with Charles, who had granted the strength that upheld her through his illness, and who if she proved worthy would at last receive her and reunite her with Charles in another and better world.

Meanwhile, she had the rest of her life to wear through. All the once golden anniversaries had been transmuted into lead: his birthday, when 'how happy I used to be on this day and how delighted those dear eyes used to look at seeing me so'; May 7th, which in 1795 'dear angel said was the happiest day he ever knew his dear dear face made everything look beautiful'; her own birthday, 'This day my Angel used to say was the best day in the whole year'; and that other best day in the whole year, 28th September, when anniversary by anniversary she recalled how 'this day I was made the happy wife of my angel'. And a fortnight before it fell that terrible anniversary, 13th September; 'A dreadful day and must ever be the most melancholy of my life.' Eight years after Fox's death she would write on that day: 'I go about as if I was happy, which God knows I can never be in this world, at least comparatively to what I have been, but we owe it to society to keep our miseries as much as possible to ourselves.'

That debt she paid, and society responded with affection and support. There was no falling off in the attachment of the Chertsey folk, to whom Mrs Fox the widow remained what Fox's wife had been, first lady of their world in esteem if not in rank. Woburn, Ockham, Woolbeding, Southill were open to her still. On her visits to London, where in 1808 she began again to spend part of the season, Whig friends were as welcoming as ever. There were comfortable gossips still with Mrs Bouverie over the tea-cups, and visits to the Opera in the Duke of Bedford's box; he who had considered Elizabeth's marriage an outrage to public morality remained a good friend to her all his life. And not far away from home, at Sunning Hill, was Fitzpatrick; old and gouty now, so stiff in movement that, Holland said, the pet crane he kept there looked in its walking as though it imitated him, but still the person with whom, more completely than any other, she could share the pleasure of reliving in quiet talk the happy days of the past.

Links with those who had been primarily her friends rather than Fox's were naturally unweakened. Among the oldest of these, stretching back beyond even the days when Mr Fox had been to her no more than an acquaintance, was a tie with two people who by birth belonged to his world rather than hers; the third Viscount Bolingbroke and his brother Frederick, now General, St John. The disgraced Viscount had during his years abroad settled down at last to domesticity, but in circumstances unlikely to aid his social redemption, for the fact that his wife was still living had not deterred him from 'marrying' Baroness Isabella Hompesch in Austria, and by 1804, when the death of the deserted Lady Bolingbroke enabled him to do so legally, the pair had several children. Bob St John represented a special tie between Bolingbroke and Mrs Fox, while the Bolingbrokes (though recognised by his relatives) were in England so ostracised socially that the countenance even of the former Mrs Armitstead might have been welcome. No such consideration, however, could have affected the entirely respectable General, who was no less attached to her than his brother. Her tie with both brothers seems indeed to have differed in kind from her other friendships; it was as if that long-ago liaison with Bully had rendered her an honorary member of his family. His sons behaved towards her with the mixture of regard and taking for granted that belongs rather to kinship than to friendship: they descended on her suddenly to stay: they reported themselves to her as soon as possible after returning from abroad: they rushed to her, or sent for her, for comfort in distress (the death of the General's second wife would be heralded by the dispatch of his younger children to St. Anne's, and announced on the morrow of the event by the widower arriving to spend the next fortnight there): and they brought up their children to look on her as an aunt.

In Mrs Fox this tacit sense of kinship may have been strengthened by her special affection for Bob, and the second Lady Bolingbroke's acceptance of her husband's bastard as a member of the family warmed that lady's first welcome at St. Anne's, but the two women got on well from the start. Lady Bolingbroke had never been a beauty – 'a little square German with broken teeth', wrote Augustus Foster of her – but she was a good-natured little soul and a devoted mother, and the two soon had established a friendship that was to survive Bollingbroke's death.

The St John children, staying at St Anne's with their parents or without them, were welcome for their own sake. Mrs Fox delighted as much in having children about the place as she had done when Fox was alive. Miss Fox and Miss Vernon frequently brought with them to St. Anne's 'the dear little Smiths', children of Miss Vernon's sister who was in India with her husband. The Albemarles lent a small Keppel for weeks at a time. The Hollands' children came, attended by such servants as Lady Holland deemed necessary and so sometimes filling up the house more than suited its mistress. 'I am at all times glad to have any of them here but I should dislike very much to have them live here', she had written to Caroline in 1807, when there were signs that the Hollands contemplated dumping their children while they toured the Peninsula, 'she does not recollect how small this House is and how one or two people with their servants make us quite full.' Harry Fox still looked on St. Anne's as his second home – for the sad reason that General Fox's return from the Mediterranean in 1807 had been followed in little more than a year by the death of his wife. Harry of course would scarcely have accounted himself a child now, for in 1808 he left Eton for Oxford. There was still however a Fox at Eton, for Holland's Charles was there now, and other young Etonians such as the younger Sam Whitbread and Townshend's son Fox were as happy as their seniors had been to come over to St. Anne's and birdsnest in the trees, or shoot rabbits under the kindly supervision of the Porter brothers.

It was for the sake of young visitors that Mrs Fox first recommenced, in 1809, her Twelfth Night parties. She had several young folk with her that New Year – Bollingbroke's son Joseph, Fox Townshend, Miss Marston's niece Emma Jenkins – and so on 6th January 'we danced in the evening young ones all very happy I dressed as Merlin Townshend as my wife.' (There is regrettably no indication of whom they supposed Merlin's wife to have been.)

However sweet the company of children, however devoted her friends, Mrs Fox could not but feel in the years after Fox's death the want not only of him but of permanent congenial adult companionship. This she should in theory have had in her stepdaughter Harriet. Harriet, though she corresponded with her mother and half-brother, had no desire to leave the social sphere in which her paternity had established her for the less distinguished society of her maternal connections. But 'Harriet is no resource', Charles had once written, and Harriet in fact was worse than no resource, for with stupidity she combined a defect most depressing in the stupid, incessant volubility. 'She makes herself so disagreeable by her love of hearing herself talking which she would do for the whole four and twenty hours if anyone would attend to her,' her stepmother once declared. Nor was her lack of her father's intelligence redeemed by his sweetness of nature. 'Miss Willoughby . . . is little removed from an idiot, and besides is jealous and suspicious,' later opined her cousin Henry, Holland's son. Mrs Fox indeed found it increasingly difficult to credit that Harriet could really have been sired by Charles. Years later she wrote: 'I wish I could believe she was my beloved Husband's daughter though she is not a person to make one very much attached to her yet from her weakness of intellect it is impossible not to feel something like regard for her.' That 'regard' could not however make her society any more agreeable.

A companion other than Harriet was needed, and that need had only to be recognised to be met. Elizabeth Marston, a daughter of that couple one of whom had befriended the young Elizabeth Armitstead, was now in her thirties, unlikely to marry, poorly circumstanced and apparently dependent on her brother-in-law for a home. A quiet, sensible, good-hearted woman, she had long been a frequent and a welcome guest at St. Anne's, and early in 1808, on Mrs Fox's invitation, she made her home there.

This addition to the household can scarcely have been welcome to the 'jealous and suspicious' Harriet. Even before it occurred, she had taken the course so often instinctively adopted by those desirous of more attention, and had developed constant and inexplicable ailments. 'Harriet poorly', 'Harriet very ill', runs like a refrain through Mrs Fox's journals in 1807 and 1808; and when they visited London the first call was usually on some well recommended physician to seek his advice for Harriet. Early nineteenth-century doctors were evidently capable, whatever their deficiencies as healers, of diagnosing hyponchondria – if not of expressing that diagnosis to the patient or the patient's relatives –, and each time Mrs Fox recorded with surprised relief that 'Dr Pemberton (or Dr Baillie) did not think Harriet so ill as I had feared.'

The ailments however continued. Harriet was unresponsive too to her stepmother's specific for health; she had no taste for exercise, and could be coaxed only into an occasional ride on the donkey kept to draw Mrs Fox's little donkey-carriage. In 1807, however, the local apothecary recommending Bath for Harriet, Mrs Fox had dutifully taken her there for two months of the winter. She herself, having no inclination towards valetudinarianism, had been bored to the point of taking a further course of harp lessons ('a miserable Harp but better than none') to pass the time, but Harriet loved Bath and Bath proved the solution to the problem of Harriet. In 1809 she settled there, returning to St. Anne's usually for some three months of the summer, and for the rest of the year Mrs Fox could enjoy her guests, and the affectionate companionship of Elizabeth Marston, undisturbed by Harriet's endless chatter.

Among the friends of Fox who were constant in friendship to his widow there was one conspicuous exception. At a party at the Whitbreads in 1808 Mrs Fox observed Sheridan, who 'seemed determined not to speak to me'; and two days later, after visiting Mrs Plumer, she wrote, 'she is a kind warm-hearted friend in which [sic] I see no difference from former times alas not so with all that call them selves friends.' The person she had in mind was almost certainly not Sheridan (who did in later years occasionally call at St. Anne's, while Mrs and Miss Sheridan passed 'a very pleasant fortnight' there in 1811), but him whom sight of Sheridan brought to mind, the Prince. After more than twenty years, it had become Elizabeth's turn to experience how totally the Prince could drop anyone in whom he had lost interest; she had not seen or heard from him since Fox's death. This hurt, for she had always been fond of him. In 1810 private hurt was aggravated by what she and all Whigs saw as public betrayal. George III sank at last into incurable madness, the long-awaited Regency came into being, the Whigs – out of power since the fall of Grenville's Administration in 1807 – prepared for the supposedly inevitable summons to office; and the Regent retained the Tory Administration.

Mrs Fox's hurt and disappointment were to slip several times into her journals. In 1814, on a visit to the races; 'I saw the Regent & he saw me but the instant he did so he turned round which I was not surprised [at] as I think upon the whole he must feel rather ashamed of his conduct to me'; while a call from the Duke of Gloucester inspired the reflection: 'I wish all princes were as amiable.' It was probably the Regent, too, that she had in mind when, in 1812, remembering as so often the dear companion she had lost, she wrote: 'had it pleased the Almighty to have spared him till now the conduct of those he thought well of would have made him suffer greatly, he was too good for this world.'

There were pleasanter events in 1810, one being the marriage of Mrs Fox's maid, Martha Goome (whose predecessor Mary Dassonville still occasionally came to visit her former mistress) to the head gardener Henry Tucker. Unlike many employers, Mrs Fox put no obstacles in the way of her servants' marrying. She was the best of mistresses. Her staff were devoted to her, and indeed it is not impossible that Martha's acceptance of the considerably older Tucker reflected in part a wish to continue in Mrs Fox's employment after marriage. They chose July 11th, Mrs Fox's birthday, for their wedding, and Mrs Fox bought 'Patty' a trousseau and gave a dinner in the Greenhouse for the guests, fifty-eight of them with the pupils from the little school she had recently founded for the poor children of Chertsey.

1811 brought distress to Fox's family in the publication of Trotter's 'Memoirs of the Latter Years of the Right Honourable Charles James Fox.' Trotter's difficult temperament had prevented his availing himself of such connections as his secretaryship to Fox had brought him, and he had sunk into poverty, in which he tried to support himself by pamphleteering. 'He was reduced to great straits,' recalled Samuel Rogers, 'and Mrs Fox sent him, at different times, as much as several hundred pounds, though she could ill spare the money.' She also – something Rogers may not have known – assumed responsibility for the education of his small son Arthur. Now however Trotter sought further relief for his indigence by writing these memoirs. The family was appalled, not so much by the portrait (of an enhaloed Fox replete with every virtue and pontificating wisdom strangely suggestive of the memorialist's prejudices) as by the constant jealous digs at Holland and the implication that Fox's death had been hastened by the administration of drastic medicines. The one favourable comment from Fox's circle on any part of the book was Fitzpatrick's endorsement of his portrayal of domestic life at St. Anne's.

Holland was outraged; and productively so, for his anger stimulated him to anticipate the full biography of his uncle he meditated writing in the fullness of time by composing (though not publishing) his 'Memoirs of the Whig Party.' The widow certainly read Trotter's book (Caroline Fox told Holland that Mrs Fox as well as Lord Ossory had urged the reading of it upon her), but her views, if recorded in writing, do not survive. They may be deduced from a subsequent reference of hers to Trotter: 'a mean low-minded wretch – that my angel and I could ever have thought well of such a person!!!' Her care and concern for his son, however, continued unchanged.

She was established in the ways of widowhood now. In outward form her pattern of life had not changed much from that of the old happy days. Still after breakfast there was, winter and summer alike if the weather permitted, the walk in the garden. There still, in the growing and planting season, she supervised and often aided the gardeners in their work. The farm commanded her interest still, for she liked to feel she was managing it herself, recording proudly, 'the sheep sheared and the Man said they were the handsomest sheep in the parish, which made me hold up my head,' or sadly, 'rain, rain and my poor Hay soaking in it.'

Within doors there was constant reading still, and music, and the letter-writing that kept friendships warm with distant friends, these occupations often broken off to receive callers. At other times she herself would be the caller, dropping in on near neighbours in the course of a morning walk, or summoning the carriage for visits to the more distant or those, such as residents yet unmet, for whom a touch of ceremony seemed appropriate. (She had no notion of setting a value on herself by exclusiveness; if told that a newcomer would like to know her, she called at the first opportunity.) Then came dinner, at which – particularly if there were house-guests to be entertained, or the dear Duke of Bedford had sent a haunch of venison – Chertsey neighbours might be present to make up a small dinner-party.

The meal would often be followed by another walk, for she was still an energetic woman who thought nothing of walking (dog-attended as ever) down to Chertsey, over Chertsey Bridge, up the left bank of the Thames to Laleham and home by way of Laleham Bridge, a circuit of three or four miles with the pull up St. Anne's Hill at the end. The after-dinner walk would normally however be around the hill or through the St. Anne's woodlands or those of the Porters at adjoining Silverlands, with the donkey-carriage available for guests whose vigour did not equal that of their hostess. Those who walked with her could not, to judge by an 1809 entry in her journal, reckon on a ladylike stroll: 'we walked in the copse a delightful evening Liz [Marston] got a fall and we were all obliged to go down the steep part on our bottoms.' And after these exertions there would again be reading, perhaps 'reading out', until it was time for bed.

In late winter or early spring Mrs Fox, accompanied by Miss Marston, spent a few weeks in London – leasing a house if she found one she liked and could afford and otherwise staying at Penton's or Hatchett's hotel –, to enjoy the theatre, the Opera, the picture galleries, the society of more friends together than could be gathered at St. Anne's, and conversation more stimulating than her good neighbours at Chertsey could provide. Often her journey home again to enjoy the blossoming time was broken by a call on the Rollestons at Battersea or the Duchess of Leinster at Wimbledon, but sometimes it was then that she discharged the sad duty of calling at Parsons Green to assure herself that all was as well as it could be with 'my poor dear Harry', her stepson. It was a melancholy business, for he did not even recognise her now, and the physical likeness to his father in this poor creature was deeply depressing: 'alas! how wretched to see him so with his dearest Father's every feature to think such a strong likeness can be without mind or any sense at all is indeed dreadful and humiliating.'

High summer was as always the time of greatest hospitality at St. Anne's, so that it was rarely that Mrs Fox and Miss Marston sat alone together in the Book Room for more than two days running. As summer ended, it became Mrs Fox's turn to be a visitor. With Miss Marston and the now often pregnant Martha Tucker she set out for a succession of short stays at the country houses of friends. These peregrinations were curiously limited geographically, never taking her north of Bedfordshire and seldom west of Buckinghamshire; though the Bolingbrokes when in England constantly visited St Anne's, and though she admitted on her first visit to them that 'Ly B. did everything to make it pleasant', she went to Lydiard less often than she was invited. Those to some or all of whom she usually went were the Whitbreads at Southill, the Townshends at Balls Park, the Ludbeys at Chalfont, the Beauclerks at St Leonards and perhaps the Bedfords at Woburn. The society of Russells, of 'the dear little Duchess' and 'her angel husband', was as delightful to her as ever it had been, even though on her first revisiting of them 'everything brought my angel constantly before my eyes, his dear Bust! surrounded by those friends he loved so much, alas what a different feel it was to go into the Temple.'

The last and longest visit of the year – the journey thither sometimes broken by a day or two with the Kings at Ockham – was, as always, to Woolbeding. The happy stays at Woolbeding became happier than ever in 1811, for the house acquired a mistress when, a conventional year after the death of Edward Bouverie, his widow and Lord Robert Spencer sealed their long love affair with marriage. Under Lady Robert's rule, the hospitable house became, in Henry Fox's later view, 'quite luxurious from the perpetual attentions of its owners to the comfort and convenience of their guests.' The day-long society of Lady Robert, her closest female friend of her own age, was itself a luxury to Mrs Fox, and within a few years of the marriage another Woolbeding enjoyment was added by Lord Robert's bestowal of the parish living on his stepson John Bouverie. From the start of her acquaintance with the Bouveries Mrs Fox had been particularly fond of John and his sister Di- 'the tell-tale Bouverie', now Mrs George Ponsonby – both of whom were regular visitors to St Anne's.* Now when at Woolbeding she could visit him at his own rectory, in easy walking distance. 'What a blessing it must be to have such a son always so near . . . he is a real blessing to his poor neighbours to whom he is always doing good.' As he was also a keen gardener, visits to Woolbeding Rectory offered an additional satisfaction to a fellow horticulturalist.

At any time during the year there might be a one- or two-day visit to London. Often on these occasions Mrs Fox stayed at Little Holland House, whose second mistress, Miss Vernon, was scarcely less dear to her than Miss Fox, but sometimes at the Great House, where Lady Holland was now creating the most famous political salon the country had ever known. Not even her husband's relatives, though in or near the house, could reckon on admission to her celebrated dinners. 'So you were not allowed to dine when there was a large party for fear you should draw off any attention from the great Lady I suppose,' Mrs Fox had once written to an excluded Caroline, and on occasion she herself,

---

Though she was now generally formal in use of names, even in her journals (even Caroline Fox, when not 'my dearest little niece', was 'Miss Fox' to her), occasional unguarded references to 'John' and 'Di' suggest that she used their Christian names – for her a very rare intimacy with unrelated adults she had not known as children. Similarly, Fitzpatrick is usually 'the dear General', but odd references to 'Fitz' suggest her likely conversational address.

staying at Holland House, was thus banished. Once, when some schoolboy friends of Charles and Henry were also staying, she was set down to dinner with them, no hardship to one so fond of the young; 'and a very jolly party we were.'

There were jolly parties again, now, at St Anne's. On 22nd September, 1812, the General's Harry – wholly orphaned since his father's death the previous year – came of age, and the event was celebrated by a grand fête there. 'All the school children and workmen dined in the Green House and a grand noise there was . . . an excellent dinner. At eight we went to the Green House where all the servants were and we danced with them I went down one dance.' (As late as her seventieth year Mrs Fox could be coaxed to join in a dance.) 'All went off very well and all appeared pleased and happy – How often in the course of the day did I feel the loss of my Angel how he would have enjoyed seeing so many happy faces.' Harry, alas, was to prove the family's disappointment. Alone in his generation he inherited the gamester disposition of his two uncles, eventually having to live abroad to escape his creditors. In the end Holland managed to make a function of necessity, and secured him a diplomatic post.

The following spring brought sorrow. On 25th April, 1813, at his London house in Arlington Street, Fitzpatrick died. He had been failing for some years, and his death cannot have come as a shock, but preparedness could not lessen the pain of loss. On the day before his death Samuel Rogers walked to Arlington Street to enquire after him and, seeing Mrs Fox emerge from the door 'sobbing violently', knew that the end was near.* For her it was the severing of a unique tie.

His will was a testament to the constancy in friendship of the buff and blue rakes of long ago. Of the five named legatees who were not his blood kin, one, Robert Price, was the son of two old friends; two, Lord Robert Spencer and Lord John Townshend, were men who had been his friends since youth; and of the other two, Lady Caroline Price and Elizabeth Fox, one certainly and one probably had been his mistress in those distant days, to remain afterward his friend into old age. To Mrs

---

The volume of Mrs Fox's journal that would have covered Fitzpatrick's death (mid-April 1813 to May 1814) is missing, as is that (May 1830 – May 1831) that would have covered Lord John Townshend's. Nothing is known that illuminates their disappearance, and it could be that in the first grief of bereavement Mrs Fox wrote more about her early associations with these two friends than she later wished to have known.

Fox he had bequeathed £1,000, to Lady Caroline, perhaps with a view to ensuring her a home should she be widowed, a life interest in his house at Sunning Hill. He was buried at Sunning Hill under an epitaph declaring him, by his own wish, 'for more than forty years the friend of Mr Fox', and Elizabeth planted ivy to grow about his tomb. After his death another date appeared in the tale of sad anniversaries, 21st November, Holland's birthday but also the anniversary of that coming of age when the Temple of Friendship was dedicated and 'how delighted my Angel was with my little Fête – the dear General too alas! both gone.'

In 1814, eight years after Fox's death, came the peace for which he had striven so long and so vainly. His widow celebrated it with a bonfire, illuminations, and a dinner in the Greenhouse for 'all the workmen their wives and children'. Peace came but not prosperity. The return from the land fell before the competition of cheap foreign corn, farmworkers' wages were cut, and industry, deprived of the markets of war and finding none of peace in war-impoverished Europe, ran into recession. Taxation rose, and the moderate inflation of the later war years steepened. Soon the old lady – living on a fixed income, trying to extend her little estate with the land purchases Fox had advocated and that were now so doubtful an investment, and increasing with increasing distress the help she gave the distressed – found with alarm that she was running ever deeper into debt. Mrs Fox had never acquired an aristocratic insouciance towards indebtedness. 'Being in debt does really make me ashamed to look anyone in the face but I trust I have not a mean heart.' She had not; that was the trouble. The state of debt that was to plague her for the rest of her life was partly due, in the opinion of one of the two people who knew her best, to her benevolence. 'Altho' her generous and charitable disposition now & then straitened her circumstances & led her into difficulties,' Caroline Fox would write after the death of her 'beloved old friend', 'yet she never squandered money in the way she was sometimes accused of but spent it in judicious repair & improvement of the estate & its enlargement by purchase of adjoining lands.'

The purchasing of land could be halted and indeed reversed. In 1817 she sold the lease of Fan Grove to the Porters (who themselves would in 1821 be forced by financial difficulties to dispose of Silverlands), and other outlying parcels of land too were sold off. Her charities she could not bring herself to reduce. She was still supporting her little school (which had given rise to the one anniversary unclouded by memories of a happier past, for every May-day the children brought her garlands of flowers). She was still paying for the education of Arthur Trotter, who was allowed to look on St Anne's as his home until at last, ready to set out in the world and fitted out at her expense, he left to take up the East India Company cadetship she had managed to secure him. She gave what personal aid she could to the local unemployed, and contributed to collections for those elsewhere; 'Mr Pembroke called for the subscriptions for the distressed manufacturers [factory workers] poor souls I wish I could relieve them all.' Nor was her charity confined to the deserving: 'walked to see old Beauchamp's children . . . it is misery to see them in such a state though they are a bad set and Rob and plunder one every day I must do something for them though God knows I can ill afford it.

Holland lent her money, and so did Lord Fitzwilliam. She borrowed from Coutts' bank, and later from Coutts's son-in-law Sir Francis Burdett on the security of St Anne's Hill. She worriedly discussed her financial problems with Miss Vernon (possibly finding it easier to discuss such matters with one who, as Fitzpatrick's half-sister, was technically of her own generation than with Miss Fox), who was soothing and lent her £1,000, as security for which Mrs Fox insisted on giving her another mortgage on the property. Her greatest fear was that she might have to give up St Anne's: 'it will wring my heart to do so, I have been so very very happy here that it seems a part of myself.' Yet she was a resilient creature after all, and would learn to live with her worries as she had learned to live with her grief.

This could smite her unexpectedly still. When in 1815 Coke, having at last brought himself to recognise Fox's widow, visited St Anne's with Albemarle and Adair: 'the sight of him for whom my Angel had so true a friendship made me nervous [a term she used with the then common meaning of 'agitated'] and uncomfortable for a little while the other dear friends I had seen so often.' When, though he had visited the house several times in the first few years of her widowhood, Charles Meyer came again after a lapse of some years: 'he brought former times sadly back to me when my angel used to be so happy reading his Homer and see[ing] me take my harp lessons with Charles.' When in 1817 she revisited Kensington Gardens, 'alas! it brought fresh to my memory how happy I was the last time I was here leaning on that dear arm the support of which made every place and every thing delightful to me.' And later that year a visiting clergyman, preaching on the death of Princess Charlotte, somehow touched her on a psychic nerve so painful that 'it was with great difficulty that I could remain in Church, alas! it brought every thing so strong before me that I believed myself at Chiswick.'

There were other, lesser, griefs. Hardly a year now passed, but carried off more of her few remaining seniors and of her contemporaries. The Duchess of Leinster had died in 1814; in 1817 died old Mrs Payne, whom Elizabeth had known since she was 'a foolish giddy girl', and in 1818 Mr Ludbey. Whitbread had taken his own life in 1815, and in 1818 Sir Samuel Romilly did likewise, both deaths horrifying Mrs Fox not by the event alone but by their nature. More poignant yet for the old are the deaths of those much younger. 1817, a year of deaths, took in April the delightful young Fox Townshend, in November Lady Albemarle at the birth of her fifteenth child, while in between fell a loss closer to Mrs Fox, that of the much-loved Bob St John. He had for years been ailing, possibly with tuberculosis of the lungs, for he had in 1816 been advised to seek a warmer climate. In August that year he had paid his farewell visit to St Anne's, and in the following June word came of his death. 'Alas! alas! dear fellow how little did I think when he was at St Anne's that it was for the last time in this world but we shall meet again in a happier and better.'

But humanity replaces its losses, and Mrs Fox was not of that nature whose power of feeling new affections atrophies with age. These years had been gladdened for her by the propinquity of her other niece Caroline, 'Catty', General Fox's daughter, who with her husband William Napier – on half-pay since demobilisation and now at work on his great 'History of the Peninsular War' – had settled temporarily at Halliford near Weybridge. They were a prolific pair, whose accessibility was the more delightful for bringing with it that of their children, and no less a delight was it to have 'Catty's darlings' bestowed at St Anne's while Catty was 'put to bed' with another little boy or girl.

Moreover, St Anne's was at this time enjoying the frequent presence of its own temporarily adopted child. The Comte de Grave, whom Mrs Fox had met during her sojourn in Paris in 1802, had a small ward whom he wished to have educated partly in England. Visiting the country in 1816 to look for a suitable school, he called at St Anne's to pay his respects to the great statesman's widow and, one cannot but feel, took the lady's measure with some accuracy. Little Maria was placed at a school near Chertsey, Mrs Fox's interest was solicited, and M. de Grave departed for his homeland, congratulating himself no doubt that his ward's welfare and happiness would be well supervised. So indeed they were. Little Maria became the pet of St Anne's. She was taken calling with Mrs Fox, brought up to play with the little Tuckers, had children's parties organised for her at the Greenhouse. The interruptions can have done her education no good, but she was only four when deposited in England, and had greater need of affection than instruction. M. de Grave left Maria seven years in England; on his reclaiming her in 1823 Mrs Fox wrote in her journal: 'It is a foolish thing to allow oneself to love any Child that does not belong to one, but there is no happiness without having something to love.'

Nor could there be for her happiness without friendship. Old friendships were kept in good repair, and new ones still were formed. Visiting Sir Henry Fletcher of Ashley Park near Walton – a carriage-calling neighbour – she met his cousin Sir John Aubrey of Dorton in Oxfordshire and took a liking to him, as he did to her, and Dorton (so well situated for a stop on the way home from Woburn or Southill) took its place among houses visited when she was touring the homes of friends. Staying in Brighton, she was introduced to the Wigney family, whose daughter Mrs Butterfield lived at Windsor, and Mrs. Butterfield began to appear among carriage-calling neighbours, and the Wigneys among those who came often to spend a couple of days at St Anne's. It was at Brighton, too, that she had the greater satisfaction of renewing a lapsed affection.

Brighton had become the second royal capital of England, a status confirmed in 1829 when at long last George IV ascended the throne. His winterings in Brighton had brought about the rise of a Brighton season preceding the London season, when the fashionable world could enjoy the pleasure of meeting itself by the sea before doing so all over again in London; and when an old lady trying not very successfully to retrench could meet her friends at the time of year when home was least attractive instead of doing so in costlier London when the buds were breaking and the birds nesting at St Anne's. Mrs Fox had spent and enjoyed a month in Brighton (still Brighthelmstone to her) towards the end of 1818, and again in November of 1821. Towards the end of November, 1823, she returned for a longer stay.

So many of her dear ones were in Brighton that winter that she had a thoroughly enjoyable time. The Hollands were there with their children, Charles the elder but illegitimate son, now in the Army, Henry the heir, and Mary, the only surviving, now debutante, daughter. The Duke and Duchess of Bedford were there for a few weeks with their children, 'the dear little Russells', and General St John and his third wife, with the children of his second marriage. The Beauclerks were there, and Lord and Lady King, and Samuel Rogers – that old acquaintance of the acid tongue, who never exercised it on her – with his sister. Mrs Fox called and was called on, dined out and was dined with; ventured – persuaded by dear Henry – on to the newly opened Chain Pier 'though a good deal frightened but ventured right to the end and a magnificent thing it is'; went, as was a common and innocent amusement of the day, to a children's dancing lesson, 'none better than my little Goddaughter Elizabeth St John'; went to the play. One day Sir William Keppel called, to tell her His Majesty had suggested that she might like to see the Pavilion. Of course she would like to see inside that remarkable building, its exterior so unlike anything seen in England before, its interior the subject of such intriguing accounts from those who had been there. So it was arranged, and on the evening of 15th January Mrs Fox met Sir William at the Pavilion. He escorted her through all the public rooms but the dining-room – then in use –, entertained her to tea, and afterward took her to see the now vacated dining-room. 'It really was a magnificent sight, and quite like a scene in the Arabian Tales.' She was beginning to think it time to depart, when Sir William said he must leave her for a few minutes. Almost immediately he returned, but not alone. Before him rolled the vast bulk that now housed the long-ago Florizel, the faithless friend, the apostate Whig, His Majesty King George IV.

As if the silence of seventeen years had never been, he 'came up to me and embraced me in the most kind and friendly way saying that he had long wished to see me and that it gave him great pleasure to have that satisfaction in short nothing could exceed the warmth of his manner and professions, he sat down and talked over old times in his former kind way said he should be happy to do anything that I wished and that I had only to make my wishes known through Sir W. Keppel. He sat with us rather better than three quarters of an hour and was really so very kind that I was quite nervous.' And, having remembered her at last, he did not forget her again. When after two more weeks at Brighton and a happy month at Woolbeding she was home again, and spring had come and gone, and her visit to the Pavilion had receded into a pleasant memory, she received on 21st June a letter from Sir William Keppel 'to say that the King had ordered him to acquaint me that he had given me an annuity of five hundred a year out of his Privy Purse.'

A fortnight afterward, Sir William came to call at St Anne's, bringing Sir Edmund Nagle with him. Mrs Fox, naturally delighted to receive them, entertained them to lunch, when they 'were much pleased with my Orange Marmelade and surprised when they heard it was made with my own Oranges.' Their appreciation was more than politeness, for two days later she received another letter from Sir William, this time to say that he and Sir Edmund had praised the marmelade so warmly to the King that he had asked for the receipt. And so the carriage was called round, and in a last quaint epilogue to the long-ago story of the Cyprian and the Heir Apparent an old lady drove to Cumberland Lodge and handed in the receipt, 'with a pot of the Marmelade for His Majesty to taste.'

Her satisfaction at this renewal of old kindness was not, financially troubled though she was, in the money alone. She was happy that she could think of the giver with affection again, and in what to her was a tribute to Charles 'God Almighty bless him and grant him health. I am sure by his conduct to me that he loved my angel Husband and regrets his loss.'

Charles Fox, to her a living presence still, to the outer world was passing into history. Monuments had risen; the Duke of Bedford had erected a statue in Bloomsbury Square, in Westminster Abbey Westmacott's florid neo-classical group overwhelmed the beholder. The inscription for the latter had occasioned Mrs Fox some worry. As early as 1820, two years before the monument was erected, Grey had composed an epitaph, which naturally was shown to the widow for her approval. Unfortunately she could not in honesty give it. Grey's production seemed to her 'fitter for a paragraph in history than for an inscription for a Monument. I am afraid my not liking it as well as many of my friends do may hurt Lord Grey which will give me real pain to do but as I was asked to give my opinion I felt I ought to say exactly what I really did feel about it.' Her opinion did cause dismay. Lord Robert Spencer was deputed to try and persuade her into approval, but in vain, for where the honouring of Fox was at issue she was immovable. The only result of his efforts was to leave her more certain than ever that the monument must bear the name alone. 'Alas! what Inscription can tell the hundredth part of the virtues of his heart and mind or of his benevolence to Mankind, no words can do it.' Fortunately she had an ally in Holland, and in the end, after three years of argument, they prevailed; the inscription, austerely contrasting with the grandiloquent statuary above, is simply: 'Charles James Fox b. 24 Jan. 1749 NS [New Style] d. 13 Sept. 1806.'

Those who had been infants when he died were adults now. Familiar names appearing in the record of St Anne's visitors might now be borne by the children of those first announced by them there. 'Mr and Mrs. Whitbread' were the son and daughter-in-law of the kind couple who had entertained 'Mrs Armitstead' to breakfast. 'Sir Henry Fletcher' was the namesake son of the Sir Henry Mrs Fox had first known. In 1823 a bridegroom brought his bride over from Sunning Hill, lent them by Miss Fox (who, inheriting the reversion from Fitzpatrick, had bought out Lady Caroline Price's interest) for their honeymoon; Vernon Smith, who had been one of the 'dear little Smiths' so often taken to St Anne's by Miss Vernon and Miss Fox to solace Mrs Fox in the first dreadful years of her widowhood. The following year the bride presented there was the wife of Holland's son Charles, Mary Fitzclarence, the Duke of Clarence's daughter by Mrs Jordan, and within a month of their visit Robert Price, Uvedale's son, appeared with his wife. The children of that quasi-family of Mrs Fox's, the St Johns, were growing up (those that survived: the Bolingbrokes lost both their daughters in adolescence) and soon would be taking spouses to themselves, their honorary aunt being duly notified of each engagement – by letter if the engagement were entered into abroad, by a personal visit if the contracting St John were in the country –, and at the first convenient opportunity the spouse would be presented at St Anne's; as, in due course, would be any fruit of the marriage.

Bolingbroke did not live to see any grandchildren by his second and happier marriage. He died in 1824, 'the oldest friend I had in the world', wrote Mrs Fox; 'I was a young giddy girl when first I knew him and never expected that he would have thrown away so much superiority of mind and body as he was gifted with for the sake of gratifying a momentary passion.' Next year a yet more painful bereavement was suffered in the death of a newer friend, Lady Robert Spencer. She had been Mrs Fox's closest friend of her own sex and age, the only other survivor of those beauties who had learned their politics in the arms of the buff and blue junto in the days not to have known which was never to have known the sweetness of life, and since the two women had met in a later, drabber age she had been a constant friend. 'To me her loss will be irreparable.'

The quiet life, the tranquil employments, went on. The stays away from home were fewer now, and shorter. Those in London were brief, and passed usually at Holland House or Little Holland House, or at Miss Vernon's house in Hertford Street. Sir John Aubrey was dead: the Beauclerks had gone abroad: Lydiard had passed to the son of Bolingbroke's first marriage, whom Mrs Fox hardly knew: the hospitality of Balls Park was diminishing as the Townshends grew old and frail. But Woolbeding, empty though it seemed without Lady Robert, was visited still, and at St Anne's the guests came and went and saw little change in the faces smiling in welcome.

The very servants gathering to receive them were mostly the same from year to year, for it was seldom that even under-servants left St Anne's, and the upper servants never. Martha Tucker and her husband, the under-gardener Scutt, William Goude the butler and major-domo, William Wooldridge the coachman, Sarah Valler the cook, they were there for life, their mistress's or their own, or at least for as long as health enabled them to serve her, and they knew that if it failed them she would see that they were cared for as long as they lived. They were all, except Goude, local folk with their roots and their kin in Chertsey; they had, except for Sarah Valler and the Tuckers (whose children lived near by with Martha's mother), their cottages on the little estate where their children were reared and they could pursue domestic life. With their mistress they were linked by ties of mutual devotion and responsibility; which in her view extended to their children, whose education and starting in life she saw as her concern, securing nominations to Christ's Hospital for Goude's son and one of the young Tuckers. The burden of this responsibility, at a time when she was harassed by debt, may have occasioned her one demurral at the prospect of further propagation by her servants: 'Ann Housemaid told me she was with Child which I am sorry for as it will oblige me to part with her and her Husband and they are both excellent servants,' she wrote in her journal one November – but she could not bring herself to dismiss them, and the following February recorded: 'Ann brought to bed of a nice little Girl.'

If it fell to Goude and Martha Tucker, the male and female heads of the indoor servants, to ensure the comfort of Mrs Fox's guests, the achievements of Henry Tucker and Scutt were more widely observed. In accordance with the pleasant custom of the day, Mrs Fox opened her grounds to those members of the public who, wishing to see them, sent in their names. The grounds of St Anne's were reckoned well worth seeing. The improvements once undertaken to delight Fox had continued, sometimes with outside aid, as when Lord King constructed a rock garden for his old friend, as a pleasure in themselves. Like all true gardeners, Mrs Fox loved to visit other people's grounds, knowledgeably assessing woodlands, flower-gardens and kitchen-gardens – these last with a housewifely as well as a horticultural eye, for she opined that the Bobus Smiths' kitchen-garden, though one of the best she had ever seen, was too large for the family. After visiting the Royal Cottage at Windsor she wrote: 'the flower-garden very pretty but I could make it still prettier,' and this was probably true, for the beauty of her creation was widely recognised. Whigs went there to sigh over the memorial she had created to Fox in the corner where he had most loved to sit, a vase with its supporting pedestal inscribed with his favourite lines from Dryden's 'The Flower and the Leaf' and with an explanatory poem by Adair; they liked to sit in the garden and think beautiful Whig thoughts, as did Lord William Russell when in 1828 he visited 'the beautiful and modest retreat of Mr Fox. The whole place inspired one with feelings of love, admiration & veneration for the memory of that friend of freedom & the human race.' Even Tories however were impressed, as was Lord Mahon, who after a visit (to the grounds, not to Mrs Fox, who he was quite sure would not welcome one of his persuasion) wrote to Caroline Fox: 'I never saw anything as pretty as those Gardens, on a little scale, & after having seen them can quite understand what used rather to puzzle me – Mr Fox's secession from politics.'

The value of garden and gardening were greater than ever to Mrs Fox as increasing age and worsening rheumatism restricted her movements. There were no long walks now. Seldom indeed did she go now on foot outside the grounds, and even within them rheumatism sometimes compelled her to make her tours in a garden-chair towed by one of the men-servants or a young male visitor. But indoor pleasures did not fail, and reading and 'reading out' were as constant a feature of life at St Anne's as they had ever been.

Though the classics figured less often than in Charles's time, the list of 'books read' maintained at the end of each volume of Mrs Fox's journal reveals a wide range of reading. Novels appear in plenty, including 'Scott's novels if they are his', and some works of another anonymous author whose unknown name was Jane Austen. Narrative poetry was perhaps read less often than before 1806, but 'The Rape of the Lock' appears, most unusually, twice, Fox's beloved Dryden is well represented, and works by Scott, Crabbe and Byron appear. History Mrs Fox clearly enjoyed, for it appears constantly, from Raleigh's 'History of the World' (the first book she took up after Charles's death) through Hume and Lingard – the style of the former being preferred – to John Halket's 'Historical Notes concerning the Indians of North America.' Books on travel too were much enjoyed, the old lady whose journeyings were so limited always considering whether she would or would not like to visit the country covered. Biography was much favoured, from Plutarch to Medwin's 'Journals of Lord Byron' and Moore's 'Life of Lord Edward Fitzgerald' (I think it was bad taste in Mr Moore to have written it nor do I think it well done dear Ld Edward's letters and some other of the letters are quite beautiful'), taking in on the way the autobiography of Benvenuto Cellini – 'very amusing though very odd.' She read 'Buxton on Prisons', and observed, 'It makes one quite long to be like Mrs Fry and her friends'; she read White's 'Natural History of Selborne', 'a delightful lounging book'; she read 'a Chinese Novel very odd and dull but it is so unlike anything else that I could not help going on with it it is called Han Thiou Chouan.'* She read regularly in French, usually novels and memoirs, and of a translation of 'Amadis of Gaul' noted: 'I like it very much but dare say I should have liked it much better in French.'

Caroline Fox often brought with her on her visits to St Anne's some book for reading aloud in the evenings, once a translation of the Lusiad, once 'Northanger Abbey'. Another time she and Mrs Fox, with a

---

*Selected Tales from the Han.

Chertsey neighbour, Lord Montford, diversified a visit by play-reading. 'Miss Fox read Alexander by Lee, Lord Montford read The Siege of Damascus, I read Oedipus Rex very horrible'. 'The Jew of Malta' was 'very horrible' too, and so was 'Tis Pity She's a Whore', but it had 'some beautiful things in it.' Not many women of Mrs Fox's time would have found them out.

Any relative or friend of hers who ventured into print could be sure that one reader would arrive at the most favourable opinion possible. She read Henry St John's play about Mary Queen of Scots and the novels of his wife Isabella; she read William Adam's 'Blair Adam'; she read William Napier's 'History of the Peninsular War', finding the details of battle rather difficult to follow, but approving the style. (She was more responsive to style in prose than in poetry, liking what she called: 'a fine strong manly style'; Johnson she considered 'a wonderfully strong writer'.) She read anything by or about the dear Russells, approving particularly Lord John's 'Life of Lord William Russell', and even more his 'Memoirs of the Affairs of Europe from the Peace of Utrecht': 'a very delightful book well written and full of information how my angel husband would have enjoyed it he would have admired the style it is just what he liked strong and simple.' She would have been delighted to know that, Holland failing in the task, Lord John was to write the first full biography of her angel husband.

In 1823 Holland had given her a copy of Walpole's 'Memoirs of the Reign of George II', which he had edited. 'A very entertaining book', she had written, 'and full of anecdotes it makes one out of humour with politics.' The Whigs generally might at that time have felt out of humour with politics in a world that excluded them from office till Whiggism began to appear rather a spiritual condition than a political reality. As the 1820s wore on, however, their offence (to which the Hollands had so much contributed), of Francophilia during a mortal war with France, sank into the past, and the reforms they so long had advocated grew increasingly desirable in the eyes of the electorate. In 1828 there had appeared the possibility of a coalition under Goderich; it failed to materialise, but hopes were rising that the second epoch of unchallengeable Tory administration might be nearing its end.

In 1830 George IV died, sincerely mourned by the one-time mistress and later friend to whom his kindness had been renewed in his last years. 'The poor King the last time I saw him he looked so well and so happy, and put me in mind of former times when he used to stop here in his way to Windsor and partake of our little dinners, he was a good-natured man and when he acted from his first and own feelings always did so kindly.' The pension he had granted her was continued by William IV. Political attention now focused on the general election that followed the King's death, the central issue in which was parliamentary reform. Reform had been part of Fox's platform in his first campaign for election for Westminster, just fifty years before, and though more urgent tasks had later been advanced above it in his programme – slave trade abolition, peace, Catholic emancipation –, all now had been achieved. Had Fox been living still his efforts would have been directed towards reform, and what should his widow do but offer her mite of support. The carriage was called round, and the octogenarian who half a century ago had been the High Priestess of Patriotism sallied forth to canvass for the Whig candidate. And to some avail, it would seem, for on August 2nd she triumphantly recorded, 'got the promise of a good many plumpers for Mr Denison', (a plumper, in the days when constituencies returned two members and electors therefore had two votes, being an undertaking to vote for one member only), and William Denison was returned for the West division of Surrey. Three months later Wellington's efforts to maintain the Tory administration collapsed, the Whigs under Lord Grey took office with Holland as Chancellor of the Duchy of Lancaster, and the two-year battle for reform was joined.

Paradoxically, it was during this period of intense party feeling that Mrs Fox made a friend among the Tories. In 1831 Lady Charlotte Greville took a two-year lease of the Montfords's house, Monks Grove, to be near a daughter who was in waiting at Windsor. Mrs Fox called, as she would have called on any new neighbour; Lord Mahon had been quite wrong in thinking she would not countenance Tories. As a matter of fact, she considered any tenants of the Montfords must be an improvement on the owners, who were among the very few people she positively disliked, describing them once as 'mean in every possible way.' (As she was too courteous to let her dislike be seen the Montfords remained unaware of it, and Lord Montford in particular was, when in residence, for ever calling at St Anne's and staying 'an unconscionable time'.) Lady Charlotte proved more than an improvement on the Montfords. Her society was really enjoyable, and rapidly proved a boon to Mrs Fox, whose Chertsey neighbours in general still tended to be 'worthy' rather than entertaining.

Lady Charlotte, the days long forgotten when she had 'caballed against' Mrs Fox in Paris, seems to have been reciprocally delighted to discover in the district of her temporary settlement such an amenity as Mrs Fox. A call at St Anne's was normally one of the pleasures afforded her house-guests; and it is fair to say that in taking visitors there she sought to give as well as to receive pleasure. Early in their acquaintanceship Mrs Fox mentioned that she had never seen the Duke of Wellington and longed to do so (Tory he might be, but some of William Napier's admiration for the hero of the Peninsular War had probably rubbed off on her), and a few days later, just as the St Anne's household and some dinner guests were returning to the drawing-room after dining, in walked Lady Charlotte with her husband, her daughter and son-in-law, Mr and Mrs Arbuthnot – and the Duke. 'I was very glad to see him and he was very civil and agreeable but looks in sad health poor man he took a cup of coffee with me and admired my place very much.' Not all Lady Charlotte's importations were so welcome, and Mrs Fox was glad that she chanced to be out when that arch-reactionary the Duke of Cumberland was brought to St Anne's.

The friendship survived through Lady Charlotte's tenure of Monks Grove and continued after her departure – much regretted by Mrs Fox – from Chertsey, which suggests that the two ladies wisely eschewed politics in their gossips together. In common with much of the adult population Mrs Fox was anxiously following the Parliamentary battles, and unlike most she was reckoning on bulletins from the front. 'No letter yet to say what is going on in London,' she wrote impatiently as the fight for the second Reform Bill reached its final crisis in May, 1832; but within a week the great redoubt of the Lords had fallen before the threat that rejection would ensure the creation of enough peers to force passage, and the last objective of Charles Fox's programme was gained.

Throughout the country the passing of the Reform Act was celebrated, with banquet, festival and dance. The Chertsey Whigs held a Reform dinner on 9th August but, well attended as it was, deemed it insufficient to manifest Chertsey's delight. On 3rd September the Act was publicly celebrated in a field near the village. 'A dinner, upon a most extensive scale, was given here to the labouring classes of this parish on Tuesday last,' wrote the 'Windsor and Eton Express' correspondent from Chertsey, 'when upwards of 3,000 persons had a substantial repast of good old English fare – roast beef and plum-pudding – served up, all hot, with a plentiful supply of strong beer . . . As the procession from the headquarters, the Crown Inn, was proceeding to the field of triumph, it met the carriage of the Hon. Mrs Fox, when a general halt took place and three times three hussas made all the streets re-echo, which were full of happy faces. The Hon. Mrs Fox, after all the company were seated, walked into the field, and appeared delighted with the arrangements.' In her journal she wrote, 'It was very gratifying to me to find that nearly the whole of the neighbourhood was there and eager to show me every civility.' This seems to have been the one occasion on which she sensed something of what she herself meant to the people among whom she lived.

The present had its satisfactions; but on 13th September, 'alas! this day always brings my sad loss fresh to my mind as if it had just happened, and fifteen days later: 'This day thirty-seven years ago I became the wife of my beloved and ever to be regretted Husband.'

There were few now to share with her memories of Charles. Lord Robert Spencer had died in June, 1831, Lord John Townshend and Lord King were to follow early in 1833. It was perhaps Lord Robert's death that precipitated in Holland, still intending to write Fox's biography one day, the realisation that those who could tell him about his uncle's youth were dropping off so fast that evidence must speedily be sought from the few that survived. One there remained who had known Charles Fox long before he set eyes on Elizabeth Armitstead, who had diced with him at Brooks's and gambled with him at Newmarket, in whom the memory of those days was living still and who was delighted to call it up for Holland; Lord Egremont. Egremont spent little time in London now, preferring to live, a patriarchal Maecenas, in his splendid untidy palace at Petworth, surrounded by children both legitimate and illegitimate and by the works of art it had been his life's pleasure to collect and commission. He was happy to respond to Holland's enquiries about Fox's early associates, and during 1832 supplied accounts of Fitzpatrick, Hare and Uvedale Price. It then occurred to Holland to wonder about another friend of his uncle's youth, the second Lord Bolingbroke. He did not know how that friendship had originated: did Egremont? Soon after he had received this enquiry, and before he had replied to it, Egremont encountered Henry St John and his wife Lady Isabella.

Of all the children of the third Lord Bolingbroke, other than his long-dead half-brother Bob, Henry was personally the most attached to Mrs Fox.* As a child (when he had been called Joseph or Joe) he had been a frequent visitor to St Anne's both with his parents and by himself, when he grew up his visits continued, and since his marriage Lady Isabella had been happy to join in his custom of spending a week or so there every few months. They had just finished one of their stays when they met Egremont, and they took advantage of the encounter to ask him to frank their bread-and-butter letter.

Egremont had seen Mrs Fox occasionally, and heard of her, during her widowhood. Woolbeding was not far from Petworth, and sometimes, visiting the Spencers, he had met her there; gossiping with Lady Robert or Di Ponsonby, inspecting the trees with a silvicultural eye, trotting off to church to hear one of dear John Bouverie's beautiful sermons, the very picture of a respectable old lady. Now however, as with Holland's letter in his mind he listened to the St Johns chatting about their kind old friend, a very different picture rose before his inward eye; a gang of young bucks invading a brothel, a bedroom door kicked open, and beyond it Henry's grandfather entwined with a beautiful girl. Of course, the friendship with Fox was already established by then – still, Holland might be interested. 'Perhaps you are not aware', he wrote, 'that Ld. B was the person who first raised Mrs Armstead from the lower ranks of her profession & introduced her into better company.' He explained how the encounter with the St Johns had brought this to mind, and then, gathering his images of Elizabeth into one affectionate reflection, he wrote: 'Mrs Fox is a very kind-hearted woman & now very religious and she seems to have taken the good qualities of God Almighty without his atrocious ones by shewing mercy unto the third and fourth generation of, not quite, thousands who have loved her and kept her commandment.'

---

*She knew him much better than Egremont, who (possibly confusing him with his cousin Henry, the General's son) referred to him as a nephew of 'the late' Lord Bolingbroke. He mentioned that Henry's wife was a daughter of the Duke of Grafton, and Burke's Peerage shows Lady Isabella Fitzroy as married to Joseph St John. Mrs Fox's journal references to 'Joe St John' indicate he was the third Viscount's son. He does not so appear in Burke, probably because he had been born before his parents' lawful marriage. Joseph apparently began to call himself Henry at the time of his marriage, when journal references to 'Joe' stop and those to 'Henry' begin.

Her loving heart was open still to new affections, and in 1833 warmed to another. In the autumn of that year Holland's son Henry brought his bride to England, and in due course to St Anne's. Henry had been living for some years in Italy (in part because his relations with his mother were easier when they had the Alps between them), and in May, 1833, he had married there Lady Augusta Coventry. The marriage was received with satisfaction by the family, for Henry was now thirty-one and it was on him that hope rested for a continuance of the male line of Holland Foxes; his brother's marriage was childless, and their exiled cousin Harry was settled in bachelorhood. Mrs Fox had expressed the family view when she wrote: 'I only hope and trust that she is a good person and that she will make dear Henry happy and that they may soon have Children.'

Dynastic considerations became trivial when the tiny, lively Augusta appeared at St Anne's. Mrs Fox was warmly attached to Charles and his wife (Lady Mary since her father on his accession had raised his younger bastards to the rank of Marquess's children), she was devoted to Holland's daughter Mary, Lady Lilford since 1829, and Lord Lilford she liked better every time she saw him, but by Augusta she was enchanted. So indeed all St Anne's seems to have been (Mrs Fox's subsequent letters to Augusta often contain such messages as 'Miss Marston begs her kind regards and Tucker and Goude send their duty'), and Augusta was enchanted by St Anne's. Long afterward, in her own widowhood, it would be her preferred home in England, and she is buried in the chapel she had built there. Lady Mary was 'Lady Mary' to Mrs Fox, and the other Mary had been 'Lady Lilford' since her marriage, but within a couple of days Lady Augusta was 'darling little Gussy', 'Henry's Fairy', 'the dear wee thing.' She was indeed a perfect great-niece-in-law, and when she was back in Italy kept up a loving correspondence and an exchange of small gifts with the old lady at St Anne's.

On her eighty-third birthday Mrs Fox had taken brief stock of herself. 'The day my angel used to say was the happiest day in all the year. I thank the Almighty that I am so well, was it not for the Rheumatism I should say there were few people at my time of life so hearty.' The rheumatism was certainly a nuisance, and a painful nuisance too, imprisoning her in the house for long periods in winter, restricting her movements so that to mount the stairs, to climb into the carriage, was a labour; but she acquired a small carrying-chair in which

Goude and one of the footmen carried her up and down stairs, and when, having struggled up into the carriage, she went out calling, her neighbours were happy to come out and sit in it to chat with her. When her rheumatism was in abeyance she was apt to forget her age. A couple of years later, when after a lapse of years William Adam came to dine and stay the night, she observed: 'I . . . found him much changed in person but in mind as perfect as ever which is a great blessing at his great age eighty-four.' It did not occur to her to put up thanks for the clarity of her own mind at eighty-five.

Others marvelled at her continuing vitality and interest in life. After she had visited Holland House in 1834, Holland wrote: 'Our old relation, Mrs Fox, has just left here after a visit of three days in which, much to her delight, she met a large portion of the Ministry and bore, I assure you, a very cheerful and agreeable part in the conversation. She is, though lame and infirm in limbs, wonderfully well; and good temper and good heart seem eminently conducive to long life, or at least to the enjoyment of it if it comes.'

She knew however that she could not expect to live much longer. For death she was prepared, but two things worried her, and late in 1835 they surfaced into the family's awareness. Miss Fox wrote to tell Henry the story. 'Who so faithful so true so affectionate & kind as our good [Mrs Fox]. The tall pyramidicus camellia at St Anne's outgrows the Greenhouse lofty as it is. Mrs Fox rather than pollard it, has through Lady Mary presented it to [the King] & it is now an ornament & an acquisition to the far-famed collection at Kew – he in return asked Ly Mary to find out what she would like him to give her as a present in token of thanks & acknowledgement – She consulted me & we agreed that perhaps a bracelet with his picture would please her best – No such thing, she has written to Ly Mary the simplest most unaffected & touching of letters – asking only an assurance from him that when her spirit has fled her remains may lie in Westminster Abbey entombed with those of her husband & then, as her property is so deeply mortgaged that little or nothing will be left when she is gone, that some trifle may be secured to the friend who lives with her. No relation but the Daughter of one who befriended her when she was a helpless Girl of eighteen. No one could read such a letter unmoved, recollecting too that the writer is halfway between 81 and 91 – I [? and Mary] could not & certainly not the Man the tender hearted Man in whose hands it has been placed.

The next letter Miss Fox wrote to Henry about their aunt was written the following summer from St Anne's, where she chanced to be staying on Mrs Fox's birthday – which had not been forgotten by darling little Gussy. 'Here I am dearest Henry & Augusta sitting down in the hottest of the Dog days, to write to you from this dear & beautiful Place where happily I find myself by surprise upon Mrs Fox's birthday, they tell me her 88th but this she does not say herself. [It was her 86th: her age is established by a journal entry on 11th July 1837, 'Eighty-seven years old.'] She is really a marvellous person, fresher & younger in her face than she was five years ago & as warm in her affections & as clear (if not clearer) in her intellects. . . . I encourage & like to indulge her in her dolce far niente, close to the open window & door of her little Drawing-room – the net curtains gracefully floating & ballooning in the South-western breeze & wafting into the room the perfume of a thousand Roses & Honeysuckles – & how often we have talked of you & your little Gussy – of her pretty letter, beautiful Bracelet & the little locket with its contents [a tress of Augusta's hair] beyond all price.'

The next year saw the death of the kindly king who had he survived her could probably have ensured Mrs Fox's burial beside her husband; and from the Privy Purse of the queen whose name was to be indissolubly associated with sexual propriety, the pension to the quondam Impure continued. Indeed Mrs Fox was Victorian in her piety and her love of domesticity – and in her now occasionally prudish responses to her reading; of 'Masterman Ready' she wrote, 'not at all a book for a woman to read.' Her reading was mostly of novels now, but it was still contemporary, and she who had been born when Fielding and Richardson were at work on their last novels now read Dickens and Fenimore Cooper. She was already acquainted with one who was to be reckoned an eminent Victorian; John Buckland, brother-in-law to Thomas Arnold and tutor to his sons Matthew and Tom, was rector of nearby Laleham and in 1833 had brought the Doctor and one of the boys (unidentified but probably Matthew as the elder) to visit the doyenne of the neighbourhood. She was greatly impressed by him, 'one of the cleverest looking men I ever saw,' acquired a volume of his prayers for use at home on the Sundays when she could not get to church, and always welcomed his occasional calls.

Infirmity increasingly limited her society to those who came to call or to stay, but these still were many. In the winter, when now she tended to live upstairs between her bedroom and the Book Room, callers were happy to climb the stairs and sit with her. Even when illness confined her to bed, intimates would be admitted for a chat; as she wrote after Lord Albemarle and his second wife had visited her at a time of illness, 'seeing those we love and that we know love us does good.' But in summer and autumn when the weather was kind and the old lady could get downstairs – and sometimes even into the carriage to go calling or to a local flower-show – the little dinner-parties were resumed, and the house-guests came and went as they had so long done at St Anne's. The widowed Lady Bolingbroke came, and John Bouverie, and sometimes his sister Di with her husband; occasionally 'Catty' and William Napier, and Lady Arran who had been Bessy Napier and one of 'Catty's darlings'; and many parents bringing their children to be welcomed and admired and petted as they themselves had been in childhood. Mrs Cope, Miss Marston's niece, came with her husband and children. The Lilfords came each year (in Epsom race week so that Lord Lilford could attend the races) with their eldest son and daughter; 'I doat upon the dear Tom and Adelaide', wrote their great-grand-aunt-in-law of these grandchildren of the first child to visit St Anne's in her time. Henry St John and Lady Isabella came with their little girl, Henry's cousin Maria Gorring, General St John's daughter, with hers, both children the third generation from Bully. And Maria's youngest brother Welbore would continue the long tradition of little boys enjoying at St Anne's interruptions in their education, for the indefatigable General, marrying for the third time at fifty-seven, had sired his youngest child thirty-four years after his eldest, and in 1839 proudly presented Welbore at St Anne's ('the General in high feather', observed Mrs Fox) before depositing him at Sandhurst.

Some visitors there were unconnected with former guests, who came simply to meet and listen to this astonishing survival from a vanished epoch. The time of Elizabeth's youth, almost as distant from the early Victorians as the Edwardian age from our own day, held a similar allure for those who, deeming themselves more virtuous, more enlightened, better conducted than their forebears, yet looked half-longingly back, across an irreversible cataclysm, to a lost world that had accorded to the fortunate a sweetness of living that never would be known again. The world before the French Revolution belonged to history, and not historians only but archivists and memoirists were seeking to evoke it in print. One, John Heneage Jesse, was now at work on the correspondence of George Selwyn. Selwyn's numerous correspondents of the 1760s and 1770s had included – the most famous of them by far – Charles Fox, and though Fox's letters to Selwyn were few and dull, Jesse could not resist the temptation to expand the short note with which he introduced each correspondent into a brief biography of this most lovable of statesmen. Having met his subject's widow, he was further tempted to digress briefly from that digression; 'Probably no two persons were ever more devotedly attached to each other, or lived on terms of more perfect harmony, than Mr and Mrs Fox. The editor, from personal knowledge, can bear testimony to the pride and affection with which Mrs Fox loved to dwell on the memory of her deceased husband, and also to the cheerfulness, the kindness of heart, and the delightful fascination of manner, which distinguished this accomplished and venerable lady.'

Mrs Fox had reached at last the tranquillity with which she could remember her beloved husband in happiness. Of the mournful anniversaries that once had darkened her year only one still cast a shadow. This was 21st November, the date which could not be forgotten because it was dear young one's birthday, her personal All Souls' Day when memory still called up 'how happy I was five and forty years this day surrounded by so many dear ones who have all left me.' There were only two people now with whom she could share a living memory of the other dear ones who had been happy at St Anne's in the far-off days of the Lady of the Hill; Adair, who always on his returns to England came down to visit her and recall old times, and Holland.

In December, 1838, she had the pleasure of a two-day visit from Holland, accompanied by 'Miladi' and by Dr Allen, that now inevitable third who had joined their household as Lady Holland's personal physician and remained as librarian and resident friend (and, in the view of the Hollands' children, widener of the wedge their mother had driven between them and their father). Miss Fox was not with them, having gone on a visit to Henry and Augusta in Italy – followed in imagination by Mrs Fox, who had got a copy of Le Maistre's 'Travels through France, Italy, Switzerland and Germany' in order to go 'Travelling with dear Miss Fox'. From St Anne's Holland wrote to his sister in renewed admiration of his aged aunt's health and good spirits: 'It is really delightful to see Mrs Fox so well and so fresh in mind & body

– really as she approaches or has reached ninety she seems more active & more alive to everything & as kindhearted & affectionate as ever. We smiled together at your fogs for she who never penetrated to Florence recollects laughing at my Uncle (who like his great-nephew used to maintain there were no fogs in Italy) at Bologna when they could not see across the street on new year day.'

Miss Fox, however, on her return to St Anne's in May, 1839, thought Mrs Fox was at last beginning to fail beneath the burden of her years. She was thinner, Caroline thought, and showed occasional signs of mental confusion. Indeed, unless Holland had misreported her, the very conversation he cites as evidence of her alacrity indicates some confusion of mind, with perhaps a long-suppressed memory surfacing in disguise. She had never passed a New Year's Day in Bologna with Charles, but on New Year's Day, 1782, she had been in Italy with Lord Cholmondeley.

Hearing and eyesight too were beginning to fail. The writing in the journal grows large and uncertain, and there appears a run of entries in another hand, probably Martha Tucker's, made from dictation. These signs of decay were however scarcely perceptible to guests who knew her less well than Miss Fox. Mrs Fox was borne up still by her powerful social instincts, and her delight in having to do with others and in making them happy. She was eighty-eight and celebrating her birthday with a party for her schoolchildren ('it gave me real pleasure to see so many poor little souls so happy'), she was eighty-nine and giving a dinner-party to celebrate Harriet's birthday, she was ninety and still glad to receive strangers desirous of seeing what had been the home and of meeting her who had been the wife of Charles Fox.

Such a stranger was Madame d'Hoogvoorst who, visiting Windsor in the train of the King and Queen of the Belgians in 1840 and learning that the widow of Mr Fox lived not far away, expressed a desire to meet her. As Albemarle's son George Keppel was a Groom in Waiting to Queen Victoria, this was easily arranged, and on 20th August Madame, Baroness Spaeth and the Duchess of Bedford were escorted to St Anne's.* 'We experienced a most cordial reception. Our hostess . . .

*When some ten years later Keppel, then 6th Earl of Albemarle, recorded his memories of this visit, he erred as to the year, which he thought had been 1838 or 1839, and combined two visits into one. Mrs Fox's Journal shows that he lunched at St Anne's with the three ladies (and his stepmother) on 20th August, 1840, and again with the Duke of Bedford (the 7th Duke, son of her old friend, who had died in October, 1839) and George Byng on 22nd August.

was in her ninety-third year [Mrs Fox's age was now commonly over-estimated] but still hale and handsome. She insisted upon showing us all over the house herself, pointing, among other things, to the tiny table upon which Mr Fox wrote his 'James II'. We all underwent a close scrutiny. When she came to George Byng she said musingly, 'Ay, good-looking enough, but not as handsome as old George,' meaning Byng's uncle and namesake, who represented Middlesex in her husband's lifetime. I reminded Mrs Fox of my games of trap-ball with the statesman. She well remembered the circumstance, and explained that when the swelling in Mr Fox's legs prevented him from walking she used to encourage him to play this game with children as a means of taking exercise; 'but', added she, 'he required no encouragement from me, for you know, my dear, how fond he was of you all.' I now learned that the Duke of Bedford was another of the boys with whom Fox had been in the habit of playing at trap-ball. We spoiled our dinners by a sumptuous luncheon. A profusion of costly wines was placed on the table. The butler, nearly as old as his mistress, [poor Goude, he was some thirty years her junior] kept constantly filling her glass. 'If you don't take care,' said the Duke of Bedford to him, 'you will make the old lady quite tipsy.' 'And what if I do?' was the reply, 'she can never be so in better company.' Turning to the old man, the Duke enquired if there were many Tories in the neighbourhood. 'Please, your Grace', was the reply, 'we're eat up with them.' '

The pleasant little socialisings went on. Henry St John and Lady Isabella spent a couple of days with her at the end of that month. Sir Francis Burdett came to call, and was welcomed. (Mrs Fox seems to have been unaware that Miss Fox's sale of Sunning Hill two years previously had resulted from his boast that as the mortgages on St Anne's Hill were his the property would fall to him on the old lady's death, a vaunt that drove Miss Fox to sell Sunning Hill in order to buy in the St Anne's mortgages with the proceeds.) John Bouverie came in September to spend a few days with his old friend; Mr Barclay, the newly adopted Whig candidate for the constituency, came to present himself to the Queen Dowager of Whiggism; on 10th September Mrs Fox counted eight callers at once in her little drawing-room. On 12th September Lord Holland, Lord Albemarle and Lord Lilford came together for a few hours: 'a very pleasant visit and made me very happy.' On 22nd October Mrs Fox underwent the heaviest blow life had still to deal her. Holland, still at sixty-seven the dear young one, suddenly died.

At first she could only cry, sometimes for herself, sometimes for the other dear ones in their bereavement. After some days she pulled herself together enough to recognise the need of remaking her will, under which (since Fox's home must stay in Fox's family) Holland was to have inherited St Anne's. Her obvious course was to substitute Henry, now fourth Lord Holland. Now however a new anxiety emerged. St Anne's, so burdened with mortgages as to be no asset financially, must go to someone possessed of the income to maintain the property; but Holland, in a final gesture of subservience to 'Miladi', had left her both Holland House and his country house for life, and all their contents and a great part of his income absolutely. Henry would receive about £2,000 a year. Distractedly the old lady worried lest her beloved home prove a burden to poor Henry, until Miss Marston wrote to, and received reassurance from, Caroline Fox.

On 7th November Mrs Fox signed her last will. All her real property, St Anne's with the hundred acres or so added to the original estate in Charles's time and hers, was assigned to Henry, while the contents were to be divided between him and his brother Charles. To Martha Tucker, 'my good and trusty servant', she left an annuity of £60, to be continued to her husband should he survive her; to Goude, an annuity of £30 and life tenure of the house he occupied, to Scutt and to Sarah Valler annuities of £12 each, and nineteen guineas to William Wooldridge. Charles and Henry Fox were appointed her executors. No mention was made of Elizabeth Marston, a silence that certainly did not reflect lack of concern or affection; the journal as well as the approach to William IV bears witness to Mrs Fox's anxiety for her dear friend after her death. The probability is that she had received an assurance that the family would look after Miss Marston, as indeed they did; Lady Holland, always at her best with dependents, was to take Miss Marston into her own household after Mrs Fox's death, and would bequeath her a legacy in her own will.

With Holland's death the vitality that had flowed for ninety years began its ebb. Mrs Fox grew feebler, suffering a malaise for which the doctor Miss Marston called in could find no cause but 'lowness and nervousness'. Callers were welcome still – she was much disappointed when Dr Arnold called one day before she was up, so that she failed to see him – but an hour or so of even the dearest company tired her. Miss Marston, herself now approaching seventy and in poor health, quietly took over the management of household and property, handling it so well that on the old lady's death it would be found that virtually no debt beyond the mortgages remained. She kept the journal, too, in her beautiful copperplate hand, until the last volume used by Mrs Fox was filled up. Virtually the last entry, on 1st March, 1841, was: 'Mr Charles St John Lord Bolingbroke's brother came to announce his approaching marriage. He is the first person who has dined and slept here since the 26 of November.'

Summer brought some recovery. The old lady could get downstairs again, venture out a little in her garden-chair, entertain a few guests. On 13th July the *Times* recorded (one day late and four years out): 'It may not be uninteresting to mention, that yesterday was the birthday of the Hon. Mrs Fox, relict of the late illustrious statesman. This Lady has reached her 96th year, and is in very good health, frequently entertaining select parties of her friends at her hospitable table at St Anne's-hill.' The summer passed, the leaves fell, autumn closed in on the quiet house where only the under-servants were young. On 5th November Miss Marston wrote to Augusta in Italy: 'Alas for poor Dandie Dinmont. Mrs Fox had him only six weeks: he died of a distemper. We are now without any pet dog . . . Dear Mrs Fox is in very good health considering her age. We live very much up stairs and it is some weeks since she has been out, this has been such an unfavoured summer . . . Poor Tucker hobbles down to his Wife's room and as far as the Green House but cannot dress himself. Goude continues to do the little that is required of him and is at present very well. I shall get Mrs Fox to sign this as if I had written in her name.' Below, in the uncertain scrawl of the nearly blind, appear the words 'God bless you both ever yours Elizth Fox.' They were perhaps the last words she ever wrote.

For now the final decline was beginning, and the spring of 1842 brought no recovery. Body, senses and mind were slowly failing together. Devotedly tended by Elizabeth Marston and Martha Tucker, Mrs Fox sank gradually towards the death that came at last on 8th July. She was three days short of her ninety-second birthday, and had outlived her adored husband by nearly thirty-six years.

Colonel Charles Fox, in the absence of his brother in Italy, undertook the funeral arrangements. Entombment beside Fox in Westminster

Abbey being now impossible, he made provision for burial at the parish church, All Saints (now St Peter's), where she had worshipped so long. The funeral, he intended, should be private, as seemed appropriate for so old a lady who as he saw it had lived long out of the world. Miss Fox, more closely acquainted than he with the feeling of the neighbourhood, suspected, as she wrote to Henry, that 'the funeral . . . however simple and unostentatious in outward circumstances will be followed by crowds of sincere mourners among the poor, & other neighbours who loved & respected her – & are not likely soon to forget her hospitality & kindness, or meet with such another benefactress.' She was right; the people of Chertsey were distressed at the thought that they might be denied their farewell to her who so long had presided over their well-being, and a deputation was sent to ask, and to secure, consent to their manifesting their own sorrow.

On 15th July Elizabeth Fox left her dear home for the last time. It was a small procession that started from the house; Colonel Fox and Lord Lilford in the first carriage after the hearse, followed by Sir Robert Adair with the rector of the parish, Henry Cotton, and then by Henry St John with Mrs Fox's solicitor Mr Grazebrook, and Charles Ives, son of the Chertsey apothecary who had been one of her first friends in the town, and by the carriage of the Duke of Bedford, empty but sent, as was the quaint custom of the time, as a token of respect. The small cortège traversed the gardens of St Anne's, aglow with their summer splendour, and passed down through the woodland to emerge on the road to the town. There, at the foot of the hill, some forty tradesmen of Chertsey, dressed in deep mourning, waited to fall in on foot behind the carriages. Slowly the procession advanced the half-mile to the town, to pass between closed shops – some of them partially closed since news of Mrs Fox's death had reached the town – through silent throngs of townspeople to the thronged and silent church.

A vault at the north-east side of the churchyard stood ready to receive the last of the great Cyprians at the end of her long and improbable course. No aspect thereof, save her long obliterated youth, was unrepresented among the mourners who followed her there. There by the vault was Henry St John, grandson of the man who had launched her upward in her career; Robert Adair, last of all the friends who had rejoiced in the golden days of St Anne's Hill when the Temple of Friendship was new; Henry Cotton, minister of the creed that had sustained and comforted her in her long widowhood; the unnamed many, 'not quite thousands who have loved her and kept her commandment'; and, at their head, the great-nephew and namesake of Charles Fox.

Notes on Illustrations

1. *The Town and Country Magazine's Tête-à-Têtes* were illustrated with portrait engravings purportedly representing the two subjects. That of 'Mrs A-st-d' with the *Tête-à-Tête* for July, 1776, is one of the comparatively few in which the woman looks like a woman rather than a wooden fashion-doll.

2. This engraving shows a company in masquerade on the promenade outside the Rotunda and Chinese House at Ranelagh Gardens in Chelsea in 1751. There would have been little change by Mrs Armitstead's time.

3. The portrait of Elizabeth Armitstead by Sir Joshua Reynolds from which this engraving was made was almost certainly that for which she sat early in 1784; Fox may well have commissioned it both to celebrate the union to which she had committed herself the previous autumn and as a companion piece to no. 4. The portrait now appears to have vanished. It must have been still in Mrs Fox's possession in 1825, when S.J. Reynolds made this engraving from it (her Journal records his visit to St. Anne's with his sister Elizabeth Reynolds in November, 1825), and presumably remained at St. Anne's Hill, to pass in due course into the ownership of the fourth Lord Holland or his brother Charles. It may have been among the pictures destroyed on the Holland House fire of 1871.

   Mrs Armitstead's identity as subject of this portrait has been obscured, not by the title 'Mrs C.J. Fox' (her name when the engraving was made but not when the portrait was painted), but by the existence of a copy, once in Sir Robert Peel's collection and now in the Tate Gallery collection, in which the copyist had added a child. This led to the identification of the sitter as, variously, 'Mrs Musters' and 'Lady Gideon'; Mrs Fox was apparently discounted, despite the existence of the S.J. Reynolds engraving, on the grounds that she never had a child. What appears probable is that the portrait of Mrs Armitstead was copied, possibly by a pupil in Sir Joshua Reynolds' studio, and the child added for some now unknowable reason.

I am grateful to Miss Elizabeth Einberg, of the Tate Gallery British Collection, for help in tracing the likely history of this portrait.

4. The papers under Fox's hand in the portrait from which this engraving was made are those of the fatal – to him – East India Bill.

5. This portrait drawing of Richard Fitzpatrick shows him in the 1790s, at about the time he settled at Sunning Hill.

6. In this portrait Fox is shown in the grounds of St. Anne's Hill; the house is discernible in the left background.

7. These two vignettes resulted from a commission by Samuel Rogers, who wished to include pictures of St Anne's Hill among the illustrations to a volume of his poems *(Poems, 1834)*. Mrs Fox's Journal records, for 17th November, 1832: 'Mr Turner RA came from Mr Rogers to take some sketches which he did very quick (sic) and beautifully – he seems an agreeable man.' The sketches are presumably those in his 'Windsor and St. Anne's Hill Notebook (also in the British Museum), from which the vignettes would have been worked up.

   St. Anne's Hill house, extended by Augusta Lady Holland during her occupancy, was demolished in 1937.

8. Mrs Fox's school was built in late 1808 or 1809; her Journal for 21st July, 1808, mentions: 'Mr Porter called we planed (sic) the new School house.' The schoolmistress she employed lived as well as taught in the house.

Sources and Bibliography

MANUSCRIPT SOURCES

BRITISH MUSEUM: ADDITIONAL MSS.

47565. Correspondence: Fox/Grey.

47568. Correspondence: includes letter from Rolleston to Mrs Armitstead.

47569. Correspondence: Fox/Mrs Armitstead: Fox/Adam.

47570. Correspondence: Fox/Mrs Armitstead.

47571/2/3. Correspondence: Fox/Holland.

47576)
47578) Correspondence: Fox/Price.

47579. Correspondence: Fox/Lord Ossory.

47580/1. CorrespondenceFox/Fitzpatrick.

47601. Correspondence: Fox/Fitzpatrick: Fox/Lauderdale.

51455. Fitzpatrick: 1802 Journal.

51467. Correspondence: Fox/Miss Fox: Fragments of pre-1806 Journal.

51468. Correspondence: includes letter from Mrs Fox to Miss Willoughby.

51475. Fox: 1802 Journal.

51476–51507. Mrs. Fox: Journal, 1806–1841.

51513. Fox: verses.

51515. Mrs Fox: Commonplace Book.

51519. Correspondence: includes letter from Coutts to Fox.

51725. Correspondence: Egremont/Holland.

51736–43. Correspondence: Holland/Miss Fox.

51794. Correspondence: Holland/Mrs Fox: Mrs Fox/Lady Augusta Fox: Miss Marston/ Lady Augusta.

51799. Correspondence: Fitzpatrick/Holland: Mrs Fox/Miss Fox.

51866. Correspondence: Miss Fox/Mrs H. Fox: Miss Fox/Lord Ossory.

51867. Correspondence: Miss Fox/Duchess of Leinster: Miss Fox/Lady L. Conolly: Miss Fox/Fitzpatrick.

51868. Correspondence: Miss Fox/Mrs Fox.

51969. Correspondence: Miss Fox/Mrs Fox: Miss Fox/Lord Mahon: Miss Fox/Miss Marston.

51975. Miss Fox: Journal.

52047/8)
52054/) Correspondence: Miss Fox/H. E. Fox.

WESTMINSTER CITY COUNCIL
Poor Rate books.

SURREY COUNTY COUNCIL
Land Tax Registers, Chertsey.
Deeds of title to lands at St Anne's Hill.

PUBLIC RECORDS OFFICE
Census records, 1841.
Wills: Fox, Mrs Fox, General Fitzpatrick.

MAGAZINE AND NEWSPAPER SOURCES
Town and Country Magazine, Covent Garden Magazine, Westminster Magazine.
Morning Chronicle, Morning Herald, Morning Post, Public Advertiser, Times, Bath Chronicle, Windsor and Eton Express.

BIBLIOGRAPHY

A. Aspinall, ed.: 'The Correspondence of George, Prince of Wales, 1770–1812' (vol. V.). Cassell, 1968.

Mabell, Countess of Airlie: 'In Whig Society'. Hodder and Stoughton, 1921.

George Thomas, 6th Earl of Albemarle: 'Sixty Years of My Life.' London, 1876.

Florence & Elizabeth Anson, ed: 'Mary Hamilton at Court and at Home, from Letters and Diaries.' John Murray, 1925.

The Memoirs of Mrs Sophia Baddeley, Late of Drury Lane Theatre, by Mrs Elizabeth Steele.' London, 1787.

Mrs Henry Baring, ed.: 'The Diary of the Rt. Hon. William Wyndham, 1784–1810.' Longmans, Green & Co., London, 1861.

Bishop of Bath and Wells, ed.: 'The Journal and Correspondence of William, Lord Auckland.' London, 1861.

Earl of Bessborough, ed.: 'Lady Bessborough and her Family Circle.' John Murray, 1940.

Earl of Bessborough, ed.: 'Georgiana: extracts from the correspondence of Georgiana, Duchess of Devonshire.' John Murray, 1955.

Georgiana Blakiston: 'Lord William Russell and his Wife, 1815–1846.' John Murray, 1972.

Horace Bleackley: 'Ladies Fair and Frail Sketches of the Demi-monde during the eighteenth century.' John Lane The Bodley Head, 1925.

Horace Bleackley: The Beautiful Duchess, being an account of the Life and Times of Elizabeth Gurring, Duchess of Hamilton and Argyll.' John Lane the Bodley Head, 1927.

Jay Barrett Botsford: 'English Society in the Eighteenth Century.' Macmillan New York, 1924.

E. W. Brayley: 'A Topographical History of Surrey.' Dorking and London, 1841.

P. W. Clayden: 'Early Life of Samuel Rogers.' London, 1887.

P. W. Clayden, ed.: 'Rogers and his Contemporaries.' London, 1889.

Ernest Hartley Coleridge: 'The Life of Thomas Coutts, Banker.' John Lane, 1920.

John W. Derry: 'Charles James Fox.' Batsford, 1972.

John Drinkwater: 'Charles James Fox.' Ernest Benn, Ltd., 1928.

Malcolm Elwin: 'The Noels and the Milbankes.' Macdonald, 1967.

Joseph Farington: 'The Farington Diary.' Hutchinson, 1923.

Brian Fitzgerald: 'Emily, Duchess of Leinster.' Staples Press, 1949.

Vere Foster, ed.: 'The Two Duchesses.' Blackie and Sons, 1898.

D. V. Glass and D. E. C. Eversley, ed.: 'Population in History.' Arnold, 1965.

John Gore, ed.: The Creevey Papers.' Batsford, 1963.

Castalia, Countess Granville, ed.: 'Lord Granville Leveson Gower: Private Correspondence, 1781 to 1821.' London, 1916.

Lord Herbert, ed.: 'The Pembroke Papers.' Jonathan Cape, 1950.

Philip H. Highfill, Jnr., Kalman A. Burnim, Edward A. Longhans: 'A Biographical Dictionary of Actors, Actresses, Musicians, Dancers, Managers and other stage personnel in London, 1660–1800.' Southern Illinois University Press.

Henry Richard, Lord Holland: 'Memoirs of the Whig Party.' London, 1852–4.

Countess of Ilchester and Lord Stavordale, ed.: 'The Life and Letters of Lady Sarah Lennox.' John Murray, 1904.

Earl of Ilchester: 'The Home of the Hollands, 1605–1820.' John Murray, 1937.

Earl of Ilchester: 'Chronicles of Holland House, 1820–1900.' John Murray, 1937.

Earl of Ilchester, ed.: 'The Journal of Elizabeth, Lady Holland.' Longmans, Green & Co., 1908.

Earl of Ilchester: 'Journal of the Hon. Henry Edward Fox.' Thornton, Butterworth & Co., 1923.

Earl of Ilchester, ed.: 'Elizabeth, Lady Holland to her Son, 1821–1845.' John Murray, 1946.

Muriel Jaeger: 'Before Victoria.' Chatto & Windus, 1956.

John Heneage Jesse: 'George Selwyn and his Contemporaries.' London, 1901.

Sonia Keppel: 'The Sovereign Lady: a life of Elizabeth third Lady Holland with her family.' Hamish Hamilton, 1974.

William Lefanu, ed.: *'Betsy Sheridan's Journal.'* Eyre and Spottiswoode, 1960.

F. Leveson Gower, ed.: *'The Letters of Harriet, Countess Granville.'* Longmans, Green & Co., 1894.

Jacobine Menzie-Wilson and Helen Lloyd: *'Amelia, the Tale of a Plain Friend.'* Oxford University Press, 1937.

Countess of Minto, ed.: *'The Life and Letters of Sir Gilbert Elliot.'* London, 1874.

Carl Philipp Moritz: 'Travels through Several Parts of England in 1872.' London, 1924.

Priscilla Napier: *'Revolution and the Napier Brothers, 1820–1840.'* Michael Joseph, 1973.

J. E. Norton, ed.: *'The Letters of Edward Gibbon.'* (vol. 3). Cassell, 1956.

Charles Piggott: *'The Jockey Club.'* London, 1794.

André Parreaux: 'Daily Life in England in the Reign of George III.' Allen and Unwin, 1969.

Loren Reid: *'Charles James Fox, a Man for the People.'* Longmans, 1969.

'Memoirs of the Late Mrs Mary Robinson, written by herself.' London, 1830.

Samuel Rogers: *'Recollections.'* London, 1859.

E. S. Roscoe and Helen Clergue, ed.: *'George Selwyn, his Letters and his Life.'* London, 1899.

George Rudé: *'Hanoverian London, 1714–1808.'* Secker and Warburg, 1971.

Lord John Russell, ed.: *'Memorials and Correspondence of Charles James Fox.'* London, 1853.

Lord John Russell: *'The Life and Times of Charles James Fox.'* London, 1866.

V. Sackville-West: *'Knole and the Sackvilles.'* Heinemann, 1934.

Mrs Steuart Erskine: *'Lady Diana Beauclerk, her Life and Work.'* T. Fisher Unwin, 1903.

A. M. W. Stirling: *'Coke of Norfolk and his Friends.'* John Lane, 1922.

Hugh Stokes: *'The Devonshire House Circle.'* Herbert Jenkins, 1917.

Dorothy Margaret Stuart: *'Dearest Bess: the Life and Times of Lady Elizabeth Foster.'* Methuen, 1955.

Mrs Paget Toynbee, ed.: *'The Letters of Horace Walpole, fourth Earl of Oxford.'* Clarendon Press, 1903–1925.

G. M. Trevelyan: *'Lord Grey of the Reform Bill.'* Longmans, Green & Co., 1920.

Sir George Otto Trevelyan: *'The Early History of Charles James Fox.'* Longmans, 1881.

John Bernard Trotter: *'Memoirs of the Latter Years of the Right Honourable Charles James Fox.'* London, 1811.

Horace Walpole: *'Memoirs of the Reign of King George the Third.'* London, 1845.

Horace Walpole: *'Last Journals.'* Bodley Head, 1910.

Nathaniel Wraxall: *'Historical and Posthumous Memoirs.'* London, 1884.

Index

Index